Learning to Be Latino

Critical Issues in American Education

Lisa Michele Nunn, Series Editor

Taking advantage of sociology's position as a leader in the social scientific study of education, this series is home to new empirical and applied bodies of work that combine social analysis, cultural critique, and historical perspectives across disciplinary lines and the usual methodological boundaries. Books in the series aim for topical and theoretical breadth. Anchored in sociological analysis, *Critical Issues in American Education* features carefully crafted empirical work that takes up the most pressing educational issues of our time, including federal education policy, gender and racial disparities in student achievement, access to higher education, labor market outcomes, teacher quality, and decision making within institutions.

Learning to Be Latino

How Colleges Shape Identity Politics

DAISY VERDUZCO REYES

RUTGERS UNIVERSITY PRESS

NEW BRUNSWICK, CAMDEN, AND NEWARK, NEW JERSEY, AND LONDON

Library of Congress Cataloging-in-Publication Data

Names: Reyes, Daisy Verduzco, 1983– author.
Title: Learning to be Latino : how colleges shape identity politics / Daisy
    Verduzco Reyes.
Description: New Brunswick : Rutgers University Press, 2018. | Includes
    bibliographical references and index.
Identifiers: LCCN 2017059103| ISBN 9780813596471 (cloth : alk. paper) | ISBN
    9780813596464 (pbk. : alk. paper) | ISBN 9780813596488 (epub) | ISBN
    9780813596501 (Web PDF)
Subjects: LCSH: Hispanic Americans—Education (Higher)—Social aspects. |
    Hispanic American college students—Social conditions. | Hispanic
    Americans—Ethnic identity. | Group identity—United States.
Classification: LCC LC2670.6 .R49 2018 | DDC 371.829/68073—dc23
LC record available at https://lccn.loc.gov/2017059103

A British Cataloging-in-Publication record for this book is available from
the British Library.

www.rutgersuniversitypress.org

Manufactured in the United States of America

Para mi mami y papi, Isabel y Jesus, por sus esfuerzos y amor
and Nancy for opening doors

CONTENTS

PREFACE

There are many ways to be Latino[1] on a college campus. I began to learn about these varied identities in ninth grade when my cousin Nancy took her sister, Jessica, and me (both high school students at the time) to an event called Raza College Day at the University of California, Santa Barbara (UCSB). Nancy was the first person in my immediate and extended family to attend college and soon became an active member of El Congreso, a political Chicano student organization that hosted a daylong event for Latino high school students on the UCSB campus. At this event, I was first exposed to the Chicano movement, the concept of "la raza,"[2] and the idea that college access for Latinos was part of the legacy of a political struggle. Feeling empowered by the events that transpired on that day, I knew not only that I wanted to go to college, but that I would seek out a Latino community on campus when I did.

Four years later, as an undergraduate at UCSB and like so many Latino students across the country, I searched for a sense of community through a Latino student organization. I attended a few El Congreso meetings, where members and leaders recalled and credited the student activism of the 1960s and 1970s for their access to resources and positions on campus. Over and over these Latino student leaders reminded us, "We are here because of those who came before us." recalling the past efforts and struggles of Chicano students. They emphasized the continued need to organize in order to keep the doors of higher education open for future Chicano and Latino students, specifically through advocacy, mentoring, and recruitment of high school youth.

I was inspired by the idea of helping a new generation of Latino students. I agreed with El Congreso's political commitments, but was discouraged by the combative nature of some members. The few meetings I attended were dominated by discussions about the inequalities facing Latinos and the importance of being socially conscious. I viewed the way some members broached these topics as contentious and conflictual. And more importantly, I saw some of these discussions as moments when one's "consciousness" and loyalty to Latino communities were questioned. My impression was that some of these students wanted to judge who held the "correct" political views and who was the most "authentically" Chicano/Latino. Politically I agreed with El Congreso, but I disagreed with the confrontational tactics of some members as they tried to get students in line with one political perspective.

Once I knew El Congreso was not the organization for me, I turned to other Latino organizations and was overwhelmed by the number of choices available for creating a Latino niche for myself on campus. At the time, Latinos accounted for almost 20 percent of the total student population at UCSB, and there were over twelve Latino student organizations. I tried Latino student organizations that were primarily social and found I was not interested in belonging to a non-political club. Eventually, I joined, Mujeres unidas por justicia, educación, y revolución (M.U.J.E.R.), a Chicana political women's organization, which also served as a support group.

Although I had not joined El Congreso, I was still sympathetic to its concerns, so I remained attentive to its activities on campus. In Chicano Studies courses, I observed Congresistas debate and argue with Latino peers who were members of Latino fraternities, sororities, and other social organizations. These arguments emerged repeatedly in such courses, where Latino students from different organizations came together. Certain Congreso members accused those of other organizations of focusing on their self-advancement and social activities rather than "giving back" to Latino communities, while members of other Latino groups accused El Congreso of being Mexican-centric, judgmental, and too radical.

Contestation occurred outside the classroom, too, particularly when it came to the graduation ceremony. At the height of the activism, El Congreso began organizing graduation for its members, and it continued to so thereafter, even as the Latino student population grew on campus and members of El Congreso were no longer the only participants. Today, the bilingual event is open to all graduating Latino students, who can invite their entire families, listen to mariachi, watch Aztec dancers, and individually express thanks in a short speech. The gathering is an intimate and culturally salient alternative to the university-wide commencement service. By 2005, however, the planning for this event had become a continuous battleground.

When I joined the Chicano-Latino graduation planning committee in 2004, a group of fraternity and sorority members sought to gain leadership positions and, hence, greater decision-making power. But even though several were elected, they were unable to take control of the graduation leadership committee because of a by-law stipulating that one co-president of the Chicano-Latino Graduation Committee had to be a member of El Congreso. With both Congreso members and nonmembers on the committee, a battle ensued over which Latino identities, politics, and symbols would be represented in the ceremony. El Congreso was intent on keeping traditions such as Aztec dancers because they noted that indigenous pride is central to Chicano identity. However, other leaders saw the dancing as "Mexican-centric" and urged the committee to consider the increasing diversity among Latino graduates. They wanted a mix of musical genres to be represented, not only those popular in Mexico, and so they sought to add *cumbia* and *merengue*. They even suggested that the U.S. National Anthem be sung because it was the most common thread shared by all members—they were, after all, Latino *Americans*. The Congresista leadership refused the national anthem on the grounds that representing American patriotism on the day of their graduation would violate its values.

Observing these prolonged meetings and intense conflicts, I was struck by the schisms among my peers, divided as they were among different Latino student organizations. I was particularly struck by how some Latinos drew upon the history of the Chicano movement as they carved out and claimed their niche on campus, while others had little regard for the movement's history. At times this disregard was by non-Mexican heritage students who felt disconnected based on heritage but it also occurred among Mexican-origin students who did not feel connected to the civil rights era activism in the United States.

I was interested in understanding how my peers understood "their/our" history as a people on campus and how that shaped their actions on campus. The experiences I had as a Latina undergraduate at UCSB informed the research questions posed and the identity formation processes examined in this book. My interest broadened when I enrolled as a graduate student in a new institution, where Latino students constituted a smaller percentage of the student body. I was curious: What were Latino student politics like on other campuses? Given that campuses differ in terms of size, prestige, diversity, and much more, how and to what extent do these differences influence Latino students' experiences?

Today, there are more ethnically based associations and increasingly varied definitions of what it means to be Latino on college campuses. Some Mexican-origin and other Latino students continue to join political campus associations, while others become members of Latino preprofessional organizations, fraternities, sororities, and social clubs. These serve diverse purposes, including fostering social networks, creating support systems and mentorship programs, and sometimes organizing students to advocate for policy change on and off campus.

Because most colleges moved to meet the social and political changes wrought by the civil rights movements by incorporating more Latino students, staff, and faculty, the context of politicizing ethnic identities has been altered. But each campus incorporates Latino students differently by adopting and implementing multicultural and diversity projects in its own way, which, in turn, shapes the way Latino students come together, organize, and understand their collectivities, as well as affecting how Latino student organizations interact with one another and whether they conflict or collaborate. This book is about how

Latino students interact within organizations on different college campuses and how these interactions shape the way these students understand their identities, their place in the United States, and how to advocate for change. The pages that follow examine how colleges create distinct contexts that serve as critical sites and incubators, where Latino communities are constructed and individual students develop understandings about those communities.

Learning to Be Latino

1

Higher Education
and Latino Students

We know that college cultures shape students' experiences. This book is about how the specific organizational environments of three distinct undergraduate institutions shape the cultures of these schools, as well as the interactions that Latino students have on campus with each other, their non-Latino peers, faculty, staff, and administrators. These interactions influence much more than the students' academic journeys. Some consequences of institutional differences are distinct outcomes on several measures, including students' identities, their sense of who they are, their collective action behaviors, and their ideas about inequality and opportunity in America. In this book, I show how the particular undergraduate institution Latino students attend shapes their lives in important ways—and how they end up learning to be Latino on campus and beyond.

Latinos in Higher Education

In 2013, Latinos accounted for 17.1 percent of the U.S. population (54 million), and this number has been growing since. Latino students also constitute an increasing racial-ethnic demographic on college campuses. In 2012, 70 percent of all Latino students enrolled in college directly after high school, exceeding the rates of enrollment for both white and black students.[1] What is more, during the 2012–2013 academic year, the number of Latinos enrolled in college amounted to 16 percent of all undergraduates nationwide and 35 percent of all undergraduates enrolled in California. Latinos are projected to have the largest growth in undergraduate education enrollment between 2011 and 2022, when their numbers are expected to increase by 27 percent (Excelencia 2015).

Thanks to these dramatic demographic shifts and projections, much has been written about the state of Latinos in higher education, garnering the attention of academics and policymakers alike. Much of this research focuses on the underachievement of Latinos, given that their attainment rates still lag behind all other ethnic-racial groups. Although the high school dropout rate for Latinos is the lowest it has ever been (13 percent), it is still the highest among all other racial groups. Twenty-two percent of Latinos hold an associate's degree, making it the most commonly earned degree among this population. In contrast to other groups, only 14 percent of all Latinos have a bachelor's degree, compared to 33 percent of whites, 19 percent of blacks, and 51 percent of Asian-Americans (Pew Research Center 2014).

It makes sense to look at what happens to Latinos when they get to college, particularly how connected they feel to their peers and their overall campus communities. Sylvia Hurtado, Adriana Ruiz-Alvarado, and Chelsea Guillermo-Wann (2015, 74) call this a sense of belonging and further define it as "a feeling of attachment and place within the overall campus community." Sense of belonging is a subjective feeling, which can result from validation in a particular setting. Historically underrepresented students' sense of belonging is influenced by campus racial climate, which in turn is a part of the institution's overall normative arrangements, or "the features of campus life shaped by structural constraints, demographics, and policies" (Stuber 2016; see also Ray and Rosow 2010), and including such factors as size, school type, curricular offerings, and programming, to name just a few (Harper and Hurtado 2007). Taken together, these arrangements and factors create specific racial climates that shape the interactions students have with one another, administrators, staff, and faculty. For ethnic-racial minorities, these climates can influence their sense of belonging on campus and, ultimately, their completion rates. Beyond this, campus racial climates can also influence nonacademic outcomes; their impact can be seen in how underrepresented students think about where they belong, and how they come to see themselves.

This book focuses on the normative institutional arrangements at four-year undergraduate institutions, where about half of all Latinos in higher education enroll. I focus on bachelor's granting institutions because I am interested in how middle-class aspirants come to see themselves within the gates of their campuses, especially as they strive to achieve social mobility through education. Latinos who have a bachelor's degree or higher also have a much higher earning potential than those with lower educational attainment, and thus are more likely to join the middle class. In 2012, individuals with a four-year degree between the ages of twenty-five and thirty-two were making a median income of $45,500 a year, while those with a two-year degree made a median income of $30,000 (Pew Research Center 2014).[2] Given their financial potential, the millennial respondents who participated in this study are also more likely to be civically engaged than their peers who do not hold bachelor's degrees (Pew Research Center, 2012). Understanding how college experiences shape Latino college students' sense of self may shed light, in turn, on subsequent patterns and processes of Latino civic development.

The Study

To understand the relative influence of organizations and divergent college campuses, I conducted a comparative ethnography of six Latino student organizations at three institutions of higher education in California: a private liberal arts college (LAC), a public research university (RU), and a regional public university (RPU).[3] The data come from twenty months of fieldwork observations at organization meetings and special events; seventy-two in-depth interviews with student members, leaders, and faculty; and eighty surveys of organization members.

The three schools studied vary by type and scholastic ranking and each is situated and embedded in a broader state (California) and national context. Located within a forty-mile radius of one another, each school occupies a different place in a stratified system of higher education and thus varyies in the resources it offers and the types of students it serves. Table 1.1 shows the diversity across the three campuses in 2008. I consider the acceptance rate, size of

TABLE 1.1

Campus characteristics*

	Liberal Arts College	Research University	Regional Public University
Acceptance rate	Less than 20%	45%	60%
Enrollment	1,500	Over 25,000	Approx. 20,000
Student-faculty ratio	8:1	19:1	20:1
Tuition	Over $30,000	About $10,000	Less than $5,000
First-generation college students	12%	25%	62%
Eligible for Pell grants	10%	30%	50%
Latino students	11%	11%	45%
Students living on campus	Close to 100%	40%	Less than 10%

* Data obtained from the Office of Institutional Research at each campus.

the student body, student-teacher ratio, percentage of students eligible for Pell grants,[4] and racial-ethnic demographics to capture the structural and cultural landscape of each campus. These factors are important because, as I argue throughout the book, they shape how students interact and, ultimately, how they construct ethnic-racial boundaries and identities, political agendas, and understandings about racial inequality and opportunity in the United States.

In my search for representative organizations, I began by collecting institutional data about all Latino student organizations on each of the three campuses studied. There were several Latino student organizations on each campus: four at Liberal Arts College, fourteen at Research University, and fourteen at Regional Public University. I profiled each organization and searched for parity in the mission and function of the organizations across college campuses. My sampling was constrained in several ways. First, I needed to negotiate access to each organization. I initially planned to include Latina sororities in my sample but was denied access (Greek-letter organizations often maintain strict codes of privacy). Second, I wanted to conduct observations on a weekly basis at all six organizations. Because this necessitated being physically present on three different campuses (sometimes on the same day), I made decisions about organizational selection based on meeting times. Given these limitations, I selected self-identifying political, preprofessional, and cultural organizations. The two organizations I selected on each campus were large, active, and stable over a long period of time (see Figure 1.1 for organizational information). Because I expected conflicts and differences between political and nonpolitical Latino student organizations, I chose one explicitly nonpolitical and one political organization (which

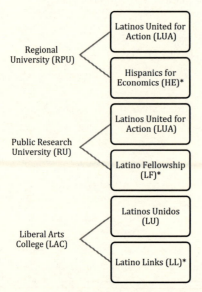

FIGURE 1.1. Organizational information.
* Indicates political organization.

claimed a political identity in its mission statement) on each campus. This sampling also ensured that I was not capturing dynamics of students only in explicitly political organizations.[5]

I simultaneously conducted fieldwork at all three campuses and all six organizations from the fall of 2008 to the spring of 2010. During this time, students on all three campuses were exposed to the same threats and provocations that Latinos experienced statewide and throughout the country. During my twenty months of fieldwork, I attended over 150 meetings, in which I sat quietly and observed. The detailed fieldnotes I wrote after each meeting generated rich descriptions of each organizational context and allowed me to interpret student interactions in their natural settings (Lofland et al. 2006). I observed *how* and *when* student organizations invoked Latino collective identities, interests, and politics. I also took note of how members deliberated during formal meetings, how members were recruited, the types of events they chose to sponsor, and how students interacted with one another.

I conducted open-ended interviews with ten people from each Latino student organization (both leaders and members). I asked respondents about their personal experiences in college, their ethnic identifications, their ideas about politics, and their attachments to their respective organizations. Additionally, I interviewed twelve Latino faculty and administrators to get their perspectives of the campus climate and student organizing. These interviews were evenly distributed across institutions. With participants' permission, I audio-recorded interviews.

Colleges recruit different types of students who self-select into the institutions that are "like" them. Thus, for example, wealthier and more academically accomplished students are most likely to apply to elite schools and to bring extensive social and cultural capital to these campuses (Radford 2014). Likewise, it is possible that the Latino students at the three different schools were already different at the outset; to examine this premise, I surveyed the entire active membership of all six organizations to acquire a broader picture of who the members were and to disentangle my understanding of the "typical" student each university enrolls from the individual biographies of student members of the organizations I studied. I asked students for basic demographic information, as well as about their reasons for joining an organization, their perceptions of the benefits of being a member, their ideas about group sameness, their individual ethnic identities, and their ideas about politics. I found that Latino respondents were more demographically similar to each other than their non-Latino classmates (see Table 1.2). Note, for example, the first row of Table 1.2, which shows the percentage of first-generation college-going students at each campus. While this figure for *all* students varies widely across the three campuses, for first-generation *Latino* students in my study, it is strikingly similar: 82 percent at Liberal Arts College, 82 percent at Research University, and 78 percent at Regional

TABLE 1.2

Student demographic profile*

	Liberal Arts College	Research University	Regional Public University
All students			
First-generation college students	12%	25%	62%
Study sample			
First-generation college students	82%	82%	78%
Third-generation Americans and beyond	9%	14%	17%
Median family income	$26K–$50K	$26K–$50K	$26K–$50K

* Based on organizational member survey.

Public University. Respondents' families fell in the same median income bracket and were alike in terms of immigrant generation. Table 1.2 shows the immigration generation breakdown of my respondents; the percentages of respondents on each campus who are third-generation Americans and beyond are 17 percent at Regional Public University, 14 percent at Research University, and 9 percent at Liberal Arts College. In other words, most students in this study are either first- or second-generation Americans and, thus, are similar in being close to the immigration experience. The students in all six organizations were predominately Mexican American, but included a few students of Salvadoran, Nicaraguan, Guatemalan, Cuban, and Puerto Rican national origin.

The Argument

Each campus environment distinctly mediated the ways that students interacted within and across Latino student organizations. At Liberal Arts College, the communal feeling of the residential campus produced instances of interorganizational collaboration between the groups studied. By contrast, at Regional Public University, the commuter campus, there was no interaction whatsoever between the organizations I studied. It was only at Research University that I found a scenario similar to the interorganizational conflict I had witnessed myself as an undergraduate, characterized by disagreements between politically oriented and nonpolitical Latino student organizations. How does each campus cultivate such distinct processes and outcomes? What aspects of each campus are formative and significant? And how do these dynamics shape students' lives in general?

To answer these questions, we must first understand the roots of Latino student organizations. It is important to remember that each campus is embedded within a broader system of higher education, which takes cues from similarly situated universities when setting normative policies and procedures. While it has become normative at institutions of higher education to develop diversity programming and initiatives, including official procedures for creating and registering as a student organization, how each campus approaches these tasks can vary in small or drastic ways (Rojas 2007).[6] Moreover, normative institutional arrangements, such as student-faculty ratio, student demographics, school size, and residential patterns, vary a great deal from campus to campus, and they can have a powerful effect on student interactions. For example, residential arrangements influence how much time students spend on campus and how much time they spend interacting in the community outside the college gates. The amount of time students spend interacting with others on campus contributes to both the development of their social ties within the school community writ large and the nature of the social boundaries between students and the external environment. The strength of social ties to people on and off campus can also influence the relative importance relationships with peers within their respective organizations has in students' lives. Students who spend more time together are likely to be closer.

In short, campus organizational dynamics create distinct contexts in which students, faculty, and administrators *interact* and *construct* meanings and understandings about how matters are conducted on their particular campus. College campuses create complex interactional environments where students are continually engaged in the *process* of understanding academic and social life. And each campus's organizational dynamics are *specific* and lead to disparate understandings on a number issues.

Imparting Disparate Understandings of Race and Politics

With their overarching goal of achieving diversity, colleges and universities in different parts of the stratified system of universities seek to attract Latino students. These students are sometimes relatively homogenous demographically (in terms of socioeconomic status and immigrant generation, for example), but campuses nonetheless shape their lives and worldviews in distinct ways. In this book, I show how the particular institution Latino students attend impart them with *disparate lessons* about racial-ethnic identity labels, racial inequality and opportunity, and politics.

Learning about Ethnic-Racial Identities

One latent function of postsecondary schooling is the transmission of lessons about race relations—where, how, and to what extent different racial and ethnic groups "fit," not only on campus but also more broadly in a national political imaginary. For example, sociologist Gilda Ochoa (2013) finds that high schools racialize Asian American and Latino students differently in ways that set them up for distinct academic trajectories. These racialization processes in schooling continue as students transition to college and often develop a stronger sense of ethnic consciousness, especially on campuses where they are the minority.[7] Given the highly stratified nature of American higher education, the lessons that college students learn about race relations are varied. *Learning to Be Latino* shows how the racial climate of three colleges cultivate particular types of interactions that influence ideas about ethnic-racial boundaries and identity-label preferences and interpretations.

Learning Political Styles

Through interactions with peers and elders on campus, students learn about and navigate the normative institutional arrangements of their campus in regard to politics. As students plan and execute strategies for collective action, they learn distinct modes of political engagement that I differentiate as *deliberative*, *divisive*, and *contentious*—modes that are cultivated interactively within specific organizational settings.

The Latino politics literature strives to trace the political interests and predict the political behavior of Latinos on a national level by looking at voting patterns.[8] Yet a focus on Latino voting behavior gets at only some of the ways in which Latinos engage in politics. Looking at the results, we might assume that Latinos make decisions and act fairly consistently or that only a few demographic variables, such as income or country of origin, make any difference. Yet a focus on Latino voting behavior gets at only some of the ways in which Latinos engage in politics. Voting behavior research does not capture the dynamic process by which Latinos come together to construct their unity, over and over again. It misses what Cristina Beltran (2010) has identified as a process of *doing* Latinidad, when Latino becomes a verb rather than a noun or adjective with fixed meaning. When it comes to Latino students, a shallow reading of Latino politics research would also lead us to think that, especially given their demographic similarities, they will act in a politically similar fashion. This misses the importance of institutional contexts. I found that students across all three campuses shared positions on and interests in issues of education and immigration, but that the ways they expressed political grievances and sought redress varied. Pundits and scholars interested in Latino politics would do well to consider how (and when) the population they are interested in learns to engage in politics, and how institutions are teaching them these lessons.

More Lessons: Views about Racial Inequality and Mobility

Each campus context is constituted through many factors including institutional wealth, programming, and the demographics of its student body. The distinct social location of each campus in our stratified system of education ensures that students leave college with differential exposure to resources and peers with varying levels of cultural, social, and monetary capital. Through each type of institution students are exposed to a unique sense of American meritocracy and inequality. In this way, each campus cultivates distinct ideas about the prospects for Latinos as a group to advance socially and economically. In this book, I show the processes through which these distinct ideas are cultivated.

By comparing how Latino youth organize within distinct organizational settings, I show how the educational system indirectly channels Latinos' perceptions of diversity, their respective communities, and their engagement in politics. These students are an important segment of the Latino population; they are middle-class aspirants. In many ways, they are a Latino elite "in the making" as they become part of the college-educated American population. Actively creating and representing Latino communities on their campuses, they may continue to do this outside the campus gates after college, especially if they go on to work in the public sector, advocacy, or politics. The students who are forming Latino collectives in school engage in a process that constantly occurs at local, state, and national levels. The contents of this book provide a snapshot of the processes Latino groups face as they seek to represent both their unity and heterogeneity while in college.

Organization of the Book

The book is divided in two parts. This first part focuses on meso-level processes of the three colleges studied and consists of three chapters (2–4), one about each campus. In each of these chapters, I paint a vivid picture of how things work on that particular campus, specifically with regard to the Latino students in the relevant student organizations. I give "thick descriptions"[9] of each student organization and explain its relationship to and place on campus. I also thoroughly describe campus-level organizational arrangements, including their programmatic and demographic dimensions. In this way, I develop a school typology that characterize the campuses contexts as follows: LAC as communal (Chapter 2), RU as conflictual (Chapter 3), and RPU as coexisting (Chapter 4). These chapters provide readers with a clear picture of how students at each site interact and how they come to understand their position on campus and beyond.

The contextual factors described in these chapters serve as the foundation for the discussions to follow in Chapters 5 through 7.

In Chapter 2, I outline how Liberal Arts College functions as a communal space. LAC offers a true residential experience; over 90 percent of students live on campus all four years. Students live in a bubble, which blocks the outside world, on the one hand, and, on the other, creates a cohesive community, facilitating interactions between students who come from diverse backgrounds.

In Chapter 3, I show how Research University is a conflictual environment for Latino students. The multicultural center offers distinct types of support for and treatment of each Latino student organization studied. For example, one of the fourteen Latino student organizations on campus has an office in the multicultural center, while the others do not. The arrangement with the multicultural center fosters feelings of connection and belonging for members of this organization. Members of the other groups feel less connected and in conflict and competition with the group that gets more resources. The Latino student organizations studied differentiate themselves and the conflict ultimately shapes their interactions.

In Chapter 4, I describe how Regional Public University, a Hispanic-serving institution,[10] draws an older, mainly working-class, commuter student body. Most students live in the home they grew up in with their families and work off campus. These students are strapped for time and spend little of it on campus other than during class. In this environment, students coexist; their relations are neither communal nor conflictual. Additionally, students report having little contact with faculty outside class, and in general, the nature of campus programming does not facilitate cohesive relationships.

The second half of the book focuses on micro-level and interactional processes, specifically focusing on three different modes in which students interact with and within their campus environment. In Chapter 5, I demonstrate how institutions of higher education create distinct racial climates. As so doing, campuses mediate the deployment and formation of panethnic boundaries and the adoption of identity labels in disparate ways. I find that each university creates a distinct Latino demographic by admitting, recruiting, and drawing students from either the local environment or nationwide. The demographic profiles of students on each of the campuses studied and the schools' efforts to incorporate Latino students produce three distinct identity formation processes. For example, the interorganizational competition cultivated at Research University leads students to identify as Latino, but in a qualified manner. The chapter extends theoretical understanding of how meso-level organizational settings influence micro-level ethnic and panethnic identity processes. Latino students appear to leave college having absorbed lessons about who they are and where they fit in the U.S. racial order, and their doing so reveals a latent function of higher education.

In Chapter 6, I identify dimensions of campus cultures that interact with students to produce three divergent forms of ethnic political expression: *deliberative*, *divisive*, and *contentious*. I employ inhabited institutional theory to explain why Latino politics take distinct forms in specific academic contexts, and suggest that strong collegiate incorporation serves, paradoxically, to suppress Latino student engagement in political activism beyond the campus gates. I find that each campus incorporates Latinos and their student organizations distinctly by providing different types of resources, recognition, and support; these paths of incorporation determine how students participate in and define their politics. The Latino campus organizations that received the *least* institutional support were *most* likely to engage in protest politics on and off campus, while those that received the *most* support were *least* likely to venture into contentious politics, instead employing deliberation and consultation. This suggests that institutional arrangements not only influence *whether* students engage in protest but also *how* they engage with politics more generally.

In Chapter 7, I note that similar meso-level processes that shape Latino students' identity formation and political styles also shape their views of inequality. I identify two master narratives that students use to understand the social location of Latinos: meritocratic and oppressive. I find that campus and organizational contexts filter students understanding of racial inequality but to varying degrees. For example, in the "bubble" of Liberal Arts College, students deliberate about inequalities and use elaborate rationales as they explain the way oppression affects Latinos. I explain how the cultural context of each campus and organization distills students' ideas.

I conclude with a discussion of how each campus produces particular understandings of a range of issues not formally considered part of the campus curricula. I note that stratification and inequality of institutions shapes Latino students in ways that are unexpected. And I review how each of the three campuses provides students with a different view of what it means to be a Latino in America, and discuss the implications of this within and beyond academia.

PART ONE

University Institutional Contexts

2

The Communal Bubble at Liberal Arts College

I entered Liberal Arts College with relative ease both physically and socially. I made my initial contact with the Institutional Review Board, which promptly answered my query to conduct research on campus and informed me that I had to have an institutional sponsor. I cold-called a sociologist to ask for sponsorship, and she quickly obliged. I then began to make contacts with Latino Studies professors, staff at the Latino Cultural Center, and leaders of Latino organizations on campus. I emailed the student leaders of two of those organizations—Genova from Latinos Unidos and Tomas from Latino Links—and they granted me permission to conduct my research. I would be attending their meetings for two academic years. I also made an appointment with Professor Nelson Tamayo[1] of the History and Latino Studies departments. I would drive to campus for the first time to meet with Professor Tamayo, and a week later, I would attend the 2008 Latino Welcome Orientation hosted by the Latino Cultural Center. Both Genova and Tomas promised to meet me at the orientation.

The LAC campus was as open as the individuals I contacted. The space had open gates and no guards, and didn't even have any parking structures. Having never spent time at a private university or a liberal arts college, I was surprised by the relative openness of the grounds. The campus is in an affluent, predominantly white, politically right-leaning community in California. I parked on a residential street in front of a private home, walked one hundred feet, and faced the campus entrance. The entrance is comprised of two tall pillars, one on each side of the street, with the name of the school imprinted on one of them. The college was built in the late nineteenth century and features uniquely Californian architecture, such as Mission-style stucco buildings, but also more "classic" buildings like those associated with Ivy League schools. With its manicured lawns and abundant trees, the campus is quite beautiful.

I found Professor Tamayo's office and introduced myself. A tall, light-skinned man in his mid-fifties, he was wearing a blazer with elbow patches that day. His immaculate office included several impressive pieces of oak furniture. I took a seat, and he began to tell me about his time at LAC. Having been there for over fifteen years, he had extensive memories of students and the institution in general. We talked for about an hour and a half, during which time several undergraduates visited. Every time a student looked in, he mentioned something personal about each one. Most of these students were his advisees, and he told me about each of their theses. The energy was very positive; it appeared that Professor Tamayo has close relationships with these students and is familiar with both their projects and their personal affairs. As an outsider looking in, I couldn't help but think that he seems to enjoy the classic professor's life as portrayed by Hollywood—elbow patches and all! He has the master–apprentice-style relationship with his undergraduate students that characterizes most liberal arts colleges, which enables him to shape a new generation of scholars and to guide them through the research process.

Professor Tamayo shared his perspective on Latino undergraduates. He said that many initially have a hard time adjusting to the climate of privilege at LAC, but admitted he had little knowledge of what students actually do socially, especially within their organizations. He did add, however, "I think they have an organization with a silly name. I imagine they do the run-of-the-mill cultural stuff, like organize *carne asadas* [barbecues] etcetera. But really, I don't know much." He suggested I talk to younger faculty, who he imagined would be more informed. This was the only time I met with Professor Nelson Tamayo, although students did mention events that he organized on campus, such as discussions about current Latin American affairs.

The following week, I attended the Welcome Week Orientation hosted by the Latino Cultural Center (LCC). The center is a two-story building, with staff offices on the first floor and a student lounge with cultural artifacts on the second. As I walked into the lounge I saw Mexican cultural artifacts such as tapestries, ceramics, and paintings. A burrito bar with flour tortillas, vegetables, chicken fajitas, guacamole, sour cream, and salsa was set up inside the lounge. There were students everywhere; I estimated between forty and sixty, several of whom were wearing t-shirts indicating they were Latino peer mentors. Tasked with welcoming the first year students, a number of these mentors greeted me, assuming that I, too, was one. They asked, "How are you? Where are you coming from?" Most moved on to greet other students once I informed them that I was a graduate student at another institution. One student, however, was intrigued and wanted to know why I was on campus. She was interested in my project and told me that she was the secretary of Latino Links and would be happy to help in any way. She asked if I knew Tomas and quickly flagged him down to introduce me. Tomas was polite, energetic, and somewhat formal. He said, "I look forward to introducing you to the members next week," and then saw someone he knew and walked away. Despite meeting Tomas as planned, I did not encounter Genova or a member of Latinos Unidos (LU) at this LCC event.

I scanned the room for the director of the LCC, Nilda Valle (we had emailed, and she was expecting me). I knew what she looked like because I had already studied her online biography and soon spotted her: a tall woman in her late fifties, wearing a pantsuit. I walked over and introduced myself. She was welcoming, insisting that she was really happy to share the LCC community with me and assist me in any way. Calling members of her staff over to meet me, she introduced Hector and Natalie, both of whom were about my age (mid- to late twenties). They handed me the LCC brochure and talked briefly about the services of the LCC, which range from mentoring to mental health support and just generally providing students with a "home" on campus. They insisted I eat and chat with the students. I obliged and spoke to several who were quite shy; this was their first big event on campus. They were first-generation college students from the local area (within a sixty-mile radius). I never encountered these particular students again, yet I could speculate as to why they appeared so timid and disoriented: they found themselves part of a broader student population that differed from them dramatically.

Who's on Campus

Liberal Arts College (LAC) is highly selective, admitting fewer than 20 percent of its applicants. It enrolls approximately 1,500 students and has an 8:1 student-faculty ratio. These numbers afford students ample opportunities to interact with faculty. The student body is predominantly white (50 percent), with the remainder distributed among Asian Americans (15 percent), Latinos (11 percent), and African Americans (8 percent).[2] Many of the students in the two organizations I studied (Latino Links and Latinos Unidos) are of Mexican or Central American origins. However, there are some Caribbean–origin students from the East Coast of the United States, and some Latin American internationals on campus, as well.

Most of the students at LAC come from affluent families. Only 10 percent of the student body is eligible for Pell grants, which are awarded to economically vulnerable students and are thus an effective proxy for measuring social class. The transition to LAC for predominantly low-income, first-generation college-going Latino students is particularly difficult, given the wealth disparity between them and the general student population. Professor Francine Paredes of the Latino Studies and Sociology departments at LAC described her impression of the transition process for students: "Being at a small liberal arts college is interesting. There's so much wealth. I think that makes it so hard for Latino students. It manifests itself in the classroom in how comfortable they are expressing themselves. I went to a big public university so my experience was very different."

Professor Paredes went on to explain that students have to interact and live with peers who are much more privileged. In the classroom, she witnesses students learning to understand each other and, in particular, first-generation students coming to realize just how much more wealth their affluent peers have. Her classes deal substantively with issues related to inequality. She shared that "racial-ethnic minority students express anger with their classmates. They are especially upset when their classmates do not live up to the things they say in class on the weekends." Both the small size of LAC and its residential patterns—over 90 percent of students live on campus for all four years—ensure that students will see their classmates most days of the week, so if they are discussing inequalities and justice issues in class, they are likely to have the opportunity to find out whether their peers live out the values they express.

Despite the gap between the mostly first-generation college-going Latino students and the general student body, respondents at Liberal Arts College reported feeling a strong community connection to their campus. Students spend most of their time within campus borders, so much so that they described LAC as their primary community. Some even considered it a "bubble" separated from the outside world. At the same time, LAC functions as a communal space and this bubble creates a cohesive community, facilitating interactions between students who come from diverse backgrounds. But what exactly is it like inside this bubble? What are its characteristics and what do students learn within it?

Resources

Liberal Arts College is rich, with an endowment of over $1 billion. The wealth is apparent in its facilities but also in its academic programming. Like most colleges, LAC expresses a commitment to diversity, and the school offers several campus programs intended to integrate ethnic minority students. This integration effort begins with recruitment: the school's large endowment allows it to fly in ethnic-racial minority recruits from all over the country. Once enrolled, Latino students are offered Latino peer mentors through a program run by the LCC, as well as the opportunity to live in Latino residential suites and even to have a Latino faculty mentor.[3] Additionally, all entering Latino students are invited to attend a Latino retreat run by the LCC.

Martiza, a student, described the retreat, saying that "I thought it was a really welcoming environment and you get to know a lot of people. It was really nice environment because you come to college and there are so many people here! It can be overwhelming. It's [the retreat] really welcoming. You go on an overnight experience with all these people and you get to know them. They really felt like the beginnings of a family." For Martiza, the Latino mentoring program and retreat had a positive, integrative impact on her transition to LAC. For other students, Latino faculty advising is also important, as Professor Paredes explained: "It's about checking in, about their classes, but way more than that. Once a week, students are crying in my office. If you look at the students I advise, they are mostly students of color." Students corroborated Professor Paredes's perspective, saying that they are able to talk about feeling marginalized on campus with their faculty mentors, who, in turn, can validate their experiences. Indeed, this relationship is a critical safe space for students' development.

In addition to receiving faculty advising, students are also networked to Latino alumni. Each academic department, as well as individual administrators, invite alumni for informal lunches designed to provide information about internships, study abroad programs, and various career tracks. A Latino alumni dinner is organized every year through the office of the dean of students. During one Latino Links meeting I attended, Lorena, vice president, said to the group: "I strongly recommend freshmen to go to the Latino alumni dinner, so you can get some internship ideas if you don't have any yet."

Classes

Classes are small and intimate at Liberal Arts College. I asked Cassandra, a member of Latino Links, if I could attend her English class with her and she agreed. There were eight students in the class. They sat at an L-shaped table, while the professor stood in the middle. She ran the class like a discussion-based graduate seminar; the class talked about a reading, and she let the students lead the conversation. The dialogue created a sense of camaraderie, with students actively and collaboratively trying to decipher the readings. Classroom climates like this are possible because of class size and pedagogical style at LAC. Students indicated that most of their social sciences and humanities classes have a similar atmosphere of open dialogue.

When I asked Professor Parades about the campus climate in general, she spoke at the length about classroom dynamics, which then led to our discussing campus politics:

FRANCES PAREDES (FP): Compared to other schools [LAC] is politically left. But for students who are more progressive, and grappling with racism, sexism, and other power structures, liberal is not enough. Students complain that some of their peers know how to talk liberally in class and live a different reality on the weekends. Other students live through the racism and classism and that frustrates them. And I don't know what they do on the weekends. I don't know if they are reproducing the very inequalities that they deconstruct in the classroom.

DAISY VERDUZCO REYES (DVR[4]): That's interesting. Are there conflicts between these students?

FP: Sometimes, ideologies explode in classrooms. We talk about topics that we don't usually talk about in mixed company. We're centering Latinos. I had a student say, "I just want to learn about the material," because students were sharing. They wanted to learn from the book.

Professor Paredes explained that students of color and first-generation college students are often frustrated with their more affluent peers because they want to spend less class time talking about how the material relates to students' lives and more time focusing on the texts. She explained the personal offense her working-class and students of color take when they feel that their life experiences are undervalued and dismissed by their peers. In Chapter 5, I further explore some of these racially charged dismissals reported by students. Also of significance is Paredes's discussion of LAC's left-leaning political ethos, which I further discuss in Chapter 6.

Social Life at LAC

Despite self-reports by Latino students of moments inside and outside the classroom of classist and racist offenses committed by affluent and white peers (more in Chapter 5), there is nonetheless a vibrant student social life on campus in which Latino students are active participants. Overall, the Latino students I interviewed reported feeling a sense of community. There are several parties on campus every weekend. Many of these parties draw on the school's alcohol funds, which can be requested by any group or club of students; the school then provides alcoholic beverages and a bartender to distribute alcohol to students of legal age. The school also frequently offers free snacks to encourage nighttime studying. Well-known artists regularly display their work, and poets and authors frequently speak on campus. LAC has hosted several visits by *Democracy Now!*, and there are musical festivals several times a year. But most relevant to this study are the four registered Latino student organizations on campus; I focus on two here.

Organizations

Latino Links and Latinos Unidos have the largest membership base among the four Latino panethnic organizations at LAC. As noted above, I gained access to the organizations with ease, simply by sending emails to the groups' students leaders—Genova of Latinos Unidos and Tomas of Latino Links. They both replied with enthusiasm and expressed general interest in research about Latino student organizations. Through my twenty months in the field, I got to know both groups intimately. At the same time, I kept in mind faculty members' diverse opinions of the organizations. Recall Professor Tamayo's assumption that they are silly and probably only host typical cultural events like barbecues. In contrast, Professor Salvador Carbajal of the Psychology and Latino Studies departments sees a very politically active Latino student culture, noting that "I think the Latino student organizations are protesting constantly, especially for the workers on campus and even against the Minutemen," a right-wing group of activists who oppose immigration.[5] And Professor Paredes took the point even further in saying that Latino student organizations are "definitely a social space, a place for cultural affirmation, talking about identity, and also a place for [Latino students'] need for politicization. And by that, I mean feeling like they belong, but also needing to make change." This professor's views about the political nature of the Latino student organizations on campus is likely tied to the overall political ethos of the student body at LAC (about which I say more in Chapter 6). However, as I will show in the sections that follow, Latino student organizations also fill a niche on campus by providing Latino diversity programming, representing Latinidad to the campus community in ways that aren't always political, and giving students some sense (to varying degrees) of camaraderie.

Latino Links

Latino Links (LL) meetings are held in a community hall, which has a kitchen where students can pick up a to-go lunch during daytime hours. From the outside, the community hall looks like a cabin. Inside are a lot of wooden chairs, including a rocking chair, a couple of couches, a piano, and shelves filled with books, mainly fiction. When I walked into the first meeting, students were sitting in a circle, waiting for it to begin. Tomas greeted me, explaining that he would introduce me later, and then started the proceedings by welcoming everyone to the first meeting of the fall semester. He identified himself as the president and pointed out the vice president, Lorena; Natalie, the treasurer; and Bianca, the secretary. Each waved as he introduced them. He asked everyone in the room to introduce themselves and say their name and their hometown. Once everyone had done so, Tomas said, "I want to talk to you a little bit about why Daisy is here. She's a graduate student at University of California Irvine and she's doing research on Latino clubs. I hope we will all help her in any way we can. Feel free to talk to her after the meeting if you have questions." I waved and smiled. Tomas continued by running through a list of agenda items and noted some of the events planned for that academic year, including open houses, activities fairs, Latino benefit dinners, a Día de los Muertos (Day of the Dead) presentation, film screenings, study breaks, ice cream socials, guest lecturers, artist visits, a Latino music festival, a Dolores Huerta visit, a Cesar Chavez commemoration, parties, and a Latino alumni dinner. Appearing to be genuinely excited about all the events, Tomas asked members to stay abreast of activities as volunteers would be needed. He then concluded the meeting, promising to get to business at the second meeting (a week from that day). Everyone quickly dispersed, with only the officers and one other person, Paloma, a freshman, staying behind. As I was getting ready to leave, she and Lorena approached me, curious about my field of study and wanting to know if Latino Links was the only group I was studying. Lorena shared that she was a sociology major and had assisted one of her professors with her education-based research. Lorena and a few other members of LL and LU were the only students among all three schools to ask about my research process; this is a reflection of the type of education students receive at LAC.

Every Latino Links meeting I attended after the first ran almost identically. Before meetings, students sat awkwardly in silence; they did not chat with one another. Members then introduced themselves briefly, stating their names and answering questions like "What is your favorite ice cream flavor?" or "What mood are you in today?" Despite these "icebreakers," the environment was never particularly friendly; students seemed reluctant to share, and some sat with their arms crossed. Instead of personal discussion, meetings were devoted to addressing logistics for the many events students were busy organizing to showcase Latino diversity on campus. I counted a total of thirty-two events in the 2009–2010 academic year. To host them, the club has a budget of around $9,000, according to Natalie, the treasurer (the sum is unusually large and a reflection of the wealth of LAC). Yet there were only about fifteen to twenty members of Latino Links at the time.

Since Latino student organizations at LAC are encouraged to sponsor each other's programming efforts on campus and even to support individual students' academic pursuits related to Latin America, outsiders often come to LL meetings to request financial aid. The requests tend to be broad. One student organization asked for and received $200 for a Latin American film festival. LL funded an undergraduate student traveling to Guatemala to conduct research; they also gave $200 for a forum with guest speakers from Honduras. A white student asked for funds to host a contemporary Latino film series. She said, "I'm bringing in documentary makers as part of my thesis and I would really like if LL would come to the film showing too." During my time in the field, LL approved all but one of the requests it received. The exception was a request from an undergraduate who wanted $140 to host a taco party. Tomas noted that the same student, who was not present at the meeting, had made a similar request the previous year and that LL had declined; he added, "The only reason she came to us was because she's selling tacos." A couple of people murmured and some laughed—a rare display of emotion at LL. They declined her request once again. Throughout my time observing Latino Links, I found the meetings to be formal and often tense, with little sign of personal connections among members, and I kept wondering the same thing over and over again: Why did these students join this organization? What did they feel they were getting out of it?

JOINING LATINO LINKS. Students said they joined Latino Links to feel connected to a campus group. Cassandra said, "I really wanted to connect more with first years so that's why I really was part of the organization." Adalberto shared Cassandra's sentiment but added that being around other Latinos was important to him: "I joined LL to be involved on campus and be around other Latino students. I always found things in common with Latinos. I heard about it through Tomas and Lorena because they were my mentors freshman year." Karla echoed Cassandra's and Adalberto's perspectives, saying, "Last semester, I was really busy with chemistry, so I said, 'No, I won't join any clubs.' This semester my roommate mentioned going to the meetings, so I thought I should go because there aren't very many Latinos here [at LAC]." Despite her busy schedule, Karla felt a need for fellowship but also a responsibility to connect with co-ethnics.

But once students joined Latino Links, their perspective on the organization shifted. When I asked members to tell me how they would describe the organization to an outsider, they consistently said they were bringing Latino diversity programming to the campus community. Adalberto said, "It's a community-focused group that puts on Latino-focused events." Lorena described it as "a student collective that focuses on celebrating cultural events and campaigns that are specific to Mexican-Chicanos and other subgroups." Natalie situated LL in the broader campus community: "We are a Latino organization that sponsors cultural and social events. We work closely with organizations with faculty and staff and committee members." Paloma said, "We bring awareness. LL is a space that, if you want something from the college, you can get it. If you want a poet to come that's not mainstream, you can bring them down and LL will help you do that. LL is a community where you work together with the surrounding communities."

Members of Latino Links were constantly thinking about their role in representing Latino diversity. Their focus was directed outward to bringing the LAC community together around Latino awareness. For example, during one meeting, Tomas discussed the group's plans to provide snacks during study hours for students. He asked everyone for suggestions on what should be offered and who should be included. Most students agreed they should welcome all LAC students and invite them to get to know Latino Links. One student said, "It's important to strengthen the bonds at LAC because I feel people are divided on campus, so let's invite everyone." The outward focus of Latino Links toward the LAC community as a whole is a reflection of the "community feel" of LAC (that students are invested in the health of the campus community) and the financial support given to Latino Links by the administration further fortifies the commitment to the campus community. Latino Links receives ample funds to host Latino cultural events on campus.

On the surface, students went along with this outward focus, constantly thinking about how they could showcase Latinidad to the campus community and planning the same events that Latino Links regularly hosts year after year, such as the Día de los Muertos presentation. But how exactly did they feel about Latino Links? When I asked students to discuss their experiences in Latino Links, what emerged were critiques about the organizational culture. Only one student, Natalie, had positive things to say about the organization: "I really *liked* the multicultural spin. It was one of the only clubs that was touching on things celebrating being Latino and having programs. We were inviting individuals and challenging the LAC bubble. We challenge the hippie culture."

By hosting Latino events, Natalie saw Latino Links as activist-orienting, challenging the dominant culture of LAC. Other students, however, had a different perspective. Adalberto, for one, expressed dissatisfaction with the lack of community involvement: "I don't necessarily like LL but I like helping out in creating Latino events. I figure that we can be doing different stuff, specifically more community service. I guess the executive board does not foster motivation for community service." Lorena went further in problematizing LL's focus on cultural events: "I feel that LL perpetuates the discrimination that happens on campus because they continue to provide Latino diversity regardless of what the campus does. And I don't think the organization has done a good job of criticizing our campus and the Latino Cultural Center. They do not support our students and LL does not criticize them." Lorena wishes LL would push the administration more forcefully to address their concerns (in Chapter 5, I will discuss instances of discrimination that Lorena mentions).

Lorena and Adalberto are the most critical members of the organization, suggesting that LAC's commitments to diversity are window-dressing. Their critiques dealt mainly with the mission of LL and its relationship to the campus and the broader community, but the most common complaint about Latino Links had to do with the nature of interpersonal relations and the organizational climate. As Cassandra put it, "I don't think LL was ever supposed to be a support organization for Latino students. I don't know if it's in the bylaws but it's more about running activities. I never really realized it until my sophomore year. I feel like there's no connection. I also know there have been divisions between former members and new members and that's created a lot of drama." Martiza similarly expressed concerns with the social dynamic:

When I first joined LL, it really wasn't a family environment. And I was in a position of having to learn how to be part of the group because I was nominated to be a historian right away. It wasn't a chill atmosphere during our meetings! I think a lot of people come here because they are Latino or Latina and they want to check it out. Sometimes they are really into it and sometimes they see strange faces and they don't know how to joke with people. I think LL needs to have a retreat within the club so that people can get to know each other and create friendship and a sense of camaraderie.

Not surprisingly, given the tense environment, LL members also reported that they were not really friends with one another. For Natalie this was not a problem: "I would say I have a couple of friends in LL. But I feel they're more business-type relationships," she said, adding, "I like it that way. I think it's good because I don't tend to cling on to a specific group of people. I really turn to other people outside the club on campus." Maritza, Karla, and Cassandra said they did not socialize at all with members of LL. Cassandra was more critical, saying that "I feel like most people have friends *outside* the organization. I wouldn't consider LL members very close friends." Karla elaborated further: "I feel connected to professors and my suitemates but not really to the members of LL. I think that there's a lot of tension between members because we're just starting to get to know each other. I think that if that goes away then we could get along. Like, I know that other people in LL are first-generation college students and we don't really talk about it."

Karla could not identify why social relations are tense in LL, but she did express a desire to talk about common experiences, such as being a first-generation college student. Cassandra also spoke of wanting more intimate conversations with members: "I once asked at a meeting if we could share our thoughts and maybe discuss what we have in common. And the president at the time said that they had talked about their experiences as Latinos on campus and some students didn't feel comfortable. It's not supposed to be a support group."

Lorena similarly reported that discussing "personal" issues connected to racial, ethnic, class, or gender identities was discouraged within Latino Links meetings and gatherings:

> The mission statement says that the Latino Links is an organization that is for Latino students to join and participate in activities or issues that affect Latino communities. There is something about being a support-based group for Latinos on campus. People just say that LL isn't a support group and they tried before and that's it. People said that we could go and talk about issues with friends but don't do it within the club space. The meetings I went to this semester, it seems they didn't really talk to each other. I think, even if you're not close to the members, having a space where you can share an experience having to do to your race or class is good but we never have any of those sessions.

Given that Lorena was the vice president it is clear that the resistance of LL to engage in "identity" and "support-based" issues was a problem; she wished to move in this direction and it never came to fruition. The reason for the organization's resistance to more personal, identity-based discussions only became clear when I interviewed Bianca, a fourth-year student who had recently resigned from her position as secretary and then left the organization due to interpersonal conflicts with another leader. Bianca explained that LL's formal, event-focused meetings and internal tensions were connected to its history:

> A few years ago, some people thought LL was cliquish because we were all friends. So, the organization tried to change our meeting and activities to make them more formal. We wanted people who were not friends with us to feel welcome. We did this because the dean of students once sat in a meeting to see how we talked about identity issues. He said some students had complained that we made them feel not "Latino enough" to be a member.

When I asked her why she thought those students might have felt that way, she replied, "Maybe it was language and music, because some third- or fourth-generation students didn't speak Spanish or know about certain music. So, we stopped talking about identity and worked on planning events because of these problems." According to Bianca's account, LL shifted from being identity-focused to being more task-oriented due to the history of the organization being labeled "cliquish." But, importantly, it was the intervention of the dean appears to have been what forced the group to shift its focus. That is, when LL peers accused each other of policing ethnic boundaries, the dean put an end to it. This led the organization to focus on planning events.

The dean's intervention is indicative of the closeness of the relationship between LAC personnel and students, but this closeness could also generate tensions in ways that became apparent when Lorena spoke of Bianca's resignation and its further repercussions:

> The woman who left the organization created a lot of animosity in the group. I think it's spewed animosity between LL and the faculty as well. Faculty began to choose sides between what Latinos were the good ones. The reason why she left was communicated to the deans and to faculty and then faculty took sides. I was personally affected by one faculty member in particular who would not speak to me, or not the way we used to. I used to be really, really, close to her. . . . After that situation happened I had an encounter with her [the professor] and she completely disregarded me and wouldn't answer my e-mails. It became very evident that she had chosen sides.

Although Lorena did not elaborate on the tensions generated by Bianca's resignation, her account of how her relationship with her former mentor-professor deteriorated as a result of events within Latino Links provides further evidence of the extent to which LAC faculty and administrators are involved in student affairs and relationships—precisely the kind of thing that happens in a "bubble."

Given all the complaints students had about social relations within Latino Links, I asked whether they would like to change the organization in some way. Some were not particularly hopeful that change could occur. When I asked Adalberto, for example, what would happen if he took a leadership role and tried to change LL, he responded: "I'm not exactly sure how to do that especially with all the events. I feel that LL already has plans. I'm not sure how plausible the kind of events I would like to do are. There are other clubs like the anarchist coalition that already do those things. So, I'm not exactly sure what I would like to do." Karla, on the other hand, was more hopeful:

> I expected the organization to have a sense of direction and know where they were going. When I got there, they took half an hour to decide what they were going to do for the next meeting. So, I thought, "Do I really need to be here?" But I thought, if I want things to change, I should stick around. So, my roommate and I met with the vice president and asked . . . for the mission statement. I hope it gets better.

As I left the field in 2010, evidence of a shifting tide had begun to surface. Latino Links decided to change their organizational structure from hierarchical to horizontal. I say more about this organizational restructuring in Chapter 8.

Latinos Unidos

The first Latinos Unidos (LU) meeting I attended during the fall of 2008 was held in the campus volunteer center office. Although I arrived on time, when I walked in, members were already discussing how to reserve a room for an event. There were eight students in the room—three men and five women. They were all sitting casually on chairs, while one young woman was at a desk with a computer. My contact, Genova, asked me to introduce myself to the group. I said I was a graduate student from UC Irvine. They did not ask any questions and quickly moved on to discuss the Día de los Muertos event they planned to hold in November. Genova said that other organizations would be donating $100 worth of some items. One woman asked, "What's the entertainment?" Genova said "mariachi," as she looked at another young woman I recognized from the open house hosted by the Latino Cultural Center (she was the violin player in the student mariachi group). She said, "I'm sure we can do it, but no one has formally asked." Genova explained that another organization was taking care of decorations and that the dining hall would be providing bread. A few members said they were upset that they could not bring the bread because they wanted to buy *pan dulce*. One student told Genova, "Next year get dibs on that." Genova suggested that the group donate the flowers, although these were expensive. The woman at the computer suggested that if they could afford only one bouquet, they should split it up across the different *altares*.

This led to a discussion of *altares*. Genova said "We have to decide whom we will dedicate our altar to. Last year's altar was dedicated to the Peruvian earthquake victims." The woman at the computer suggested, "We could dedicate it to those people who died in Mexico during the Independence Day celebration." The violinist asked, "Did they die because someone shot a gun up in the air?" The woman at the computer clarified, "It happened because a grenade was thrown into the crowd." The violinist made an alternate suggestion; perhaps they could dedicate the altar to "immigrants that cross over and endure violence." She elaborated: "Some immigrants . . . were hospitalized last week after crossing. Some people are calling for a protest against the U.S. hospitals helping them." Genova said, "Let's take a vote." The woman by the computer interjected, "I really don't care either way; whatever people decide is fine with me." A few students quietly said the immigrant idea sounded good. The group decided their altar would be dedicated to immigrants. The violinist remarked, "I'm sure someone will have an altar for Selena." Genova and the others started laughing. The violinist said, "That altar was intense last year, they played the Selena movie all the way through."

The meeting adjourned, and I stayed behind to talk to Genova and introduce myself to other students. They were approachable and polite. I learned that the violinist was Josiana, Ana was on the computer, and that one of the male students was named Bernardo. I also learned that they had a horizontal organizational structure and were essentially leaderless. They had about ten active members and a budget of about $2,000 a year. This is notably less than Latino Links, which has established a very large and expensive cultural event on campus and receives extra funds in support.

Every Latinos Unidos meeting I attended after this one varied. The meetings were held in different rooms and they rarely started on time—sometimes beginning earlier than stated and other times later. I also noted that they had a hard time convincing students to volunteer for their programming events. It was essentially three women doing most of the organizational tasks. Genova and Ana discussed problems with the group's organizational structure and, indeed, by the end of that spring semester, they began to change it. Before this happened, I saw Genova at a Latino Links meeting (this was the only campus where members of the other organization attended a meeting of the other, which supports the notion of a friendly and collaborative environment between Latino organizations). After the meeting, she said to Tomas, the LL president, "Props on your club. It's really organized." Tomas said, "Thanks, I can't deal with the collective stuff." The change at LU began with outlining the officer positions and expectations and establishing six leadership positions: two co-presidents, a secretary, a treasurer, a public relations officer, and a historian.

Ana, who helped to lead the restructuring efforts, discussed the new arrangement for leadership: "I know it's a little weird because the group is so small, and I know we can only add so many positions without having everyone doing something." Genova, who also led the restructuring, explained the impetus for the change: "I feel like we have more of an organization now, before it used to be more like a group of people and whoever wanted something done needed to do it. The structure has changed." Ana elaborated: "Last year, I feel like me and my friend took on most of the workload. I think it was just too stressful and it takes a lot of your enjoyment out of it. Even if you want to continue, you're not going to be interested anymore if you do all the work." Ana was strongly in favor of change because she personally carried much of the responsibility for organizing. But even students with less workload saw the need for change. Selena shared her sentiments:

> I was really in favor of creating a structure for LU. I feel like the organization was so diffuse and I completely understand the reasoning behind eliminating hierarchy. But we had gone to the point where we were no longer productive. I feel like no one was accountable for stuff that needed to get done. People thought that because they didn't hold a position that it wasn't up to them. At one point, we decided that everyone would have a week where they would lead the discussion. But it was not sustainable because not everybody would come to the meetings consistently. We opted for a structured co-president and secretary model and we wanted a very institutional approach, we want to be more efficient. The plan is to go back to the elimination of hierarchies eventually. I feel like it was really necessary to get things running. I think that it's created more structure in meetings.

The overall assessment by members was that the organization has improved. After restructuring, a consistent pool of students attended each meeting, tasks were delegated, and agendas were set for the meetings. I also noted more efficiency in managing the details of the various programing events LU hosted. Meetings, however, remained largely the same after the restructuring. Members continued to discuss the details of events such as deliberating who to honor on Día de los Muertos and often went off on tangents. But whereas meetings at Latino Links also tended to focus on events, at Latinos Unidos the climate was much friendlier. Planning often involved members joking with one another. For example in 2009, they talked about the Selena altar of 2007 yet again. One of the freshmen girls said, "Didn't they make an altar to Selena one year?" Several students broke into song, "Bidibidibumbum." The room filled with laughter.

Although LU members were friendlier with each other than LL members were, LU members still focused their energies externally, planning events to expose the broader LAC community to Latino culture. During a fall meeting in 2009, for example, they discussed the organization's budget. Genova said, "We have over $1,700 left over. Contingent upon our balance, we will give money to Prof. Paredes for her event, but we need to plan. I think we should put on a big LU event." Cristina suggested, "We could have a Little Miss 15 Dance like the 'My Super Sweet 16' [TV] show." She added, "We can educate people about the *quinceñera*, for people who don't know what they are or didn't get one. We can have tiaras and cake, and have a special money dance." They all seemed to be very excited about the idea of having a *quinceñera* party. Javier asked, "Do we want this to be a party or like come learn about Latino culture?" Cristina said "Both." They discussed making *recuerdos* (gifts/souvenirs), having a cake, and dancing a waltz. Soe asked if they would play *banda* and maybe *merengue* or *bachata*.

On another occasion, members talked about hosting a Latino film series for the campus community. They talked about screening *Ladron que roba Ladron*, *Antes que Anochezca*, and *Sin Dejar Huella*. Bernardo asked whether they could bring snacks. Josiana suggested that they also have *churritos* and other *botanas* (snacks). Walter asked, "Do you mean like pork grinds?" Miranda said, "No, they aren't pork grinds but they are kinda orange?" Josiana adds, "I just think we should have Latino snacks." They decided on *agua fresca* or *jarritos*, chips, and cookies. Both the discussions about *quinceñera*-style party and the snacks for the film series reflected students' desire both to celebrate and enjoy their culture and to package and share it with the broader LAC community. These two goals drove most of LU's activities.

Like Latino Links, LU also dealt directly with administration and faculty, inviting them to LU events and supporting their endeavors, as noted above regarding their donation to Professor Paredes's event. But they also challenged the administration when their needs were not met. For example, LU took issue with the Latino Cultural Center (LCC) over Latino graduation and addressed their concerns to administrators directly. In 2010, for example, they sent the following email to the dean of students:[6]

Hello Dean Foster,

We received your email minutes before our LU meeting began. Thanks for your support. Like you mentioned, LU has been working on Latin@Grad and we were very excited because this was going to be an event designed by us, for us. Our concern is that our work will be dismissed and that LCC will take over the event and not take into account student input. Of course, we will want to keep as much of our ideas about the ceremony, and based on how the senior celebration has been handled this year, we will definitely want you and/or Natalia

Vera at a meeting with Nilda Valle and Hector to assure that this is a true collaboration. Can we schedule a meeting for this Monday, April 19, at 4:15pm, pending that you, Natalie Sandoval, Nilda Valle, and Hector are available?

In solidarity,
Latinos Unidos

The tone is direct and assertive; they clearly expected the administration to be responsive, even suggesting an exact time to meet. In another email, they addressed the director of the Latino Cultural Center directly, demanding that the students employed as mentors through the LCC meet with them and expressing a desire for more programming from the mentors:

Hello Nilda and Latin@ mentors,

As the programmers of Latinos Unidos, we would like to have a discussion about the role of Latin@ mentors and the work that we expect them to do on campus. We are disappointed that LU has had to be at the forefront of collaborating with the Latino Cultural Center, programming at Liberal Arts College, and outreaching to Latin@ students without the support of the mentors. We understand that, like the rest of us, you all are busy, but by taking up the paid position you are making a commitment to provide programming and services for the Latin@ community. It should not be our sole responsibility to program when there are people who are paid to do this. Can you all meet Friday April 16, at 4pm to talk about these issues?

In solidarity,
Latinos Unidos

They felt empowered to ask for their needs and the perceived needs of the Latino community on campus as a whole. Institutional players responded, and meetings were held.

JOINING LATINOS UNIDOS. Like new members of Latino Links, new members of LU were recruited via their assigned Latino mentors and upper classmen. Vanya explained, "I'm a freshman and I heard about it the first week through my mentor. He mentioned it, he's not part of it but he is thinking about joining too." Similarly, Genova shared, "I found out about the organization because I was paired up with my mentor, a sophomore, and she told me about it. She was Latina and also Muslim, so she didn't know if she wanted be part of a Latino group because she identifies with her Muslim religion a lot." The LCC-assigned mentor served as bridge to LU membership for several students. Other upperclassmen also connected new Latino student arrivals to Latinos Unidos. Ana told me, "My roommate and I became really close friends to seniors that were part of the LU. I was invited to the first meeting [and] they really made me feel comfortable." LAC students get close to upperclassmen, who invite them into the organizations. This mingling of students across different class levels is facilitated not only by the LCC mentor program, but also by the college's residential pattern: with 98 percent of students living on campus, they have ample opportunities to interact.

Furthermore, students stay in LU for several reasons: the connection to their peers, the desire to be involved, and a sense of commitment to making the Latino presence known on campus. LU members feel connected to one another, something that was evident when I asked them to tell me about their friends on campus. Ana said, "I feel close to friends that are in LU but I still call other people on campus friends," while Selena explained:

> I do enjoy myself at the meetings, it's not like it's purely an extracurricu-lar thing. Two of my really good friends do attend the meetings. After the group meeting we go back and talk about things. I don't think every-one in the meeting is really, really comfortable with each other in order to really say that we are really close and that it serves a total social pur-pose. But overall, I would say a little more than half of my friends on campus are Latino. I have a very ethnically diverse friend group. I have my Latina girls and then I have my multicultural friends.

Selena's words capture the social and interpersonal dimensions of LU well. They are friendly with one another and kind. However, they are not a completely cohesive and connected group. In contrast to the students at Research University (discussed in Chapter 3), for example, LU members do not provide each other with "a home away from home." But they are much friendlier with one another than members of Latino Links.

Beyond friendship, Josiana felt LU served a cultural purpose for Latino stu-dents themselves. She said, "I think it's really important to have a Latino organ-ization. Special places like this because there aren't that many Latinos on campus. We can do things that we think are fun and because Latinos are so diverse, we can learn about other Latinos." But seeking a cultural refuge wasn't the reason students stayed in LU; more than anything, members of LU wanted to be involved and saw part of a being in a Latino organization as performing a service. Cristina explained, "I kind of felt a responsibility to be in the club because of what the club does. As a Latina I thought I should try to be involved and help out the Latino community or whatever it is that LU was doing." Selena, on the other hand, was a bit critical of the sense of involvement students gain from their membership to Latinos Unidos: "I think LU provides a space for a limited cross-section of the Latino population to feel like they're active," she said. "I feel like it satisfies some sort of 'I am an activist Latino.'" She went even further to say that "I feel like the organization is sort of social but not in the way I thought it would be. I thought LU would be the most important community-building element in college. And it continues to not serve that purpose for me. I've gotten that in different organizations and communities at LAC." Selena is only one of many students at LAC who reported finding a sense of community at LAC broadly and not necessarily through their Latino organization.

Inside the Bubble

On the campus grounds of Liberal Arts College, students live close together for four years. They are connected through various forms of programming, residential patterns, ethnically based activities coordinated by the LCC, and relationships with faculty. In short, LAC students' social ties within the campus are high. Students are very busy with course work, programming, and other relationships on campus, so they spend little time off campus. Latino Links and Latinos Unidos have amicable relations. The boundaries between the organizations are minimal and being part of one organization does not preclude one from belonging to the other. Both organizations are focused on bringing Latino diversity to the broader LAC community, as summarized by Table 2.1. These organizations serve the same purpose and are similar, albeit one has a friendlier environment than the other.

Within the communal bubble, Latinos Unidos and Latino Links continue to evolve their organizational forms. During my fieldwork, LU switched from a nonhierarchical to a hierarchical structure, while LL began to move in the opposite direction. Of the six organizations studied, only those at LAC played with organizational styles, which is a testament to the left-leaning political ethos of Liberal Arts College (which I further describe in Chapter 6). On a campus where students pride themselves as being left-of-center and politically sophisticated,

---

TABLE 2.1

Inside the communal bubble of Liberal Arts College

Strength of student social ties within campus	High
Description of external campus boundaries	Rigid and enclosed
Description of internal organizational boundaries	Minimal and nonexclusive
Description of role of Latino organizations	Contributing to diversity on campus

it makes sense for them to consider alternative organizational forms. The students are experimenting with structures and agendas as they interact with faculty and administrators—sometimes asking for their assistance, other times demanding that they address their concerns. With the support of the "adults" on campus, these Latino organizations are invested in serving the LAC community and exposing it to who Latino people are. Chapters 5–7 show how Latino students showcase Latinidad within the bubble of LAC.

3

Conflict at Research University

Research University is located in a mainly white and Asian American, upper middle-class, politically conservative neighborhood. The neighborhood consists mostly of new real estate developments and is the epitome of suburbia, with manicured lawns and pristine roads. You can find virtually every corporate chain restaurant within a five-mile radius of campus and several high-end shopping malls within a ten-mile radius. This campus is relatively new, having been built less than one hundred years ago. Several of the buildings on campus were constructed to be sustainable and are made from recycled materials. During the two academic years, I spent at RU, there were on-going construction projects. On the periphery of the campus there are several large parking garages, but parking is relatively difficult to find and costs $8 a day. About 30 percent of the student body commutes. Wedged in between campus buildings is an open space that serves as a campus quad, where vendors sell merchandise and students blast music, set up club booths, and advertise their events.

RU is ranked among the top twenty public universities nationwide. It is a moderately selective school, accepting approximately 45 percent of applicants. Obtaining access to RU as a research site entailed a highly bureaucratic and long Institutional Review Board (IRB) process, and, as at the other campuses, I needed a faculty sponsor in order to conduct observations and talk to students. I reached out to six of the fourteen Latino organizations on campus: a fraternity, a sorority, a women's social-cultural club, a preprofessional organization, and the two organizations featured in this study, Latinos United for Action (LUA) and Latino Fellowship (LF). The Latino fraternity and sorority denied me access. They were reluctant to allow an outsider into their organization because, as one student told me, "The stuff we do is confidential." The women's group and preprofessional group allowed me access, as did Latino Fellowship, a co-ed social-cultural club, and LUA, a political organization. To keep the gender dynamics as equal as possible across my cases, I chose to study only co-ed organizations, and chose Latino Fellowship over the preprofessional organization because their meeting times did not conflict with those of LUA. LUA was crucial in my study because I was interested in the identity processes occurring in explicitly political organizations. Gaining access to LUA was not without challenges, as I describe later. First I discuss the demographic profile of the student body and other institutional dynamics of RU.

Who's on Campus and Why This Matters

Research University enrolls over 25,000 students, many of whom relocate for college. About 40 percent of students live on campus, including most first-year students and some second-year students; most juniors and seniors live in the surrounding area. Only 30 percent of enrolled students are considered permanent commuters, or those who do not relocate for college. The student body at RU is approximately 50 percent Asian American, 25 percent white, 11 percent Latino, and 2 percent African American. The Latino student members of the two organizations I studied, LUA and Latino Fellowship (LF), reported feeling racially isolated on campus mainly as a result of their underrepresentation. Only one student disclosed encountering overt racist remarks from non-Latino peers on campus (discussed in Chapter 5).

Most did, however, share an overwhelming sense of culture shock. For example, Suyeli, a member of LF observed that "there are only whites and Asians here. You feel lost. You feel like you stick out like a sore thumb. In LF, you see yourself in the members and you feel like you can connect. You know where they come from, and they have the same background and the same struggle." Suyeli highlights the hypervisibility that many Latinos on campus feel and the critical role her LF membership plays in her life on campus. Virtually, every student I interviewed at Research University shared similar stories of finding refuge in their Latino student organizations. Thalia, a member of LF, said her transition to RU "was . . . really hard" and that "LF made all the difference."

Organizational membership helped students deal with academic challenges as well. At times, students connected their sense of culture shock to their perceptions that they were not college-ready. Belinda, a member of LUA, explained: "Of course, you get a culture shock when you walk into classes and the majority is Asian. It was very hard. I guess, I didn't come from a very good high school so my writing wasn't good and my study ethics weren't, I guess, on point for college. I kind of had to learn all of that as soon as I got here and it was hard." Liliana, a member of LUA, also felt underprepared. She said: "I had a really difficult time transitioning to college because I went to a subpar high school. I had bad writing skills. I spent a lot of time trying to fit in and then realized I couldn't use my dinosaur computer. But then I found LUA and they helped me make

sense of my reality." For Liliana, finding a community in a Latino student organization helped her feel less alone and better able to cope with her academic struggles. Facing new educational environments, Latino students described experiences
of isolation and insecurity in the classroom. The underrepresentation of Latinos
gave my respondents a feeling of not belonging. Externally ascribed as "other" on
campus, they found refuge in Latino organizations. Students described their
respective Latino student organizations as "a home away from home, and a
family," and they considered co-members some of their closest friends on campus. RU students reported that their organizational experiences are their most
significant campus connections and social ties, a theme I address again this
later in this chapter.

On Academics

Unlike the Latino students at LAC, those at RU did not list faculty among the
critical components in their transition to campus life. In fact, academics rarely
came up during interviews and organizational events and meetings. The size
of classes at RU plays a role here, as there is a 19:1 student-faculty ratio and several
large lecture halls that seat over three hundred students. Students described
feeling anonymous in these large classes, and none disclosed having a close
relationship with a faculty member. On the other hand, at RU, most classes with
more than seventy students have a teaching assistant who is more likely to know
undergraduates by name.

Only two students mentioned academics or faculty during our interview.
Evelyn, a member of LUA, expressed disappointment with the education she
was receiving at RU. She explained: "The schoolwork hasn't been that bad. It's
really disappointing. I thought we were going to have really interesting discussions and talk about issues. I had a totally different perception about college.
People barely know your name here. The TAs, not to be mean, but sometimes
they just talk and talk and talk. Academically, it's been disappointing." Evelyn
was the only student to express disappointment in the lack of rigor or interesting discussions. Evelyn's feeling of "people barely knowing your name" is, however, comparable to other students' inability to name professors with whom they
had close relationships. Jennifer is the only student who had regular contact
with faculty, and this happened through her position as departmental representative of LUA in the Latino Studies department. LUA has had a student representative within the department (previously, a program of Latino Studies) for
over twenty years and LUA is the only student group to have such a position.[1]

DVR: You're the department rep? What's that like?

JENNIFER: It's ok, but I know they don't want us there.

DVR: How do you know?

JENNIFER: They haven't expressed it to me specifically. But in the past, other reps have been told that they don't want LUA taking over the meeting or trying to change things that they don't want changed. Some of the professors question why LUA would be at the faculty meeting. Some professors have asked me "What is the purpose of you being here?" So, we explained to them that we're willing to help the department; we are not trying to change things. I've gotten to know the professors a little more. I've learned how to speak to people a little better ever since then. I've gotten some communication skills. I do get asked for my opinion sometimes. They ask us why students drop classes and they ask us about evaluations.

Jennifer is treated with suspicion by some faculty and asked mainly to remain quiet during meetings. However, Jennifer's experience as representative to the faculty gave her real benefits, such as improving her communication skills. This type of skill development is a constant in LAC's small classes and within their student-faculty relationships. However, Jennifer's experience is unusual at RU.

Faculty confirmed students' sentiments about the student-faculty relationship. I asked RU faculty the same questions I asked professors at LAC. Recall that LAC's Professor Paredes spoke in depth about her students' experiences in the classroom and their overall transition to campus. I asked Professor of Latino Studies Hector Jasso, who has taught at RU since 1969 (when he was hired as a graduate student), to speak about the contemporary Latino student.

DVR: What are the Latino students are RU like?

HECTOR JASSO (HJ): I get the sense that the question of immigration is much more salient. They are more interested in immediate issues. When I was growing up, the transnational was not a question. I went back to history—the Mexican American War and racism. Our socialization was that; we had a barrio consciousness. The police and schools were the problems, not *la migra*. It was very localized. Now we have to take a broader look. I find students accepting the broader look. It was not something that would have resonated in 1971.

DVR: So you think they're really interested in immigration issues?

HJ: Yes, it's a real concern for them.

DVR: Other than their political concerns, what are the students like? Like, how do you think they look to you as a Latino faculty member?

HJ: I have no idea what students want from me.

Professor Jasso spoke about his curriculum and how he believed it resonated with students. However, when probed to discuss students further, he had little to share. Given the 19:1 student- faculty ratio at RU, it is not surprising that faculty had few close relationships with their undergraduate students.

Multicultural Resources and Programming

Research University, like LAC, promotes diversity through several programs available to Latinos and other underrepresented students. First, there is a Latino residential hall on campus. Samuel Navarro, the academic counselor who runs the hall, explained that he admits between fifteen and twenty students per year on the basis of their application essays. He runs programming about Latino culture, and residents engage in community service such as beach clean-ups. He also indicated that he admits non-Latino students as well, observing, "I didn't want the house to be a LUA house or a Chicano house exclusively." Beside Samuel Navarro, there are also a few other Latino staff on campus, including a dean, an associate dean, and a high-level administrator.

Ernesto Telles, the associate dean, runs a summer program for first-generation college students, which is intended to track them into graduate schools. This program gives the students research experience and prepares them for understanding what graduate school might be like. This selective program, which serves about twenty students every summer, is not exclusively for Latinos. Telles explained: "I've been accused of making it a Latino organization. It's two-thirds Latinos. I demand they do research. They [the students] want to be in sororities, etc. I just want them to expand their experiences. I want to get them to leave home. Go to graduate school." Ernesto Telles is committed to mentoring first-generation college students, many of them Latinos, and getting them into the graduate school pipeline. However, he can admit only twenty students a year, just as Samuel Navarro can host only twenty students a year in the Latino residential hall. Thus, while Research University offers great programs, student seats are limited. Moreover, while some students are not aware of the opportunities, others who are may not receive mentorship through the application processes. In contrast to their peers at a place like LAC, Latino students at RU are not automatically pulled into these programs and other non-ethnic professional and academic programs.

Research University has a Multicultural Center (MCC) that recognizes five core student organizations, one representing each of the five major minority groups on campus (Asian American, African American, Native American, Muslim American, and Latinos). LUA is the official Latino organization, and it has ties to the campus activism of the late 1960s and 1970s and, therefore, a historically protected role in the MCC. The MCC provides LUA with meeting space and an office and expects it to represent Latinos on campus, as well as to lead and plan Latino Heritage Month, Día de los Muertos, and Latino graduation. As a result, LUA leaders typically have a close working relationship with the staff of the MCC and even hold paid internships within the center. By contrast, Latino Fellowship has no standing historical tie to the MCC. LF is primarily a cultural organization and collaborates with the MCC only to schedule meeting space

and add its events to the Latino Heritage Month calendar. Nor does it have a
designated office on campus. The MCC's differential treatment of LUA and other
Latino organizations on campus unintentionally fosters competition for resources
among Latino student organizations. The conflict between LUA and LF shapes
their interactions and leads them to differentiate themselves along political
(Chapter 6) and identity lines (Chapter 5). Students at RU construct identities
(Chapter 5) and worldviews (Chapter 7) within a climate of intra-Latino organizational conflict.

Organizations

Latino Fellowship (LF) and Latinos United for Action (LUA) have both been active
on the RU campus for at least fifteen years and have the largest membership
base among the Latino organizations there. In the process of gaining access to
LF and LUA, my initial contact was similar with both organizational representatives whom I emailed; they responded promptly. LF was open and excited about
the prospect of my attending their meetings, while LUA treated me with quite a
bit of skepticism. Both organizations, however, were described by their members as "a home away from home, and a family." Students considered co-members
their closest friends on the RU campus. Students in both groups reported that
their experiences as members of these organizations create their most significant campus connections and social ties. In the following sections, I will say
more about my initial entry into these organizations, how that reflected their
respective organizational culture and history, and how students feel about their
"campus homes." I also discuss how these "homes" develop as exclusive spaces
and how tensions between the nonpolitical and the political organization remain
a constant.

Latino Fellowship

I contacted Cruz, the president of Latino Fellowship, before the fall 2008 semester
began. He responded promptly and invited me to join the first meeting of the
semester, which was held in the conference room of the Multicultural Center.
As I approached the room, a tall young man was holding the door open and greet-
ing everyone with a hug and kiss on the cheek—including me. He then asked for
my name, and when I told him, he said, "Wait, are you the grad student?" I said
yes, and he said, "Oh wow, I thought you were a freshman." I chuckled and assured
him I wasn't. He then asked me to join everyone and indicated that he would be
introducing me. I sat in the back of the room, in the last of four rows of chairs,
providing seating for approximately 60 people.

The meeting began with the leadership (the board), wearing blue jeans
and t-shirts with a pirate printed on them, introducing themselves to everyone.
The president, secretary, representatives for external and internal affairs, and

treasurer introduced themselves. Once they had all stated how long they had been part of LF, their majors, and year at RU, they called me up to introduce myself. I told them about my research and encouraged them to talk to me about any questions or concerns they might have. Cruz asked the attendees to give me a round of applause, which was pretty loud. (I counted about 60 people in the room at this point.) He then encouraged all students to get to know me since it was nice to have a graduate student around. After I sat down, a young woman made an announcement about raising money for the Boys and Girls Club, which needed funds to buy soccer equipment. The president interjected, reminding members that "it's not mandatory." The young woman passed around a collection box.

Next Cruz and Mireya (the external affairs representative) played a video, which was about ten minutes long and presented various scenes in which the board members acted. The video showed how college and high school are different and alike by juxtaposing a scene of a mother waking up her daughter for school and a student going into a friend's dorm room to wake her. It also included a scene in which people were trying to learn how to dance *bachata*. Another scene, with the *Friends* theme song playing, showed group members assisting others with their homework. Then each of the board members shared his or her favorite memory in Latino Fellowship. When the video ended, there was a knock at the door. Cruz said, "Oh, it looks like some of our homeboys from [Latino fraternity] are here." A group of young men came in, and one said, "Can we serenade you?" Cruz asked the group, "Should we let them?" Everyone clapped, and they began to sing. They had two guitars and six of them sang "Vale mas un buen amor," a Vicente Fernandez song that is also the theme song of the telenovela *Fuego en la sangre*.

When the Latino fraternity singers finished, and now twenty minutes into the meeting, Cruz asked everyone to introduce themselves by saying their name, year, major, where they are from, and a highlight of their summer. With around one hundred people at the meeting (more students had trickled into the room), this took a while. Most students said their highlight was going somewhere local—within a two-hour drive—usually to a beach town, or getting good grades, or coming to a summer bridge program for first-generation college students. I took notice of two very different responses from two girls who didn't appear to be Latinas but rather looked phenotypically white. They mentioned getting a new Acura TL and going to Barbados to learn how to surf. They were outliers and did not attend subsequent meetings.

After all the students had introduced themselves, Cruz said, "LF is a cultural group that experiences unity through cultural diversity," and added that the organization is fifteen years old. The secretary, Gloria, then explained that in honor of the anniversary, they wanted to have a *quinceñera* theme for their winter formal and that they had chosen pirates because they like a pirate song that mentions the number 15. Gloria continued to list all the social events the board had planned for the academic year: night club parties with a group at another local university, a three-day winter retreat, and a karaoke night with the Chinese Language Club, where LF members would sing Chinese songs while the Chinese students sang Spanish songs. Mireya explained that LF would also be doing more community service. Cruz interjected again, saying, "There's no obligation to participate." Cruz joked about LF as a good place to "check each other out," emphasizing that men and women could meet here.

Once LF's activities for the year were listed, the officers sent students on a scavenger hunt. At this time, Cruz came to the back to talk to me. He was very friendly and told me that the important thing to know about LF was that it is a "no commitment, no obligation" organization. He explained that while there are many organizations on campus that either have fees or are political, LF likes to create a very open space, and it requires nothing from their members. He emphasized that the group wanted to have many more intercultural events in the coming year and build more connections with other cultural groups on campus.

Every subsequent meeting had a playful and light-hearted tone and was organized similarly. The meeting always began with introductions in which students gave their names and their majors and then answered a specific question, like what is your favorite ice cream flavor? What place do you want to visit most? What is your biggest turnoff? These changed every week. They then discussed upcoming events and ended each meeting with either a game such as a scavenger hunt or charades, or a cultural presentation about a specific Latin American country. A student with heritage from that country usually brought in artifacts from home and food to share with the club members.

After the initial meeting attended by almost a hundred students, there were usually about twenty to forty people in attendance at subsequent meetings. I asked Cruz about the membership base, and he responded: "We have forty active members, more or less. They come to at least half of the meetings throughout the year. Inactive members—I would say we have about a hundred or hundred and twenty—people that go to our events, people that go to our parties, people that are associated but drop off every now and then." The proportion of students who attended Latino Fellowship meetings was only about a fourth of the total students the group reached with their social events and programming. LF hosted a party at a night club every academic term, held a winter retreat for members, and hosted a day-long event called Encuentro Latino showcasing Latino culture to the campus community once every academic year. Mireya explained the funding sources for LF:

> We don't get money from the school. We do all of our fundraising on our own. The only thing that they do give us money for is for Encuentro Latino. It's a free event open to anyone on campus so we ask for funds,

but they don't say like "Here's eight hundred dollars for Encuentro Latino." We have to give receipts and get reimbursed. All the money we have is because we raised it on our own; club events, TV tapings, selling food, and like the LF formal that's a fundraising event. All the money that we raised throughout the year is to put on events and also for next year's board.

Thus, the funding stream for both LF and LUA differs from that of the organizations at LAC, which make annual budget requests, providing a tentative list of itemized events for the upcoming year and receiving funds for the amount requested. As we see in Mireya's explanation above, LF must request funding on an event-by-event basis and then provide receipts for reimbursement. At RU, these requests are presented to the student government, which controls a pocket of money for student programming. LF makes only one request per year and this is for Encuentro Latino.

When I asked members what they considered to be the most important event LF puts on, Gloria said: "Well, it depends. A lot of people go to Winter Retreat. The members start to get to know each other in the fall. And in the retreat, you get to know each other intimately and you do form tighter bonds. But it should also be Encuentro Latino because it's during this time when we bring cultural awareness to the campus." Gloria believes that the winter retreat is the most significant event LF hosts because of the friendships cultivated in that space. However, she has a sense that bringing cultural awareness to the campus should be put at the top of the list. This is the official message about LF, even according to Associate Dean Ernesto Telles, who observed, "they bring culture but not in a political way." Other students also communicated LF's role in raising cultural awareness while emphasizing the importance of solidifying friendships.

DVR: What is the most important event LF hosts or does on campus?

MIREYA: First thing, I would say, it's a social club. It's not for protesting, it's not for a specific career like psychology or business. It's just to, you know, hang out, to have somebody kind of from your own background. It's a very open club because we don't just have Latinos; there are some other ethnicities too. We're very welcoming. We don't just want to learn about you, we want to learn about where you come from. Cultural presentations are in our motto. It defines us; we are social; we're cultural. So pretty much those are the main themes we focus on. It's so the members learn and be aware and pretty much learn something about different cultures and experience something different.

Differentiating LF's programming from that of other Latino organizations on campus and emphasizing that LF is not political or preprofessional, Mireya underscored the role of culture and acceptance. Another student, Lissandra, expressed similar thoughts when asked the same question:

> I think we make friendships and try to be very culturally aware about accepting other people, and we accept people no matter who they are. We try to unify and make sure that people feel comfortable with each other. We try to make sure people know a little bit about culture. We think that people should know each other and have a second family here. And we really try to provide awareness. We do party as well but we do a lot of bonding.

Lissandra echoes Mireya's words about acceptance and emphasizes how friendships are cultivated through bonding, even using the words "second family."

I continued this line of questioning with others, including Cruz.

DVR: What is the most important event LF hosts or does on campus?

CRUZ: I think our goal is to promote cultural diversity. Rather, I'm sorry, to promote unity through cultural diversity and awareness. I think we do a good job at that because I think by becoming aware different cultures, of different ethnicities and everything, I think they [members] become more comfortable with it and, because of that, that kind of brings diversity. It brings people to get along better.

Although cultural diversity awareness is a stated goal of LF, the LF respondents overwhelmingly mentioned the winter retreat as the most important event. The cultivation of friendships trumped showcasing Latino culture to the campus writ large. As Cruz explained:

> By far, the most important and the most fun thing we do is actually our winter retreat. Latino Fellowship is just a social organization, really. Like I've been saying, there's no affiliation with anything. It's just to be, just to be social, that is the epitome of what the organization is. It's a family, it's a close unit. What happens at retreat, there's no mistaking it, it's what the organization is actually about. I've been to three of them and I want to say that I've been to at least maybe a hundred events that RU has sponsored [and] our retreat is by far the best I've ever been to. Whether I was part of it, part of the committee or whether I was just there. The activities that we have, just the talks that people have, the sharing that people, the friends that you make, it's three days but the friends that you make there usually last. I mean, for me, I made a couple of friends my second year and I'm still friends with them.

Pablo echoed Cruz's enthusiasm, saying that "the winter retreat allows us to bond. During the day, we have a bunch of activities. They're kind of silly games." What he emphasized, though, was that the connections you make in LF are very different. You get to know people very personally. We always bond after the retreat. It's amazing; you get to know people really well. You might see them all quarter but [at] retreat you become good friends. Like my friend, Mark: we didn't really know each other, but after retreat we lived together.

Even outside of conversations about the retreat, members raved about the bonds they felt with each other. Tania explained:

I've noticed that LF is something that's very, very different than what anyone else can offer. It's hard to explain—like the bonds that you make with the people. These people are people that I'm going to talk to for the rest of my life. It's a family environment. LF is like my home away from home. Every time I'm stressed and I think, ok, who can I call? It's someone from LF, like Cruz. Every time I need something, every time I'm super stressed out.

Like Tania, other students also highlighted the supportive role of LF. They also replied in similar ways when I asked them how embedded LF was in their social life on campus and if their friends were in the organization. Thalia said, "Yes, it's a family away from home. All my friends are in LF and we hang out a lot. And we see each other around a lot." Similarly, Gloria said, "All my friends are there. It [LF] does define me because it's the people I like being around." Mireya said about LF, "Yeah that's how I met most of my friends so LF has a very strong relationship with my social life." In reply to another question, about how LF shaped students' experiences on campus, Cruz offered:

When I came in, I wasn't too caring, I wasn't too affectionate. Spending a lot of time with people that are in organizations, just being in a friendly environment has kind of helped me become that person. I think that's probably the biggest thing, just being social, just being friendly, being affectionate toward anybody, and I think that's just the personality of the organization. We don't have any kind of, I guess you could say, try-outs, any requirements or anything and that's mostly because if your personality doesn't fit a friendly, welcoming personality, then you kind of leave it on your own and if it does, you stay, so I think that's the biggest way that Latino Fellowship has reflected me or I reflect Latino Fellowship, rather.

And within this friendly environment LF has also created a light-hearted atmosphere where joking and banter, sometimes including sexual innuendo, are commonplace. There is constant heterosexual flirting. When I asked students if LF members date one another, most said that they don't but that they do flirt. "Maybe some of the guys think about it, but I don't see any dating," Cruz observed. "They do flirt though." Pablo confirmed, saying that "I don't date in LF, but I check out the girls. They're cute!" Lissandra added that "people sometimes hook up," and Deidra said that "I think some people in LF date each other. I think it's a little weird. I think people do kind of hook up too."

Although LF seemed like friendly utopia for its members, I wanted to make sure there were no hidden disagreements. Only one member of the leadership, Gloria, acknowledged any, but her description of them made it clear that they were logistical, not earth-shattering. "As a board we do have some different opinions. We rarely fight since it's mostly girls on the board. At the beginning of the year we were stressed out because we had no money. But we made up all the money with fundraisers." Moreover, insofar as there is any tension in LF, it is external tension, owing to its relationship with LUA, which is a very different kind of organization, as I quickly saw.

Latinos United for Action

Latinos United for Action required me to meet with the leadership board before allowing me access to their meetings. I met with the co-chairs, Liliana and Lalo, the fundraiser chair, the external chair, the internal chair, the secretary/historian, the outreach chair, the community and labor chair, the social-publicity chair, and the student services chair in LUA's office, located in the MCC. The office, which is labeled with LUA's name on the outside, has two desks, three chairs, and many politically motivated and Latino posters on the walls. All of the leaders crammed into the room and somehow managed to close the door. They began the meeting by asking me about my research interests. Liliana took the lead in asking questions. I mentioned how I'd like to know how student groups were organizing across groups and campuses. They informed me that several years ago, a graduate student had gotten involved in their organization and "infiltrated."[2] They explained that the "infiltration" led them to lose members and have lots of tensions. Lalo said, "We want you to be here because we think this seems like important research, but we can't have another infiltration." I emphasized to the group that I was not there to sway or shape their organization in any way. One of the students asked if I could stay quiet and maybe sit in the back. I conceded: I would be a nonparticipant observer. After they were thoroughly convinced of my commitment, they welcomed me to attend the second meeting of the school year.

Before leaving the MCC, Liliana stayed behind and told me that I had met most of the leaders with the exception of the leaders of support groups for women, men, and LGBT students. She said they had about thirty to forty active members. I also learned that LUA raised most of its funds but also received some money from the student senate for programs that are open to the entire campus. A week later I attended the meeting, along with approximately forty-five students. LUA had an agenda printed on a white board, which read: "Intros—new people, Reports, Ice Breaker, Workshop, Announcements." I arrived a bit early, so Liliana and Lalo greeted me, telling me that after all the committees made their reports, I could address the group and tell them about my research. I thanked them and sat in the back. They then removed all the chairs so everyone could sit on the floor. There was a television at the front to the room. I watched members as they walked in and noticed the majority were wearing Converse sneakers, blue jeans, and either organizational t-shirts or t-shirts with EZLN logos.[3] Several students also carried *morrales*.[4] Once the room was substantially full, the leaders began the unity clap, a ritual associated with a variety of unions and movements.[5] All members joined them. Carlos (external chair) took the floor and greeted everyone. He invited the approximately ten people who had not been at the previous week's meeting to introduce themselves. Then Liliana announced that there would be a multicultural leaders' retreat (hosted by the MCC) during the upcoming week and that it would cost $60 per person, so all those who wanted to come should find a sponsor. Lalo announced that Estelle had had a birthday the week before and brought out a card that people had signed the previous week. He handed it to Estelle and asked everyone to sing happy birthday. Liliana announced that the Latino Studies open house would happen later that week and there would be a *son jarocho* (folk music)[6] performance.

Next, each chair stood up and gave an update. First, the internal chair, Maximiliano, urged people to run for the legislative council (RU's schoolwide student government). He advertised the open secretary position, which paid $77 a term. Second, the student services chair, Alicia, announced the organizational mentorship program. She asked anyone who had participated in the program to speak about their experience. One woman in the back said, "My mentor and I got along great; she and I are still good friends. She introduced me to the organization and she's about to finish grad school. This is a great way to make lifelong contacts." Alicia then told all who were interested in the mentor-mentee program to contact her after the meeting and fill out an interest sheet. Although mentorship programs are created by staff at Liberal Arts College, Research University does not provide such a program, so LUA members create their own. Then Alicia told everyone about the interest in creating a notes, tests, and book archive for members of the organization and asked everyone who had resources to contribute to see her after the meeting.

Next, Liliana requested that the leaders of the three support groups (men, women, and LBGTQ) stand up. They were introduced but did not say anything. Liliana announced that the outreach chair was not at the meeting, but that, later, she would bring information about the high school program. The community and labor committee chair, Evelyn, spoke about the boycott against Forever 21 (a retailer of women's fashion), explaining that the company "has been giving money to the mayor and now they [Forever 21] want a local farm's land." She added that people were looking into the donations made to the mayor and that she would bring more information to the next meeting. The fundraising chair announced an upcoming *carne asada* (barbecue) and said she would pass out volunteer sheets soon. Lastly, the co-chairs urged all members to attend next week's meeting because it would be the annual organizational open house.

The group then transitioned to an ice breaker. The leaders gave all students a sheet of paper and told them to walk around the room and get to know each other's names and write those names on the paper. This exercise went on for fifteen minutes. When it was over, the co-chairs stood in the front and asked members to discuss what it means to be Chicano. The community and labor chair, Evelyn said, "Chicano is a very political word, and it's not just a Mexican American. It's someone who fights and talks about issues such as sexism and the Forever 21 stuff." Then a young woman in the back raised her hand. She said, "I'm Central American and I used to think that only Mexicans could be Chicano, but now I identify as Chicano because it's about fighting for equality."

After this statement, Maximiliano, the internal chair, went to the front of the room with another young woman. He transitioned the group into the workshop of the day, telling the members that it was time to discuss the Chicano movement of the 1960s and 1970s. He explained that "the Chicano movement was several acts and some are unconnected, but they all fought against oppression." He listed a few, including the student movement, which fought for educational access," but chose to speak in greater depth about the United Farm Workers movement, which fought against exploitation and poor living conditions, and to describe its five-year strike and coalition with the Filipino Farmers Union. Then, a young woman spoke about the fortieth anniversary of the East Los Angeles high school protests by student who demanded better conditions in school[7] and showed about ten minutes of a video about them on the television in the room.

After the video both Maximiliano and the young woman attempted to start a discussion about it. One young woman in the back said, "I wonder what their goals were and if they achieved any of them?" One young man said, "I went to school in south central LA and I didn't get a good quality education. The schools aren't good and I know that the students adapt and they act up. But there are still a lot of problems in schools." Liliana spoke up and said, "Well, the movement was able to change the racist tracking, but there is still a lot of vocational training in urban areas, less AP classes in urban schools and a lot of military recruitment." Carlos stood up in the front and mentioned the fortieth anniversary of the student movement. He explained that "it started when the Olympics were going on in Mexico City and stuff was happening all over the world." Carlos asked everyone to break up into groups of five. He asked people to discuss their view of Chicanismo before and after the day's discussion.

I picked one group to observe. One young man said, "I'm from Ecuador and now I know that Chicano isn't just for Mexicans; it's about political values to change and work together for same goals." Evelyn said, "I used to think it was a nationalistic term, but now I see it as political goals and higher education." Another student said that "people are friendly here and they took me in, and we are working together for the needs of others." The fourth student in the group said, "It's not just about the social and family but about struggles." Carlos asked each group to report to the whole group. One student said, "You never hear about the Chicano movement, mostly the black movement." Liliana said, "I used to think that Chicano was a negative word especially since my parents are from Mexico and they said it meant ungrateful. Now I think it's about workers' struggle and education." A young woman from a third group said, "I learned that this organization isn't just about Mexicans, but it's how it portrays itself. But if we were in New York, it would be more Puerto Ricans. Like, for example, it portrays Mexican issues like Día de los Muertos, although it's open to people of all backgrounds." Liliana raised her hand and said, "Just to add, people all over Latin America celebrate Día de los Muertos." Carlos interrupted and asked people to attend the Día de los Muertos planning meeting and said the LUA meeting was officially over. Despite the workshop about Chicanismo and a favorable review of the label, few students I interviewed used the word to identify themselves. (I say more about this in Chapter 5.)

Latinos United for Action is self-described as a multifaceted organization that works on several issues. In Evelyn's words, "We are a cultural, social, political, and educational organization. We do outreach and social events. My emphasis is outreach but we also do workshops that are educational and fundraisers. We do go out and do club events." Evelyn understands LUA as an ambitious organization that promotes a vision of itself as serving multiple purposes on campus and beyond. The outreach that Evelyn mentioned is to the community outside the campus. And when she said, "We do go out and do club events," she was talking about socializing. Gilda similarly described LUA as "a social, cultural, political, and educational organization that works toward helping on issues that Latino students face in the community and on-campus." She further noted that "it's also about educating the campus community about these issues, and I think it's also about fighting for social justice. I think it's a form of campus retention because it makes people feel connected to the campus." Lalo continued in a similar vein, boasting: "What don't we do? We are a student organization that promotes culture and promotes programs about higher education. We put on events to get students of color into higher education. We try to promote awareness about political issues and culture on campus. There are two avenues that we do: promote things on campus and try to get more students into higher education."

When I asked students what they considered to be LUA's most important activities, Carlos replied:

> I would say our high school day-long event. This is the organizational event that we work hardest [on]. Because at RU we have to have programs that are geared toward students on campus, but this event is for potential students. It takes a lot of preparation. We let people know that we are here to help and we prepare them. What they need to know to get into college. It makes you feel really good that they really appreciate it and they send emails and look forward to seeing us next year if—when they graduated and get in.

Like Carlos, Evelyn also expressed excitement with the outreach work LUA did with high school students. She said, "I'm in love with our high school program right now. Students who are interested slightly in going to college, that program is a great success for them." LUA members saw their outreach programs having results and impacting the lives of the Latino high school students they sought to serve. Deidra, who was a member of both LF and LUA for a year, also recognized LUA's efforts to focus on promoting educational attainment. She observed, "I think they [LUA] try to focus on higher education stuff. I know that they really focused on getting other Latinos into education. I know they also mentor high school students during the day-long event."

In addition to the perceived positive effects of LUA on high school students, members also detailed many positive influences on their own personal development. Liliana, the co-chair, claimed to have gained organizing skills, learning to work under pressure and "how to get things done" within LUA. She added, "I learned about my leadership potential, which will help me throughout life." Other students, too, saw LUA as having an impact on their approach to work and even helping them find a path forward after graduation. I asked Alicia, "How important has LUA been to your overall undergraduate experience at RU?" She replied: "It's been super important. It's been a huge priority. I've grown here a lot and I have really found my passion. And I really like working with my community. I think now, leaving RU, I will always be an active member in my community. It's really helped me get in touch with my cultural roots. Even though I came from a predominantly Latino community, I found out a lot more here about my culture." Alicia has gained connections to her cultural identity and community and has declared a lifetime commitment to these connections. Alicia's words confirm Associate Dean Ernesto Telles's perception that LUA "fortifies identity."

Other members saw their experience in LUA as also helping them build their resumes. Gilda said:

> I think it's been essential in getting access to different knowledge of developing as a leader. It also gave me knowledge about how the university

system runs and it gave me access to mentorship. I know that all of these positions helped me and prepared me for graduate school. When I got to college, it was more like I had just made it. It [LUA] gave me all these opportunities to become involved and kind of develop skills as a person and as a leader. When I look at my resumé, I think, "Wow, I guess I have done a lot and it's because of LUA."

Similarly, Kenya credited LUA with her development: "My experience would've been a 180 without LUA. I think for personal growth it's been very important. I think for my education, it's been very important but it has affected me academically. I think if I wasn't in LUA, I would be doing much better academically." This drawback squares with Ernesto Telles's observation that "the students that are successful do not get involved in these student organizations. And I don't know what that means." Telles had a particularly negative assessment of LUA, which I discuss in more detail later in this chapter. For her part, Evelyn called attention to the workload that the LUA leadership faces, and this may be a reason why students who are actively involved seem to suffer academically. She said:

> Some of the older members feel like they've already paid their dues to the organization and they've left. I think that leaves the newer members without guidance. I think part of LUA is very stressful and you get tired. I think LUA is about growth, and some people feel like they've gotten enough from the organization and they want to expand, and I think that's the point of graduation. I know some people are doing research and they're really sucked into the research. I mean I wanted to do research too. But I need to put something into the organization.

Evelyn, like Kenya, may have suffered academically as well due to her leadership in LUA. She had chosen the organization over research experience, and for her, as for other leaders, this also meant feeling pressure to keep up LUA's ambitious programmatic agenda.

Aside from such drawbacks, LUA is similar to LF in serving as a "home away from home" for its members. Gilda talked broadly about Latino student organizations, saying, "Regardless what they do and what they define themselves as, I think their unwritten goal is to give students a place to feel home on campus and they develop leadership and really think it is important." Lalo commented that "LUA is a sense of *familia*. A lot of my friends are in LUA. And I have a lot of close friends in LUA and most of my friends at RU are in the organization." This was also true for most members of LUA. In Belinda's words, "All of my friends are in LUA." Evelyn echoed the point: "All of my friends at RU are part of LUA. I don't really have many other friends at RU that are not part of organization." Kenya agreed: "All of my friends are in LUA. I think few of us have friends outside of LUA." Carlos observed that while he had some friends from home, "I would say 75 percent of my friends are in LUA."

Although LUA appears to be a safe place and a home for its members, the organization had quite a negative reputation on campus. I asked members to talk about this. Gilda said, "Before I joined, I heard really dumb things like 'They're crazy, radical, and racist.' I heard that we were Mexican-centric. It was a lot of stupid, negative things that really had no merit." Evelyn expressed similar ideas: "When I tell people I'm in LUA, they think I'm crazy. They think we hate all white people. They think we are racist group." Like Gilda, Evelyn asserted that these critiques of LUA were unfounded. In the next sections, I describe the various difficulties that LUA faces, given its negative reputation.

Tensions between Latinos United for Action and Latino Fellowship

Membership in both groups, Latinos United for Action and Latino Fellowship, was seen as incompatible by Latino students interviewed. The exclusivity of these organizations was partly a result of university programming. Each organization occupies a different space on campus based on its history and structural incorporation. Latinos United for Action (LUA) is a national student organization, founded during the civil rights era, with chapters across the southwest and an explicitly political mission. LUA has a historical legacy and is formally recognized by the administration at Research University as evidenced by the campus resources available to LUA in the Multicultural Center and the MCC's recognition of the LUA as the representative Latino organization on campus. LUA's and LF's differential access to campus resources fuels their competitive and often antagonistic relationship, as do organizational sagas of what Deidra called "old beefs," but without going into any details.

When I began my fieldwork at RU, I met three young women, Deidra, Guadalupe, and Micaela, who joined both Latino Fellowship and Latinos United for Action. Guadalupe said of her experience with both, "They know I'm in both groups. Latino Fellowship members say, 'I didn't know you were radical.' LUA members say, 'Oh, you like to party, too.'" Each group perceived the other as quite distinct from itself. As a member of LF and LUA, Gloria noted, "I've heard that LF and LUA don't get along. Because we're on different sides of the spectrum. Some of our [LF] members are in LUA, so I don't think there is drama. We're just more social, social cultural, not political, radical." Eventually, though, both left LUA with negative feelings, as did Deidra, who in her second year had both joined the board of LF and taken charge of planning the Día de los Muertos event for LUA. The latter, however, became fraught with conflict and led her to leave LUA. As she outlined the circumstances, she represented LUA at the meeting of the United Latino Organizations (ULO), an umbrella council of all Latino organizations on campus which met once every academic term to outline all the events that each of the Latino organizations was planning. When ULO began to plan a combined Día de los Muertos event, its advertising flier in particular angered LUA, as Deidra explained:

> The flier said LUA presents Día de los Muertos with the support of the United Latino Organizations. They [LUA] got to the point that they were really upset with me. The president said this had never happened before. I was part of more than one club so I didn't have a problem with it. I didn't really understand it. But they made a really big deal about doing that. Then they pulled out their old LUA school binders to talk about how Día de los Muertos will always be theirs. I guess that LUA wants to hold onto that event. But ULO wanted to make it bigger.

While Deidra felt that including the name of ULO on the advertisement should be no problem, LUA members used their records to prove their historical precedent in planning the event on campus. The reaction of LUA leadership ultimately led Deidra to leave the organization. "This made me feel like I'm obviously not a member of LUA. They made me feel like it was my fault and I messed up. I think they're afraid that people will slack off. They always say things like 'We have to pick up your slack.' I think it's the same thing at Latino graduation, because LUA is in charge. But I think, 'Why can't another organization plan it?' Their answer is 'It's always been LUA's event.'" Other students also perceived LUA as holding onto events and not collaborating with other Latino organizations or ULO. Lissandra, for one, thought that

> certain LUA members are not the nicest. I once said something to a girl that knew I was in Latino Fellowship and she was not very friendly. I don't even know why people don't like each other. That's drama that happened before. I won't get into it. Sometimes I would say, "Oh come to this event, we're having a fundraiser," etcetera. One time I went to LUA meeting and they noticed I was new and they asked me to introduce myself. I was there for a while and I kind of feel bad because I had to leave. I started working at the Grill and one of the girls told me about the meeting. But she also told me that she didn't really like things that LUA would do and say. I remember going to a meeting for Day of the Dead and they said something really rude. They didn't want anyone to help them plan the event. I thought, "Seriously, this is why no one likes you and you wonder why people don't want to support you or include you in things." I also know someone else who had a really bad issue with them.

Lissandra had a lot to say about LUA. She talked about LUA's bad reputation on campus for not being "very nice," but despite this she attended a meeting. She also talked about LUA's resistance to collaborating with ULO and the organizations within it. As the president of LF, Cruz, too, wanted to collaborate with LUA. He said, "We've been talking to them a little bit. One of their events overlaps with our Encuentro Latino, and I think we're going to see probably what we can negotiate events and dates, maybe collaborate a little bit." The groups did eventually coordinate dates for their events, but they did not collaborate. One group hosted its event a day earlier.

What did LUA members make of Latino Fellowship, and vice versa? Jennifer, a member of LUA, said, "I went to an LF meeting once. I didn't really like it as much. It didn't really feel like there was a purpose. It seemed mostly social. Which is ok, but I wanted purpose." Evelyn, a member of LUA offered a broader critique:

> Before, going to college was about educating yourself and doing stuff for your community. But the media now talks about college as partying, joining sororities, and getting drunk every night. And it's not really like that, and people who do it every night, well I don't think that's a good experience. In Latino Fellowship, you do nothing but socialize. We have a member that goes to both meetings, and she says that in LUA, she actually has to think about things and that turns off a lot of people. I think they're leaning towards Latino Fellowship because they want to socialize. Everybody has different needs. I wanted to become more politicized.

Evelyn's view of LF as being merely social was also shared by other members who felt alone in organizing for Latinos on campus. Kenya, a member of LUA, said "I look at the black political organization and they have the support of their Greek organizations. We [LUA] don't really have the support of anyone else. I think it's just us doing all this active stuff on campus. Latinos on this campus will avoid us because we are political." Like Kenya, Gilda, another member of LUA, was also disappointed with the lack of solidarity around political issues:

> I feel like the Latino community on campus can use its power. They could get a lot done if they united. Like for example, we could do a campus campaign on the Dream Act. I think maybe we should do a rally, but sometimes they think having rallies are too crazy. We brought it up in a ULO meeting and they said that it was cool but then nobody wanted to do it. And then somebody had the idea of doing a Latino festival and we just had different booths. It was a like pulling teeth to organize it. Nobody wants to put the work in; everyone's so apathetic. I think it's because these organizations don't have a political component and mostly they're just social and they just want to work for their own population. They don't want to contribute to the campus community per se. I really

wish we could've worked together and done something because I think that would have been such a powerful force if the whole Latino community did something.[8]

When I asked Gilda whether ULO could be a site for collaboration, she said: "All the Latino organizations on campus get together once a month under ULO. And I think it's really frustrating because people just give announcements. I think that we had meetings just for the sake of meeting because we didn't put on any events together; there's only one barbecue at the beginning of the school year. LUA serves as a liaison to everything that is going on campus. LUA is so active in the Multicultural Center and student government." Gilda expresses the feeling of many LUA members that they are pulling most of the weight of representing Latinos politically on campus. Members and leaders of LUA are intent on keeping their commitments to advancing social justice for Latino communities, and as they focus on this goal, ideology takes over as does their concern with organizational integrity. They scrutinize other organizations for not doing enough or perhaps advancing Latino causes in ways that conflict with their ideology. Despite their well-intentioned actions and hard work, even some Latino administrators held negative perceptions of them.

Latino Administrators' Perceptions
of Latino Student Organizations

Latinos United for Action had conflicts and tensions not only with other student groups but also, at times, with some administrators. I interviewed two Latino administrators at RU. One is an associate dean, Ernesto Telles, and the other is an even higher level administrator, Lorenzo Flores. Both reflected on their own experiences as students while talking about the students they now serve. While they hold complex views of Latinos and the Latino community, at times they trod close to stereotypes. Ernesto Telles talked about the gendered inequalities within families:

> I talk to these Latinas. For example, I had one student. She was so depressed. She went to DC for graduate school. She said, "This is the first time I haven't slept in my bed. I miss my mom." I asked her, "Does she cook for you, *te plancha* [does she iron your clothes]? *Te lava los calzones* [does she wash your underwear]?" This is 2010! It's the same situation as my mother. The boys can do anything. He can have a 2.1 GPA and his family will support him going to law school but not the daughter.

Telles is expressing his perception of Latino families' failure to support their daughters' educational endeavors. Lorenzo Flores also blamed Latino culture for the educational attainment rates. He said: "Other cultural groups take their education more seriously. We do it on the surface level. Soccer trumps going to the library every time. There is not enough academic cultivation within our culture writ large. I'm not trying to blame La Raza. I think a major part is institutions' roles in opening up for us. But I'm not blind in our role getting here." Flores's view combines both structural and institutional issues but does not shy away from the perceived cultural component he thinks is a problem. Moreover, he is aware of how structure shapes his relationship with students. Replying to my question about his relationship to Latino student organizations, he said: "I used to have relationships with the organizations. They invited me to speak, etcetera. I have more relationships with individuals now. That's how the institution works. It promotes relationships with individuals, individual student leaders. It's the meritocratic model. Notice how it handles protests: it doesn't do well. They give individual grades not group grades."

Both Telles and Flores were college students in the late 1960s and lived through the Chicano movement. Both viewed today's student through the lenses of their own experiences:

ERNESTO TELLES (ET): I could never understand why the rhetoric of the 1960s is relevant to the rhetoric of the twenty-first century. That's what LUA students do.

DVR: Can you say more about that?

ET: They're still talking about internal colonialism, the periphery, imperialism, colonialism. In class I say, "Look, we know there is racism and discrimination; the question is, what are we going to do about it? How are we going approach it with a public policy agenda? Who are the leaders and how do we educate? My concern is if we have a student for two, four, or five years, between classwork, research, community service, and student organizations, what should they come out with? They shouldn't forget who they are. History should be corrected. I deal a lot with Mexicans. At many of the conferences I go to, Mexicans talk about the northern population. Even Mexican governors from Baja, etcetera, say, "These people think Mexican American War was last year!" Attitudes! If you look at extremes here—look at Latino Fellowship. They have totally different attitudes and rationalization for purpose. I've always had a little bit of trouble with the rhetoric. I will support them either way, no matter what.

Telles emphasizes that LUA uses what he thinks is outdated rhetoric. He uses his relationships with contemporary Mexican leaders to strengthen his argument. Regardless, he does take seriously his task of supporting all Latino organizations. Flores shared similar perspectives: "I was at the planning of El Plan de Aztlan. Is Aztlan still relevant? I think we need whole new ideological perspectives and tactics to unite our population. We don't even know how to refer to our population." Flores was directing these comments at LUA. He explained further.

LORENZO FLORES (LF): LUA is the only surviving 1960s student organizations overcoming SDS and SNCC. I knew all of the individuals, Cesar Chavez, Corky, Reies Tijerina, I supported them and worked with them. They contributed immensely to the unification and politicization of a people to take on societal oppressive practices. It only went so far. And it fragmented. There is a proliferation of Latino student groups. These movements shaped the way we judge Latino leaders.

DVR: How so?

LF: We ask are you Latino enough? Chicano enough? Do they represent the issues of our people?

Flores then explained that he often is judged by students, as Kenya, a member of LUA, confirmed, describing an incident that troubled the group:

Lorenzo Flores is coming next week to our meeting because of a comment he made last week. There was a speaker talking about racism and education. He was a really good speaker. Flores comes in to introduce him and says, "It's raining," and then he said, "Ha ha. Look, I'm all wet and I won't say anything if you call me a wetback." The speaker was talking about racism! Nobody laughed, and then he went to ULO and wouldn't apologize for that joke. . . . We asked for a written apology and he said no.

I asked Flores to explain how and if he is challenged by Latino students.

DVR: What do you think about students questioning your performance as a high level administrator and as a Chicano?

LF: What can I think about it? Do your homework! The perception that I have must not be different from an eighteen- or twenty-year-old. My perception as a Chicano activist now is different from theirs. My ideas have changed as I've engaged in change at different levels in my life. Each generation has to determine how they are going to define themselves, how they are going to connect their energies as human beings. It's a continuous conversation with lots of pitfalls.

Telles held similar perspectives about LUA, commenting, "I talk to LUA and I say something wrong, and they stop talking to me. Then they invite me again when they forget." I asked him to talk more about the "wrong things" he says, and he responded: "I'm not interested in rhetoric. You don't have to convince me about the Mexican American War, you don't have to convince me of Aztlan, about immigration. I just want reasoning. You are part of the top percent of California! Don't isolate yourself! But there are some that are totally committed and some students will follow them. There is a variety of views on campus and the rhetoric used. They're so desperate and factionalized. And it's 2010 not 1969." While Telles did not appear to be hopeful that the divisions among the Latino students will dissipate, Flores has a slightly different perspective.

LF: We were pioneers. We had a passion for bringing in a new generation of Latino students to campus. I don't see that anymore.

DVR: You don't?

LF: I do but it's played out somewhat ritualistically.

DVR: What do you mean by that?

LF: They may not be addressing the real issues because they are following templates of previous generations. It might have worked then. They need new ones.

DVR: Like what?

LF: Using technology: it costs so much more to go to college. They should be preparing students to save money for college. And this might sound contradictory, but they should be talking to students about what the role of higher education [is]. It's not an *ipso facto* job training degree, not at the research university. It's more of a leadership development opportunity with networking opportunities. It's not the end.

Flores continues to think that Latino organizing is important. He sees work to be done, but he believes LUA needs new templates. He reflected on his experience: "I began my work as a young Chicano activist against police brutality. Police were never charged with killing Chicanos. And I started my work in higher education. I think if we continue to get educated we will have an intelligentsia to guide the movement and our people." For Flores, Latino student activists are essential for the creation of the intelligentsia, but in his assessment they need a new vision. Despite their perspectives on Latino student organizing, Telles and Flores do not have strong or close relationships with them or interact often with them. It is also ironic that these veterans of the Chicano movement find LUA's rhetoric irrelevant and counterproductive. It remains unknown how the critical assessment of Latinos United for Action might shape the organization's overall reputation with other Latino organizations on campus. The critical views of these administrators might be trickling down.

Inside the Conflicts: The Latino Community at Research University

Inside the gates of Research University, most students live on campus for the first two years and then choose to relocate to the surrounding areas for their

TABLE 3.1

The conflictual environment of Research University

Strength of student social ties to campus at large	Medium
Description of external campus boundaries	Semi-permeable
Description of internal organizational boundaries	Differentiated and exclusive
Description of role of organization	Family away from home; identity

final undergraduate years. This makes the boundaries of RU semi-permeable. Ideas and people travel off and onto campus, and students are integrated and connected to campus through organizations. Thus, they do not feel totally alienated from campus, but then they do not talk about RU as their community the way LAC students do, and so their social ties to the campus as a whole are moderate, when compared to LAC and RPU. Table 3.1 provides a summary of conflictual climate of the RU campus.

At RU, the main purpose of Latino student organizations is to be a "home" for their members, and this role is critical, given the impersonal dimensions of RU—large classes, lots of students, no faculty-student relationships, and Latino underrepresentation. Students' time is occupied with organizational activities. They have strong friendships within their organizations, and fellow members are often their only friends on campus. The boundaries of organizations are, in effect, closed, and membership is exclusive in practice (since we know three women tried but failed to reconcile dual membership). This becomes evident in the relationship between LUA and LF, which is exacerbated by the MCC's unequal treatment of the groups. However, some of the intergroup tensions live on because of institutional memories and the stories students tell about the organizational conflicts. There is organizational continuity at RU, perhaps because it is not a true commuter campus and students join groups for four years, but perhaps also because both LUA and LF are highly structured and hierarchical. They keep records and are able to keep stories alive. Within the campus grounds of RU, the negative perceptions of LUA and LUA's fraught relationship with LF live on. And RU continues to provide a conflictual context for Latino student organizing.

4

Coexisting at
Regional Public University

Regional Public University is nestled in the mountains, right off a major highway, in a historically Latino, mainly Mexican neighborhood. There are two ways of entering the campus: on the east side or west side. One entrance leads to the College of Math and Science and the other to the College of Arts and Letters. Many students are unfamiliar with both sides of campus; they usually take courses and park on the side where their major is housed. As Jackie, a member of Hispanics for Economics, said, "I'm always on this side of campus; I don't really know what's on the other side." Buildings are surrounded by more than ten parking lots, and parking is relatively cheap and can be paid by the hour.

I first went to the campus to visit the Institutional Review Board (IRB) office because an online form was not available. As I walked on the Arts and Letters side of campus, I noticed a few students sitting outside a student union, a big square building, which, I found out, had just been opened. Inside were two fast-food franchises, and other rooms were still under construction. A stairway in the middle of the union led to a series of offices on the second floor, including the Multicultural Center. I walked into the center and was greeted by a student employee at a front desk. There are four student resource offices housed within the Multicultural Center: Asian Pacific Islander, Chicano and Latino, Pan-African, and Gender and Sexuality. The resource offices had some decoration on the walls and pamphlets outlining what they provided, such as study space, computers, workshops, and a list of affiliated student organizations. I was familiar with the organizations listed on the Chicano-Latino pamphlet because I had already found a similar list on the Office of Student Life's website.

There wasn't anyone in any of the rooms, so I grabbed a Chicano-Latino pamphlet and went to the IRB office, where I was instructed to fill out the form and turn it in in person. Expecting to need a faculty sponsor, I turned to Assistant Professor of Sociology Walter Chen, whom I knew through a mutual friend, and emailed him before my first visit to the RPU campus to arrange a meeting. We met in his office, which he shared with another faculty member. He told me that most sociology professors shared offices. The building looked as if it hadn't been renovated since the late 1980s. Pieces of the ceiling were falling down, and the lockers in the hallways appeared to be relics of the past. Chen described his heavy teaching load, of up to seven courses a year and lamented that he did not have more time or resources for his own research. He invited me to attend one of his undergraduate sociology classes at some point in the semester.

Reaching out to four of the fourteen Latino organizations listed on the student life website, I purposely included Latinos United for Action, as it was the only Latino political organization on campus and I was also studying another chapter at Research University. I received only two responses from the remaining three organizations I contacted. I corresponded with leaders from both groups: one was a Latina social support group and the other was Hispanics for Economics (HE), a group with a preprofessional focus. To keep in line with the other co-ed groups in my sample, I chose HE. At HE, I was in contact with Yvette, who was listed on the webpage as the president of the organization, and at LUA, with and Gilma, who was listed as its president. Yvette invited me to attend the next meeting of the semester. Gilma invited me to meet with her. I did both.

Who's on Campus

Regional Public University is the least selective school in my study; it accepts approximately 60 percent of its applicants and enrolls approximately 20,000 students. It has a student-faculty ratio of 20:1. RPU students are mostly local, nontraditional, and low-income. More than 50 percent of the student body is eligible for Pell grants. Regional Public University is also a Hispanic-serving institution, enrolling many first-generation college students of Latino origin. Moreover, Regional Public University is located in a Latino enclave. RPU's student body is 45 percent Latino, 20 percent Asian American, 10 percent white, and 8 percent African American. The Latino majority at RPU distinguishes its racial climate from those of Liberal Arts College and Research University. RPU respondents did not report experiencing racial isolation even when pushed to discuss instances of discrimination or prejudice (more in Chapter 5). For example, Amalia, a member of LUA, said, "I feel comfortable in most of my classes. The demographics are similar to my high school."

Regional Public University is a commuter school: fewer than 10 percent of students live on campus. Most live with family in the predominately Latino communities in which they grew up, and they work off campus. These students are strapped for time and spend little of it on campus other than during class. For example, Teresa, a member of LUA, explained, "I started working at community college. I work four days out of the week, including weekends. I balance full-time school and part-time work. It's a struggle." Ernesto, also a member of LUA, described his schedule: "I work in the morning and I come to school in the afternoon so I never really joined an organization until later for that reason." Due to time constraints, few students participated in events on campus and thus RPU had the least vibrant student life among the three campuses studied. On this topic, Amalia, who doesn't work and is one of the few students who live on campus because she relocated from over six hours away, commented, "It's hard to make friends with people here because they don't live on campus. I don't have a car. I can't go visit anyone." Given that most students spend little time on campus outside of class, and there is little interaction between students and the organizations studied, their environment is predominantly one of coexistence. Additionally, students reported having no mentor-like relationships with faculty, and campus programming does not facilitate cohesive relationships.

I asked all students to talk about what they considered to be their community and describe what and who were included in it. Of the students at all three campuses, only RPU students referred to communities outside of campus. Many of them took this question as an opportunity to discuss the service they provide to these outside communities. For example, Alex, a member of LUA, said, "I give a financial aid workshop at my high school. I helped them fill out their FAFSA [Free Application for Federal Student Aid]. I especially helped the undocumented students. I talked to fifteen families about what to do for college. They had no idea what to do, and their sons and daughters were seniors." Likewise, Hector, also a member of LUA, talked about service: "I was involved in a Latino coffee shop. They were offering free English classes for the community and I did help with that." And Yvette, a member of HE, followed suit: "The city has this program where they choose three houses that they have to fix. They belong to elderly people. I was able to participate in that and it was really cool because I got to meet people that I would probably never have met." Other students talked about their involvement in church. Amalia, the residential student, said, "I'm still connected to people back home. I'm not part of any community organizations here. I am part of the church at home. I used to read lectures at mass. I only go to church when I visit my uncle around here because I don't have a car." Sara, a member of HE, also noted, "I am involved in my church and I do some work with the youth."

Ernesto, Mayra, and Josefina talked about their neighborhood and parents. For example, Ernesto, a member of LUA, said, "My community is where I see myself influencing the people around me. I feel that work and at home, I feel that's my community. My mom has a relationship with all the neighbors, and all the neighbors have gone to my house. She says, 'Come in,' and there are a few random people at my house. My mom talks to all the moms. I feel connected because we know that we want to do the best for the community." Mayra, a member of HE, talked about service in similar terms: "I volunteered at my niece's school. My niece is sort of like my daughter because my sister worked a lot. I really wanted to meet her teachers and make sure that I knew what she was learning. My family does a lot of volunteer work with the church. On the street where my parents live, people do know each other and they're connected." Like Ernesto and Mayra, Josefina, a member of LUA, also has connections in her neighborhood. She spoke very proudly of her community.

> Yes. I love where I live. People talk bad about the 'hood and the ghetto, I hate the word "ghetto." I love being here. I love walking down the street and saying hi to people and recognizing their faces because I've lived here so long. I like saying "Buenos dias, que le vaya bien [good morning, I hope you have a great day]." I know other neighborhoods are friendly, but, like, I really like this community. I know a lot of people want to get out of the 'hood. When I was in high school, people would not come to my house; they said they were going to get shot up in my 'hood.

RPU students were the only ones to talk so deeply about their families, neighborhoods, and local organizations. This is likely due to the locus of their social ties and networks, which are off campus rather than on campus, in contrast to LAC students, who live on campus all four years, and RU students, who usually relocate to the neighborhood surrounding campus while they attend.

When prodded to talk about their transition to RPU, many students indicated that they transferred from a local community college. Joel reflected on his arrival at RPU: "This is my first year here because I transferred from community college. In community college, I was part of an economics organization so I joined HE to continue to be part of a club that was economics-based." Joel went on to explain that his transition to RPU was not easy. "I am the first person in my family to go to college. I felt really isolated entering RPU. I had a very bad experience. I didn't have correct advice in picking my classes. I have had a bad experience here. I asked for some help and people weren't very helpful, at all! I kind of had to figure everything out on my own because people are, like, 'Look at the wall; that's what the information is' at the counseling center." Joel laments the lack of guidance he received at RPU, especially while seeking answers at the counseling center.

The academic advisor for Hispanics for Economics, Carlos Cedillo, is also an academic advisor for the Business Department. He attended the first HE meeting of each school year, sitting at the back of the room and announcing advising services. When I spoke with him about the students he served, he said, "Unfortunately, many of our students have no models or guidance. They come to HE for any information they can get. I see them in my office and they are hungry for knowledge to navigate their time here." Hector, like Joel a transfer student and member of LUA, also described a tough transition. "I had a sluggish transition. I think for a lot of Latinos, they don't make it past their first or second year, unfortunately." And Alex, a traditional student, likewise commented that "it was a really big transition for me because I had to figure things out for myself. For example, knowing where to sign up for classes. I grew up a little bit. I learned how to find certain things. I now know how to find books at the library—like it's four floors! And I can find books." While Alex did not know at first how to maneuver through the institution, Teresa lacked guidance earlier on, through the college application process. Yet she also described her transition quite differently from the others:

> I am the first person in my family to go to college. My transition to college was scary because I didn't know anything about it. I didn't have an older brother or cousin to tell me how to do it or how to apply. I got accepted to RPU as a freshman but didn't come until I transferred from community college. Academically, everything came pretty easy. I have been pretty lucky in terms of professors. I've only had to challenge myself a very few times. Everyone says I'm pretty crazy for saying that and that I should be proud of it. I haven't really been challenged, but I've always been into school.

Compared to Teresa, who was one of the few students who found her courses easy, many others were more focused on challenges in the classroom. For instance, in referring to the placement exams required of all entering students, Antonietta, a member of LUA, said:

> It was a difficult transition because I never practiced for the exams. I guess it was kind of my fault. You take the test, get the results and then from there decide the classes you have to take for English and math. English, they gave me really low. I did advocate for math because they told me that I needed to take a really, really low math. I was like "I think all that math is basic so I think that I should go to another level." So, what I did was I took the exam again and got into the next level.

In an interview, Joaquin Tovar, the chair of the Chicano-Latino Studies program, said that "the problem with our students here is their preparation. Ninety percent of students have not passed the placement exams for math and writing. The public school system has not prepared them for their college education. They have been trained in the model of sitting back and waiting for me to divulge the truth. Sixty-five percent of students are women and many are single mothers." As Tovar continued to talk about the challenges of teaching the RPU student population and the difficulties students faced in their transition to RPU, he fixated on the lack of guidance before their arrival on campus. Many students struggled to learn how the bureaucracy worked; others lacked academic preparation. But unlike students at Liberal Arts College and Research

University, RPU students' transitions were not marked by experiences of racial underrepresentation and isolation.

Resources

When primed to discuss relationships with faculty or administrators, students mentioned only their organizations' academic advisors. Carlos Cedillo, who served as the advisor to HE during both academic years of my study, was the only staff person that HE members mentioned during the interviews. Several talked about meeting with Carlos for advising. I also noted the way Carlos interacted with students during the HE meetings he attended at the beginning of each school year. He appeared to know them and laughed and joked with many students; at times, he appeared to be flirting and leering at some of the young women. His interactions were very informal. LUA changed advisors from one year to the next. The first year the advisor was Armando Gonzalo, a part-time lecturer at RPU who was also a doctoral student at a local university. Armando attended one meeting and helped plan one of LUA's big events by providing musical contacts for it. The students referred to him as Profe Gonzalo and joked with him as well. Despite the friendly rapport that students had with Carlos and Armando, they were also very deferential to these advisors. The second year, Belem Hernandez, Associate Professor of Chicano-Latino Studies, served as LUA's academic advisor and attended one meeting at the beginning of fall semester. Students had a more distant and formal relationship with her; several had taken her introduction to Chicano-Latino Studies course. I heard her name only one more time when, during an LUA meeting, Josefina asked the group if it could co-sponsor an event in which she was going to be discussing her research of a Chicano movement archive.

In addition to meeting Carlos, Armando, Belem, and Joaquin, I also interviewed Ester Figueroa, Associate Professor of Chicano-Latino Studies. She was curt in our interview, which lasted only twenty-five minutes. She had little to say about students, other than two graduate students whom she was mentoring and taking to a professional association meeting to present their research. She did not disclose relationships with undergraduate students.

I also followed up with Walter Chen and attended his sociology of race-ethnicity course. The classroom was located in the same building as the sociology department. There were about fifteen students sitting in the room, but more trickled in as Walter arrived. The room eventually filled up with about twenty-five to thirty students. Walter pulled out a piece of chalk and wrote the term "internal colony" on the board. He asked the class, "Do you remember last class, we discussed this term? What does it mean?" A black woman quickly raised her hand and said, "Oh, that's about the Puerto Ricans, Mexicans, and black people." Another student, an Asian American man, interrupted: "Also Native Americans!" Walter asked, "What about them?" The black woman again jumped in, saying, "Something about how they're treated in the country, unfairly?" "Yes," Walter continued. "It's the idea that these populations are treated similarly to colonies. Remember, it's in your reading." He then asked the class to break into two groups, reread the text, and then discuss it. Meanwhile, he and I chatted, and Walter observed, "Yeah, a lot of these students really struggle with the reading, you know? It's a comprehension issue a lot of times." Walter echoed Joaquin Tovar in lamenting the under-preparation of students, yet both also flirted with deficit-oriented evaluations of their students (assuming their students were ill-prepared for college).

Like all public institutions, RPU has a commitment to diversity. RPU has a Multicultural Center, which I visited during my first time on campus, and an Educational Opportunity Program (EOP), which has been on campus for over thirty-five years. RPU's EOP offers a summer-bridge program for freshmen and provides counseling services, but of the twenty students I interviewed, only one had used its services, and many students did not know what the EOP was.

As discussed earlier, the Multicultural Center houses four resource centers, which provide students with information about the campus, employment, and other opportunities, as well as a space to hold meetings. The Chicano-Latino resource office occupies a small room with three tables and is staffed by a student employee who sits behind a desk. There are flags of every Latin American country on the walls and a mural painted by a local Cuban artist. A few more paintings decorate the plain white walls: one is of an agricultural worker in the fields; another is of bright sunflowers. There are also a few *veladoras* (candles often found in Catholic churches, many times featuring a saint) and skulls representing Día de los Muertos. LUA held all of its meetings in this room.

Organizations

Gaining access to these organizations was easy. My identity was not questioned or scrutinized by LUA as it was at Research University. Gilma, the president of LUA, invited me to meet with her, and Yvette, president of HE, welcomed me to attend the next HE meeting. In the following sections, I talk more about the actions, dynamics, and roles of these organizations on campus. The primary issue shaping how these organizations function is the commuter identities of students. Teresa, a member of LUA, explained: "I know it's pretty difficult for students to join a group because some students have two jobs. So, time and energy runs low. People can't be as involved as they would like to. But the organization makes you feel a little connected to campus and helps you get to know staff and what's going on campus."

Given the lack of student life on campus and time constraints, these Latino organizations at RPU fill institutional gaps in student services, primarily focusing their energies on giving students information about resources and opportunities on and off campus and providing a semblance of student life. However, Latinos United for Action and Hispanics for Economics had *no interaction* with one another—neither *cooperation*, as at Liberal Arts College, nor *competition*, as at Research University. These organizations coexisted.

Latinos United for Action

The Latinos United for Action chapter at RPU differed in many respects from the chapter at Research University. Mostly notably, when I got in contact with Gilma, she was struggling to revive the organization. Since no organizational meetings were scheduled, she invited me to meet her on campus and discuss the status of LUA. I found her outside the Multicultural Center, and we chatted outside of a Starbucks. She began by telling me that in community college, she had had a boyfriend who introduced her to Latinos United for Action, so when she arrived to RPU, she looked for the campus chapter. This is what she found:

> When I got here, it was destroyed or inactive. It's been really hard. The student union was torn down so there was no visibility for the organization. It was really hidden in the basement. Some people have explained it to me in that way. People also say there was an "infiltration." This is what I heard; it's all secondhand. I heard that LUA was pretty big and had many members, but there was a rally against immigrant rights close to the border and some students got arrested and they were members of LUA. I guess someone in LUA pushed people to be a little more radical, and because of this person, they got in trouble so they really thought that this person was an infiltrator. From what I found out later, this person was part of a progressive party movement; they were more like a communist or socialists. And from what I've heard, his tactics were a little more radical, and LUA didn't want to associate with something like that.

Gilma related LUA's institutional memory as told to her by the remaining members when she first arrived on campus. The idea of LUA being "infiltrated" resonates with the experience of LUA at Research University. While Gilma could not report directly on the "infiltration" incident, the hearsay surrounding it reflects the kind of suspicion that followed this type of political organization.

Gilma also noted that when she arrived, the group was small, with fewer than ten people. "The atmosphere was very unwelcoming when I would go to the meeting," she added. "I felt like I didn't know anything. There was a hierarchy. The members of LUA acted like they knew everything." By the time we met, however, these members had graduated, and as Gilma explained, "It's pretty much only been me lately, because LUA died on this campus for, like, the last two years." She felt optimistic, though, since some students expressed interest, and she said that she would contact me when the first meeting was to be held.

She did as promised, and when I walked into the resource center, there were three students sitting on the tables, each reading something. I asked if they were there for the LUA meeting, and when they said they were, I introduced myself. They did not ask follow-up questions. Gilma walked in twenty minutes late and apologized. The first meeting consisted of three students, Gilma, and me. They talked about the importance of having an active chapter of LUA on campus and emphasized the need to recruit members. Gilma asked each of the three students to bring someone new the following week. But the two subsequent meetings were similarly attended, and no real organizational business was discussed. By the fourth meeting, Gilma said to me, "I feel bad telling you to come because we have such a bad turnout, but then I think it's good for you to see how we're struggling. I don't think the students think that it's necessary to talk about issues because they think everything is ok." When I asked, "What do you mean, issues?," she replied, "It is hard 'cuz Latinos are 60 percent on campus and they don't think it's important."

As the semester progressed the group grew to between six and ten regular attendees, including Gilma. They began to think about organizing their first event, a Día de los Muertos booth, where they would sell food to raise money for the organization. As Gilma saw more members consistently attending LUA meetings, she suggested, during a meeting, "I think we should have roles, because I am a very disorganized person and I want LUA to go on even if I'm not here." Only Anthony responded: "I don't think we should focus on that because the semester is almost over. I think we should focus on what LUA is about and recruiting." They spent 2008–2009 rebuilding their membership base and left the question of leadership for the next academic year.

One day, Cesar, a transfer student and LUA member, told me that "some LUA chapters have hierarchies but we don't." Antonietta interjected: "Maybe we should, but we don't." She continued, "Right now, we are just focused on recruiting; we need more members." Cesar added, "Yeah, we have, like, four to five members who take upper division courses or are close to graduating, so we need more new members." These upcoming graduations were part of the challenge of maintaining an active organization at RPU. Because many students transfer from community college, their tenure at RPU is often shorter than the average four or five years at most colleges. Without a stable leadership to continue organizational operations from one year to another, it was difficult for LUA to maintain organizational memory. RPU's LUA chapter lacked continuity.

Given the organizational continuity problem, many meetings were dedicated to recruitment strategies, which often emerged from conversations about what LUA was as an organization. At a meeting during the 2009 spring semester, Gilma shared: "I heard the LUAs on UC campuses are better because they are more organized and they have more money." Antonietta said, "I'll have to ask my brother about that." Gilma said that she had many ideas about organizing LUA. She would like to form committees, create a youth outreach program, and talk to members about how they might benefit from joining LUA. Anthony agreed with the youth program. He said that LUA is essentially about retention and access. Alex asked, "How are you recruiting members? Have you tried other organizations?" Anthony asked Alex, "From your experience, why do you think students don't join organizations?" Alex explained that time constraints are the biggest obstacle for students. He thought that the organization should be flexible with meeting times.

Anthony asked the group if they would agree to meet a couple of times over the summer to brainstorm and plan for the fall to make sure they recruited members early on. Alex suggested that they recruit through Chicano-Latino Studies classes. Anthony said, "We've asked Chicano-Latino Studies professors in the past, and they never help." Antonietta added, "Maybe we can make it clear that we don't need financial support, but we want them to come to our speaker events." Antonietta added more about recruiting, saying, "Here, where there are 50 percent Latinos, it's harder to recruit." Gilma interrupted, and said she would like to have a multicultural event with other organizations in order to attract new members. Anthony asked, "How will a multicultural event help promote a Chicano identity? The problem is that so many students already don't identify that way." Gilma responded, "I think we need to show that LUA is multicultural and not Chicano-centric. People think we are radical, but they shouldn't just think that about LUA. I like how some of the frats are organized. They are social and friends." Cassandra responded: "But frats are not conscious, so that's another issue. Let's not go there."

As LUA members strategized about their recruitment strategies, they also navigated what they perceived as a stigma of being militant. Alex explained: "Whoever wants to join us is welcome. We will not deny anyone the right to be at our organization because of his or her background. People think that LUA is radical, and we want to reclaim our lands for Chicanos only. But why would we do that if we know that other races and other people of color are going through the same thing? Why would we oppress other people of color? We have to help each other out." Ernesto also talked about the stigma of LUA: "If I could change one thing about LUA, I would show that we are not political or radical. For some reason, people think that LUA is just radical, like back in the sixties, like the movement." Amalia talked about the stigma: "I heard that LUA were brown supremacists, and I was so confused."

Conflating radicalism and militancy, these students thought of LUA as focusing only on the advancement of Chicanos and Latinos, at least in the past. For their part, they sought to emphasize openness. Alex said: "When people think of LUA, they just think of Mexico, and they don't want to join because they think we are only open to Mexicans. But we're open to Guatemalans and other nationalities. We want to promote higher education and support other groups at school that are fighting for something that's needed, like the budget cuts." LUA members at RPU, as at Research University, were concerned with the progress of Latinos in higher education. They did not hold regular thematic workshops designed to educate their membership on issues, as did the RU chapter. However, they did talk about educating each other about various kinds of issues and increasing their awareness and consciousness.

At a meeting during the fall semester of 2009, Anthony read excerpts of the founding document of LUA and then asked the group to discuss it. As they prepared to do so, Erika, who was in the army, interrupted the group and asked, "What is the point of this exercise?" Anthony answered, "Well, we are going to recruit people. We want to make sure we are all on the same page that day so we can answer any questions." Erika responded, "Yeah, but when we are recruiting, we need a pitch-line and we need to show people the activities that we are doing. I wouldn't join an organization [that didn't have that]. Talk is good but it feels like you're not doing much else." Adriana, a master's student in Chicano-Latino Studies, responded: "I think it's important that we figure out who we are as a collective so we can be strong and on the same page. We need to help each other out in becoming conscious. Like, I might be in one level of consciousness and someone else might be at *indigenismo*," meaning that that individual was versed in a critical perspective that focuses on the history of the Americas and the social location of indigenous peoples. "Master's students can help everyone else become more conscious," she added. Erika then pointed out, "I have a lot of experience recruiting and it works when you're more organized and I see no organization here." Rafael responded, saying "I'm sorry that you don't feel any power here and we have no hierarchies and maybe it's your military background. But I transferred from a community college to be here. I feel a lot of power in this room with my *compañeros* [comrades] because we're trying to figure out what we want to do about everything affecting our community." Erika's reply was "most of us are seniors and we will not be here next year. It's important we get more people to join." Adriana said, "I agree, but let's figure out who we are first."

The same discussion dominated the first semester of my second year in the field. What was LUA? How would they draw more students? The answers to these questions were not clear. When I asked Ernesto, "How are you recruiting members?," he replied, "We give them a flier. We tell them the name of the organization and just give them a flier. I tell them to feel free and come give input to the organization. I don't really know about the history, so that's all I say." Ernesto, then in his third semester attending LUA meetings, still did not know the history.

LUA continued to struggle with organizational continuity. Students did not learn from one generation to the next about the mission and purpose of the group because LUA did not require much of its members; nor did it have a formalized leadership structure to pass on institutional knowledge. However, this was exactly what Hector liked about LUA.

> I really feel like these people are not going to judge me because I missed a meeting. I know people prefer if we had more dedication, but they will take what I can offer. I think if people aren't respecting other people's ties—people have kids and they have jobs—then that's a problem. I don't like it when people frown upon when you can't make it to an event. . . . I don't think you should put that pressure on them.

While Hector preferred the light commitment, by the middle of the fall semester of 2009, the group had decided to choose an official president in order to get more done. Josefina explained: "As of right now, I'm the president because we did the paperwork, but I was really against it. But I'm also honored to be the leader. They wanted me be leader, but I don't like the hierarchies. I think we should be an organization where we are all on the same level. I think, obviously, we're not on the same level of consciousness. I don't want people to say that I have the *palabra* [word] or I get to facilitate." Despite accepting the leadership position, Josefina made it clear that she was against hierarchies and that she did not intend to have the last word or be the only one to lead the meetings.

Josefina did indicate that she would continue to focus on recruiting members. "At RPU the chapters are always really small and sometimes plan stuff and then the group dies out. I want to change that." But she also recognized the challenge of being at a commuter school: "My best friend goes to school in Iowa and they're all forced to live on campus. When they go back to their dorms and people can say, 'Hey what are you doing now' and everyone knows what he or she is doing. And it's really easy to encourage people when you know see them." As she notes, residential patterns at another type of campus can lead to higher participation rates by students (in the chapters that follow I discuss how these patterns play a role in Latino student life). In addition to recruiting, she expressed a desire to do more activities. "Last year, we only had El Día de los Muertos. I want to do more than that. We're going to do a Mexica New Year celebration."[1]

During the 2009–2010 school year, LUA held two different fundraiser sales on campus. They held a bake sale and sold nachos and *aguas frescas* (cold drink made from fruit), and used the funds raised, along with money from student government, to host their Mexica New Year celebration. Alex recalled, "I think Mexica New Year was interesting; a lot of people went, about 100 people went."

That year, LUA also hosted a Día de los Muertos booth on campus. This was the extent of the group's on-campus activities that academic year.

JOINING LATINOS UNITED FOR ACTION. As LUA struggled to expand its membership, I asked members to talk about why they joined the organization and what they got out of their time in LUA. Alex and Ernesto were recruited in a Chicano-Latino Studies course. Alex said, "I thought it was interesting and sad because they only had four members. And this school is where the movement really began." Ernesto commented: "I had classmates that were very active and intellectual. They invited me, dragged me into the organization. I consider them very intellectual. That's how I started joining. They were in Chicano-Latino Studies courses. They were outspoken about certain issues. And they shared their thoughts about it. They could talk the issue out. They had events going on and invited others to come and help. I thought I could help and just asked what they were working on." Ernesto was drawn to LUA not only for the prospect of helping, but also for the "college experience," as he put it: "It's a good space to communicate with people and create events. Having the space to communicate and talk about certain issues and *be part of something*. And LUA is one of those groups that being part of it gets you *the college experience*. It's good to help you get through college and get skills and network. I think LUA makes it easier for a transfer student to become a university student."[2] Ernesto feels connected to others on campus through LUA. He sees LUA building his skill set and networks. Hector expressed similar sentiments. "I feel like, as an undergrad at this school, that is commuter school, you don't really have a social network. You meet a whole network of people when you join the club. It gives you the college experience, which a lot of people lack here." Teresa agreed. "It's important to be active, not just be commuters. It [joining LUA] helps promote school spirit. It's good to learn about others on campus and know who else is here."

To summarize, members of LUA were recruited during recruitment drives when the organization tabled and in classes. They talked about LUA as a pleasant disruption of their routine of going from their car to class and then home or to work. They believed that LUA was giving them networks and skills and the college experience. By contrast, the LUA chapter at Research University provided a "home" and had a very clear and organized political agenda.

Hispanics for Economics

After exchanging emails with Yvette, the president of Hispanics for Economics during the 2008–2009 academic year, I was invited to attend the first meeting. It was held in the building that also houses the Business department. Every student I saw in the halls was either Latino or black. As I stood outside the meeting room, which was a classroom, I saw a group of young women and one young man waiting outside the room as well. I asked them if they had seen Yvette, and they told me that she wasn't there yet. I asked, "Are you in the executive board?" They replied, "Yes." I told them that I was the graduate student from UCI, and they seem to know who I was. They asked, "Are you Daisy?" I said yes and walked into the meeting room with them. Sandra, the membership officer, wrote the word "announcements" on the board. Within a few minutes, the list was complete, and the room was full of students. Saul, the vice-president, and Sandra read the announcements aloud. He mentioned the three upcoming socials with students from four local universities. He asked people to please sign up for the beach clean-up. Then Sandra interrupted. She was sitting in the first chair from the door and in the front. She reminded people to please pay their membership dues, explaining that they would receive their HE t-shirt once they did. Next, Marta, HE's publicity officer, said, "I want to make a shout out to our advisor, Carlos Cedillo, who is an academic advisor in the department. You should all go see him!" Carlos smiled and stood up from the back of the room and walked up to the front. He shook Marta's hand and addressed the group. "Thank you, Marta. I am available to all of you. If you have questions about courses, schedules, or you just want to figure out what you're doing here. Come see me!" Students applauded, and he returned to the back of the room.

Marta then took the floor and informed everyone that they would begin their recruitment incentive. She told the members that if they brought a new member to the meetings, they would get a Starbucks card in return. Next, Saul began to discuss a few more plans for the semester. He mentioned their national umbrella organization and a baseball game fundraiser. Selena added that this would be a great chance to meet Latinos from all other campuses. She also said that they would have a reading volunteer event. She asked Jackie, the group's media designer, to elaborate. Jackie told the members that in honor of Dr. Seuss's birthday, there would be an event to read to elementary school children. She asked people to sign up to volunteer and told them that the school was nearby.

Saul pleaded with members to join a committee. Sandra mentioned all the committees: publicity, social, membership, community service, and fundraising. Then Marta asked all the members, "Who hasn't signed up for a committee? Why not? I want to know why people don't want to sign up. It's not going to take all of your time, I promise. And it's not very hard." She went on to explain what her role as the publicity officer was: "I want to plaster the campus with posters of HE to make our presence known. If you joined this committee, I would need help doing this." No members responded.

Then Saul said, "The speaker is supposed to be here by now. Sorry that he is late." A young man in the crowd raised his hand and asked, "So what do you guys usually do when a speaker is late, which I'm sure has happened before?" Saul responded, "Well, it happened once, two years ago, and we had an icebreaker instead." Another young man asked, "So do you always have speakers?" Saul said

"Yes, and food, which the speakers usually sponsor, but someone needs to pick it up, that's why our president is late." Selena interjected: "It's raining; that's probably why they are late. But keep in mind that we need people to join committees so they can pick up the food."

The young man who asked the speaker questions said, "I was asking if you always have speakers because I was wondering if you ever have workshops." Saul responded, "Yes, sometimes we have resume tips workshops." Marta interjected, "But the speakers are almost never late; like, next week Telemundo will be here; then JPL [Jet Propulsion Laboratory]." The speaker was still nowhere to be found, so Sandra suggested that everyone in the room introduce themselves (say their favorite music, major, and year). I introduced myself to the group at this time. Among those students present, there was a club promoter and a salsa dancer who both offered their networking skills and connections to the group. There was also an older gentleman who said he had been an actor for many years and had just come back to college. He said he acted in *Zoot Suit*. Another young man said he played in *una banda Sinaloanse* (which performed regional music from the state of Sinaloa in Mexico). Marta asked him what his instrument was, and he responded, "Accordion, and I sing." Once everyone had introduced themselves, Sandra said she had personally baked a cake for all members with birthdays last month. Then someone in the crowd asked, "How many members do you have?" Saul responded, "Thirty-nine members, not including the ten executive board officers."

After this question, the speakers finally arrived: an Asian American woman and a white man who were, roughly, in their forties. They were soaking wet. The woman introduced the man as her boss and soon-to-be-president of the company. He thanked her and said, "I am so glad to be here at the HE because my company is launching in Mexico next week. We need young Latinos like yourselves to work for us." As he continued to talk about his company, I realized they were pitching a pyramid scheme. He said things like, "We aren't like corporate America; our company is about residual income. We help others; it's relationship-building." He later spoke about their product, a video phone, which he called an "insulated field."

When the speakers were done, everyone went into the other room to eat pizza. I looked for Yvette to introduce myself. She apologized for their disorganization and said speakers are usually not late. I told her they were very organized and that I had not seen any other group that brought in so many speakers. She responded, "Thank you," and went on to explain the organizational structure. HE has ten officers: president, vice-president, media officer, treasurer, secretary, internal affairs officer, external affairs officer, web design officer, and community service officer. She also confirmed that they had forty-six paid members during the prior semester. She was optimistic that this year would draw similar numbers.

Unlike LUA, HE does not have a recruitment issues, and they keep binders for each leadership position, which they give to the newly elected officer every year. They also maintain a club website. They hold fundraisers, some of which (baseball games, for instance) are held off campus, and club parties. They also receive money from student government, which funds most of HE's requests, although they rarely exceed $100. Yvette explained: "The student government on campus funds us most of the time. Whenever we have a fundraiser, we spend around one hundred dollars. They have basically funded every event that we've catered on campus, with the exception of the first one, because we turned in our paperwork late, but for the most part they've always funded our events."

HE continued to be highly structured and formal throughout the two years I spent in the field. Mayra, the 2009–2010 president, explained the changes she made when she became leader: "I feel like we've hyped up our professional aspects. For example, we have PowerPoint now. I did that because I have really sloppy handwriting and didn't want people to see. I really think that we promote more campus events, like, for example Homecoming. I always tell people, this is where your fees go, you pay for it. You need to go to these events."

JOINING HISPANICS FOR ECONOMICS. Mayra, Yvette, and others on HE's executive board recruited students by emphasizing how open they were. Yvette explained, "You know we're a professional organization. We're not biased towards any culture. We welcome all majors and all ethnicities and we encourage them to visit our website, [which] tells them more about us." Like members of LUA, the leaders of HE also emphasize that they are open to individuals of all backgrounds (which I talk more about in Chapter 5). However, unlike LUA, HE has a website and resources for potential members to look at to help them decide if they are interested in joining the organization. During recruitment, officers talked about the resources they offered members, including their speaker series, networks, and skill-building workshops.

Members talked to me about the skill-building and networking benefits of joining HE. Sandra, the membership officer, said: "I think what really makes us stand out is our networking. We have the largest membership base in any of the organizations in the School of Business and Economics. We bring speakers; they talk about getting a job or how to have a successful interview or what kind of attire to wear." Students acquired information from the speaker series. Sara reflected on this: "I think they [HE] offer great opportunities by bringing the speakers and giving us good information. I have learned a lot through the club. For example, I didn't know they had social events where you get to meet corporate employers." Students found the connections made to be very valuable. Jackie commented, "Networking is the most important thing for professionals and nonprofessionals. And they do that here." Mayra thought the speaker series was more significant than creating connections because Latino speakers operate as possibility models for Latino members: "I think by bringing Latino speakers, there's inspirational aspect and it's very important. I think it's especially important when we bring Latino people in high executive positions. I would want our members to say that they were inspired by Latino leaders."

HE also transmits professional skills. Mayra shared: "We try to educate our members and provide them with the skills that they're going to need when they go on to graduate or interview. But it's not only a business organization. We also create an environment where we are approachable for academic reasons and other reasons. We ask members to tell us what they need." Yvette is a testament to the skill-building imperative of HE. She observed, "I think I grew a lot as far as being able to market myself, market my school and market my organization." Students also learned more about campus resources in general through their membership. Mayra encouraged students to go to homecoming and other campus-wide events. They also explored the other side of campus. Sara said, "I never knew about the other side of campus and the resources on that side of campus. And even when I found out there was a new student union, I would never go take a look." She shared that through the encouragement of HE she decided to explore the student union.

Like members of LUA, HE members feel that the organization gave them the "college experience." Mayra commented, "I wanted to make memories in college. I didn't want to come to college, go to class, and go home. I really wanted that experience because I'm a transfer student and I feel that I'm a little older, but I never wanted to feel like I graduated without that experience." HE broke the routine of going to class, then home or to work for many students. Sara shared, "I had nothing else to do after class so I would just go home instead. I was not comfortable staying on campus and studying here." Sandra similarly shared: "I really felt disconnected from school. I think it's really boring when you just go to school and go to class. And when class is over you just get your car and go home and don't know anyone." Jackie commented, "I didn't know anyone. I would just go to school, go to work and go home." Hispanics for Economics gave students connection and integration on campus, just as LUA did for its members, but HE did not serve as a "home" the way that the organizations at Research University did.

Coexistence at Regional Public University

Regional Public University differs from Liberal Arts College and Research University in many ways. Some are related to the availability of resources on campus, but the commuter dynamics are what make RPU so distinct. Since most students live off campus in the communities where they grew up, they maintain strong relationships to the people they knew before college. These relationships continue to be their main social ties. Because most students commute from class, to work, and then home, their social ties with others on campus are weak. Students cite communities off campus as their main and most significant

TABLE 4.1

Commuter culture at Regional Public University

Strength of student social ties to campus at large	Low
Description of external campus boundaries	Open and permeable
Description of internal organizational boundaries	Minimal and nonexclusive
Description of role of organization	Instrumental connections

communities. The boundaries of RPU are open as students go in and out (as discussed earlier many students transfer into RPU and they many have a shorter than four-year tenure on campus). The campus does little filtering of their ideas, identities, and politics as you will see in the chapters to come. Table 4.1 summarizes these campus dynamics.

Students join LUA and HE to break the commuter routine and gain the "college experience." However, they also claim to gain skills and networks, which were not mentioned by students at LAC or RU. RPU students cite instrumental connections as benefits to joining an organization. These differ from the kinds of connections sociologist Janice McCabe (2016) observes in settings where students gain academically from friendships and activities such as peer-editing assignments. For RPU students, on the other hand, gaining information and access to resources and opportunities on campus and beyond are crucial. On a campus with little student life, students interact only minimally with other students outside of class. Latino student organizations fill a niche on campus by letting students know what resources they can find at RPU, like the student union or the homecoming activities. HE and LUA meet on opposite sides of campus and have no contact with each other. They coexist on the RPU campus.

Because the racialized organizational setting of RPU also matches the adjacent community outside the campus gates, Latino students do little relearning of their ethnic-racial knowledge as compared to LAC and RU students. There is more cultural similarity between RPU students' home lives and campus lives than between RU and LAC students' home and campus lives. This has real consequences, which I discuss further in the chapters to come.

PART TWO

Student Interactions and Meaning-Making

5

Who We Are

(Pan)ethnic Identity and
Boundary Formation

Given that all the students in this study are part of a Latino student organization, how do they conceive of their unity?[1] What do they believe they share with one another? How do they understand what it means to be a Latino student on their campus? I explored these questions through ethnographic observations of student interactions during organizational meetings and in-depth interviews in which I asked students what they thought about different labels and which they preferred for their own self-identification. Consider the following responses from students at each of the three different campuses. Selena, a student at Liberal Arts College, explained, "I identify as Latina because it's the most all-encompassing term. 'Latino' allows for panethnic identification and doesn't distinguish between citizenship statuses. Someone in Argentina could be just as Latino as someone in Chicago. It allows for difference while retaining a cultural tie." Deidra, a student at Research University, similarly identified as Latina but described it differently, saying, "I say 'Latina' although I'm light-skinned. My parents are from Mexico." In contrast, Josefina, a student at Regional Public University, rejected the Latino label completely, stating, "I don't use 'Latino' or 'Hispanic.' They are racist terms. 'Hispanic' means Spaniards to me and it reminds me of colonization. I think it puts too many of us together. You can be from Nicaragua or Mexico, anywhere. It reminds me of people thinking we're fiery and other stereotypes, like in the media. I try to refer to where people are from. I try to be more specific." These remarks reveal the speakers' individual efforts to negotiate a sense of identity using existing categories and terminology, but more broadly, they are also representative of the pattern of responses of students at the three different colleges.

Selena, the Liberal Arts College student, connects with "Latina" as a broad, all-encompassing term that espouses solidarity. For her, the label "Latino" highlights the heterogeneous nature of Latinos—she even notes the category's inclusion of various nationalities—while simultaneously providing a framework that finds unity in that diversity. This differs from Deidra's understanding of "Latina" at Research University, where the category seems to come with implicit boundaries and assumptions against which she feels compelled to qualify her own identity. When she mentions that she may not fit all of the markers of a Latina (such as skin color), Deidra reveals an understanding that the label comes with specific phenotypical criteria. Meanwhile, Josefina, at Regional Public University, rejects any single panethnic category or label precisely because she sees so much heterogeneity among the Latino population. Indeed, from Josefina's perspective, any effort to impose overarching criteria or terminology has oppressive implications. These student observations capture the patterns that distinguish each institutional environment; Selena, Deidra, and Josefina voice the views largely shared by their campus peers. I identify three distinct patterns of self-identification that corresponded closely with the campus students attended: inclusive Latino identification signifying solidarity above all at LAC, qualified Latino identification mediated through specific organizational membership at RU, and the rejection of panethnic identities in favor of national-origin identification at RPU.

Selena, Deidra, and Josefina share similar socioeconomic backgrounds and are all second-generation Americans. Attending college at the same time and in the same geographic area, all three are integrated into a community of other Latinos through a college club on their specific campus. Yet they express distinct preferences and understandings of various identity labels. The crucial difference is the particular campus context in which they are embedded; each campus creates a distinct and specific environment for students as they interact with one another, members of other organizations, the student body at large, faculty, administrators, and even the community outside the campus gates. Within these settings, students are ascribed statuses and then, through various and ongoing forms of interaction, actively construct their own sense of who they are and to which community or communities they belong. It is a dialectical process of identity formation, through which external ascription and self-identification co-create ethnoracial understandings and categories.

This chapter examines how students respond to ethnoracial ascription as they co-construct and negotiate their own ethnoracial understandings and identities. First, I discuss students' subjective experiences on campus to explain how they understand the racial climate therein. I draw from interviews and ethnographic observations of student interactions during meetings. It is notable that the amount of data is not balanced across campuses. Students at Regional Public University had very little to say about racial marginalization, while students at Liberal Arts College spoke in-depth on this topic. This does not reflect an absence of racial inequalities at RPU per se as much as does the difference in how students come to know and talk about their ethnoracial experiences.

Second, I describe how subjective experiences within each racial climate shape how students interact with one another and form understandings about boundaries and identities. I lay out the three different patterns by which students deploy panethnic and ethnic boundaries, specifically, as they adopt and define identity labels: inclusive Latino identification signifying solidarity above all, qualified Latino identification mediated through specific organizational membership, and the rejection of panethnic identities. The three identification patterns reveal distinct racial socialization processes on each campus. Campus contexts provide distinct breeding grounds for specific ideas and understandings of Latinidad. At Liberal Arts College, students learn about ethnic-racial identities mainly through external ascription in the form of racial microaggressions, tokenization, and marginalization, but they maintain rather fluid boundaries of Latinidad among one another. More clearly, they recognize the heterogeneity among Latinos and allow individuals to define boundaries as they wish. Their number one concern is solidarity. Because LAC Latino students recognize their heterogeneity and hold solidarity as a goal, they maintain fluid boundaries of Latinidad within their communities on campus.

At Research University Latino students deploy ethnic boundaries constantly. Within Latino United for Action and Latino Fellowship students make assumptions about what an "authentic Latino" does, wears, and believes in. In LF, these messages are delivered through humor and banter, while at LUA the messages are delivered through discussions, mainly political. Both of these boundary deployment strategies shape how students identify and perform Latinidad. Because students espouse particular understandings of what it means to be Latino, they feel a constant pull to qualify their identities—to prove that they are indeed, Latino enough. Ethnic identity performance has interpersonal consequences for Latinos at RU. Choosing how to display who they are amongst their Latino peers has high stakes.

By contrast, at Regional Public University the lessons learned about ethnic-racial identities are mostly unexamined. Unlike students at LAC and RU, students at RPU did not disclose instances of external or internal Latino boundary deployment on campus. How these students choose to perform their identities have little consequences for their interpersonal relations on campus.

The sections that follow explains these observations in greater detail.

Essential Vocabulary for Understanding Identity Formation

Before delving into the students' experiences, it is useful to define some terms and talk about identity formation in general. I mentioned the dialectical nature of identity construction above; this is what Brown and Jones (2015) have called *ethnoracialization*. It is a process that is a result of both *ascription*, which is externally imposed, and *self-identification*, which is agentic. Ethnic boundaries are intrinsic to the processes of ethnoracialization. Ethnic boundaries tell individuals to which groups they do and do not belong. It is through interactions with other individuals and with institutions that we learn where these lines are drawn and, in turn, where we belong and thus who we are.

In everyday life, individuals confront sociopolitical parameters shaped by race, ethnicity, gender, and class. Ethnoracial boundaries can be overt, like Jim Crow laws in the South, or they can be covert and symbolic, operating as often subtle cultural norms and expectations. Consider, for example, a Latina interacting with a group of white friends who respond with disbelief when she is not familiar with a particular musician; she learns in that moment that her cultural knowledge is distinct (and, all-too-often, considered inferior). Such boundaries communicate difference and similarity to individuals, telling them who they and others "are." Such understandings shape the groups with whom people socialize, how they form social networks, and where they see potential to organize for collective interests.

Externally imposed boundaries can be deployed at the macro-level by nations, when particular groups are excluded from government benefits, as was the case for African Americans and Mexican Americans who were treated quite differently from European immigrants during the New Deal (Fox 2012). However, boundaries can also be drawn at the meso- and micro-levels. At the meso-level, institutions such as schools and universities, voluntary associations, and many other types of groups can choose to exclude or include people of particular ethnic, racial, gender, and class backgrounds. Boundaries may be drawn and deployed within organizational settings simply in order to acknowledge difference, but not necessarily in order to exclude others. Moreover, these boundary deployments can also occur in small groups or one-on-one interactions at the micro-level.

Although ethnoracial boundaries are products of social structures such as the law or policy, ethnic groups and individuals have agency in terms of *when* and *where* they deploy and patrol such boundaries. The Latino youth in this study confront ethnoracial boundaries created by the university, their white peers, and their Latino peers, but they also draw ethnic boundaries that include and exclude one another. In addition, individuals exert agency in their own self-identification—which label(s) they adopt to describe themselves and when and where they use them. When the students featured in this book decide what to call themselves, they choose from the labels available on a national scale to designate people of Latino national origins. But their choices are also embedded within and shaped by specific local contexts (such as their home community, campus, and family) which influence how they come to understand these labels. As clusters of cultural meaning, ethnic labels and categories are not static entities, but rather constantly negotiated understandings that take on different inflections and emphases in different contexts. And as Selena, Deidra, and Josefina's observations demonstrate, students in different spaces arrive at varying understandings. This is significant in that Latino students are likely to carry with them competing and disparate understandings of Latinidad outside of the campus gates especially after graduation.

In this chapter, I demonstrate how students interact within the racial climate of their campus and develop a sense of where and with whom they belong—on campus, within their organizations, and broadly in the United States. The differences across campuses, I argue, are not coincidental, but rather shaped by the particular dynamics that prevail in each space. I identify the various factors that shape identity formation on each campus (see Table 5.1). Table 5.1 outlines these factors and their different results. Rows 1–3 compare the characteristics that contribute to a campus's racial climate: racial-ethnic composition of student body, residential arrangements, and diversity programming. These

TABLE 5.1

Boundary and identity formation across campuses

	Liberal Arts College	Research University	Regional Public University
1. **Student body demographics**	Majority white and affluent	Majority Asian American and middle class	Majority Latino and working class
2. **Residential arrangements**	Residential campus	Mixed residential campus	True commuter campus
3. **Diversity programming**	Abundant, guaranteed funds for diversity events	Funding available for diversity events; organizational competition	Minimal funding for diversity events
4. **Inter-organizational dynamics**	Cooperative	Competitive	Coexistent
5. **Self-reported experiences with racism on campus**	Micro-aggressions	Culture shock and some micro-aggressions	None
6. **Intragroup ethnic boundaries**	Solidarity above all	Based on culture and color	Based on gender and family arrangements
7. **Most common identity-label preference and meaning**	Latino (solidarity)	Latino (but qualified) and some Chicano	National origin

characteristics are external to the student organizations examined and, together, create the organizational contexts within which students interact with one another. Row 4 describes the intergroup relations of the Latino student organizations studied on each campus—how the groups view and interact with one another. Row 5 then compares how the campus and organizational characteristics in Rows 1–4 shape students' racialized experiences on campus. In Row 6, I summarize how my respondents construct and define ethnic boundaries on each campus. Finally, Row 7 illustrates the preferred identity label of the respondents on each campus.

Liberal Arts College: Inclusive Panethnic Identification and Cooperation

As described in Chapter 2, Liberal Arts College provides a community-oriented ethos, such that students often describe feeling integrated in the LAC community. Fittingly, Latinos Unidos and Latino Links, the two Latino student organizations I observed at LAC, have a cooperative relationship. During my time in the field, I observed members of one organization attend the meetings of the other. For example, Lorena and Adalberto (members of Latino Links) attended at least two different Latinos Unidos meetings, and Ana and Genova (members of Latinos Unidos) attended a few Latino Links meetings. During these meetings they offered support for each other's upcoming events. The members of both organizations also shared similar sentiments about being a Latino student at LAC. Students shared experiences of initial culture shock, marginalization, continuous tokenization, and frequent microaggressions.

Given the prestige of LAC, the affluence of the student body, and the low percentage of Latinos on campus, many of my Latino respondents faced a difficult adjustment to campus life. During a late spring semester meeting, the president of Latinos Unidos, Fabian, asked members to introduce themselves and answer the question: "Why did you choose LAC? And did the issue of how many Latinos are on campus matter to you?" The responses were varied. When it was her turn, Jane said, "I'm from East LA so I didn't know that having no Latinos on campus would be an issue. I was used to everyone being Latino." In contrast, Soe said, "It was a non-issue because I always knew that most colleges have little Latinos. And I didn't even consider the colleges that do have many Latinos." Vanessa jokingly called her an elitist. Jovita echoed Jane's comments and said she did not know that having very little Latinos on campus could be an issue. Jovita shared that she considered attending a college on the East Coast until a school counselor informed her that there would not be many Latinos, especially not Mexicans. Fabian shared that he was deciding between Swarthmore and LAC. He said "I really considered Swarthmore because they have many more

Salvadoran students and at times, I think I am an honorary Salvadoran because of my close circle of Salvi friends." This conversation reveals several perspectives that students brought to their college decision-making, and, with the exception of Soe, most considered the representation of Latinos on campus important. That is, most students were primed to think about and consider this underrepresentation before even stepping on the campus grounds, and this consideration likely shaped their experience from the onset.

Once enrolled at LAC, the Latino members of LL and LU faced the reality of being part of a small community of Latinos on campus. Students' early encounters with a new cultural environment, white peers, and university personnel left many feeling out of place. Many of the Latino youth at Liberal Arts College are also the first in their families to go to college, and for many, this is their first time living in a non-Latino community. These "firsts" lead to feelings of disorientation and culture shock and, coupled with Latino underrepresentation, students feel racially marginalized on campus, at least initially. Many also reported dealing with tokenization. They talked about the pressure to be "the diversity" on campus and being singled out in class to give the "Latino perspective" on various issues. Paloma, a member of Latino Links, shared: "I think that the school claims that they have diversity and they use us to have diversity. At times, I feel that I am the school's diversity. I think that the school uses us to lure students. I don't like that very much. I'm the only Latina in my political philosophy classes." Several students disclosed their experiences with alienation and culture shock upon arriving on campus. Paloma, for one, became aware of her difference as soon as she met her suitemates: "My suitemates were okay. Most of them were white and they talked about things that I couldn't connect with. Like, they talked about their vacations and I had nothing to add. My family didn't go on vacations." Everyday conversation quickly revealed the classed differences between Paloma's lived experiences and those of her more affluent white suitemates.

Other students shared similar stories of initial culture shock. When I asked Bianca, a member of Latino Links, about her transition to LAC, she exclaimed, "I felt racially-isolated at first." Vanya likewise described a frustrating interaction with a white suitemate to illustrate how a sense of not-belonging and racial isolation could develop: "The other day I was in the restroom and my suitemate was telling me that she was talking to her mom about where she would live after college. I told her that I'm expected to go back home. She asked, 'Why do your parents expect that? Didn't they go to college?' I told her they didn't, and that my uncle went to college, but he stayed home. She was so shocked. She was so shocked she had never met anyone that was first-generation college student. I told her to expand her lens." Latino respondents at LAC often expressed a disappointment in their white peers' reactions; they believed that their white peers too often assumed that everyone shared the same experiences and outlooks and, in doing so, invalidated non-white, first-generation college-going and working-class students' experiences.

Such assumptions constitute a type of microaggression. *Microaggressions* are a subtle expression of racial and other types of stereotypes through interactions; they can occur as a microinsult, microassault, or a microinvalidation (Solórzano, Ceja, and Yossa 2000; Sue 2010). These microaggressions are not trivial; they are consequential. Latino students at LAC communicated several experiences of racial microaggressions, which further challenged their fragile sense of belonging on campus and shaped the ethnic boundaries they constructed and deployed with one another. In the face of microaggressions from non-Latinos on campus, LAC students attempted to promote solidarity first and to avoid emphasizing internal boundaries or differences.

For some students, microaggressions led them to question whether they even belonged on campus. For example, Karla shared: "I get the feeling that a lot of these colleges just accept us for being Latino. Because my SAT scores were not stellar and sometimes I feel they just accepted me because I'm a Latina. And people treat me that way. One of my suitemates has a full ride here and she wasn't born here, she's Latina. My white suitemate wasn't accepted to all the schools that my Latina suitemate was. The white girl told me she is really upset that the other girl got into those other schools." In asserting that she did not believe her Latina friend was deserving of a full scholarship or admissions to the other schools, Karla's white peer called the Latina student's qualifications into question. This racial microinvalidation made Karla question not only why her friend received admission and scholarships, but also whether race and ethnicity played a role in her own admission to LAC. Racial microinvalidations came in other, less explicit forms too, as Martiza explained: "I've experienced racism on campus. There was an event on campus, and it was at the same time that we [Latino Links] had an event. We were returning a cart and this white woman asked us if we were part of the janitorial staff. She thought *we were* the staff and I told her we were students here. I didn't realize what she was saying until my mom said, 'That was racism, *mija.*' My friend and my mom were adamant that it was racism." Maritza grew up in a predominantly Latino neighborhood in Los Angeles and attended a private high school with mostly Latino peers. Liberal Arts College has been her first experience in a context in which she is an ethnic-racial minority. She did not recognize the racist undertones of the white woman's comments until her mother and her friend pointed them out. But once she came to understand that to others her body read as janitorial staff, not as a student on campus, the experience of racial microaggression reduced her sense of belonging on campus.

And yet, there were instances of more overt racial aggressions on campus, as Lorena disclosed:

> My mother and I went to the school garden to pick fruit because I received an email from the school that fresh fruit was available and they didn't want it to go bad. We picked oranges and lemons and we had two bags. We were putting the bags in the truck and one of the directors of the garden started yelling in Spanish "Alto! Alto! [Stop! Stop!]" Then he accused us of intending to sell the fruit on the street. He called us orange-pickers. I told him I was a student and showed him my ID, but then he asked why I took so much fruit and I mentioned the e-mail. Then he said that the fruit is only for community members and we're only allowed to take two or three oranges. And I was very, very upset.

Following this incident, Lorena wrote to one of the deans of the university asking for an apology to her mother for being stereotyped as a poor, uneducated immigrant who did not belong to the university community. At the time of our interview the dean had refused to write an apology, but had questioned the director of the garden. Unfortunately, this was not the only instance of racial targeting of Latino students. During a fall LU meeting in 2009, Fabian told the group: "Apparently someone put a sign up by a dorm this weekend that said that 'LAC has been white since its founding, Mexicans cook, clean or conform.'" He criticized the Latino Cultural Center for excusing the comment by saying it was a disgruntled employee rather than an attack on Latinos. Fabian proposed that Latino Unidos engage in some action against the racist sign but members did not respond to his proposal and quickly moved on to the next agenda item.

Some LAC Latino students also encountered racism right outside the campus gates in the predominately white, conservative, and wealthy community where the school is located. During one Latino Links meeting, Gerardo shared, "Yesterday I borrowed my friend's car and went to fill up at the gas station across the street. This truck in front of me almost hit me, then he rolled his window down and said, 'You immigrant scum, you are taking all my benefits and you probably wanted me to hit you so you can send the money to your family.' I felt so riled up and shaken. I wanted to bring it up, and tell everyone that there is racism!" Paloma, the president of LL at the time, asked him, "Do you want to do something?" Harriet added, "You should write an article." Paloma added that "the local town is not like campus." The campus, she said, is "a little weird, like a bubble." Soon after Paloma's comment the topic was changed to other agenda items. During another Latino Links meeting Natalie told the group that a restaurant across the street from campus was scheduled to host a meeting with Jim Gilchrist and the Minutemen, a nativist vigilante group,[2] but that LAC students and community members called in complaining to the restaurant management, who ultimately decided to close the restaurant on that day.

Keeping the Boundaries of Latinidad Open at LAC

In the face of culture shock, tokenization, marginalization, microaggressions, and instances of overt racism on campus, Latino students at LAC discussed their experiences with their Latino suitemates, faculty, peer mentors, and at times, fellow members of Latino student organizations. Liberal Arts College has several programs in place to integrate Latino students in the campus and to help them acclimate. Once enrolled at LAC, each new Latino first-year student is assigned a Latino peer mentor and connected to the Latino cultural center. Each LAC student is assigned a faculty advisor, and since many Latino students choose one of the few Latino faculty on campus, these faculty are often overburdened. Still, students found them very helpful. For example, Bianca indicated that Latino faculty played a critical role in helping her to feel less racially isolated. She said, "My Latino professors encouraged me, they told me to get out of my comfort zone and not only stick to my kind." Small ethnic studies and sociology seminars also served as spaces for students to discuss their identities and the racial climate on campus. LAC's student-faculty ratio ensures that there are many small classes which foster feelings of safety and intimate discussions.

As discussed in Chapter 2, Liberal Arts College also supports Latino student organizations by giving them ample funding to organize cultural events on campus. This, in turn, facilitates solidarity and cooperation among the Latino student organizations, which are further encouraged to share funds and co-sponsor each other's events. Latino Links and Latinos Unidos did so, whereas inter-organizational cooperation did not take place at RU or RPU. Moreover, at LAC, there were no antagonistic feelings toward members of other Latino organizations. These inter-organizational relations along with the racial climate shaped how panethnic boundaries and identities were constructed.

The racial climate of LAC with its predominantly affluent white demographic and occurrences of racial microaggressions, coupled with its community ethos of LAC, shaped how students understood Latinidad and its boundaries. The students of LAC chose to deploy expansive and inclusive boundaries amongst each other given the at times hostile environment on campus and off. For example, during one LU meeting, Fabian asked members to indicate whether they spoke Spanish. When all indicated that they did so, Fabian expressed his surprise and noted that another member (not present at the meeting) did not speak Spanish. This interaction underscored that one did not have to speak Spanish in order to belong to the group.

Indeed, if anything, Latinos at LAC were vigilant about remaining open and hyper-aware of the risk of being Mexican-centric. They wanted to ensure that they were inclusive and open to non-Mexican members and cultures. Latinos Unidos especially took issue with the Latino Cultural Center's (LCC) focus on Mexican-related issues and outlined their grievances in a letter:

Although we understand the Chicano focus of LCC is founded in the location of the southwest—we feel that it is for the betterment of the Latino community here on the campus that LCC address the other significant segments of the Latino population in the United States, which include Caribbean, Central American, and South American groups. By hosting special events, speakers, and identity workshops that deal with the Latino identity beyond Chicanos and Mexican Americans, we feel that this could be achieved.

Members of LU complained about not only the Mexican-centric programming but also the age of the staff and their political leanings. They felt that the staff was conservative and too old to understand the issues of the contemporary Latino student at LAC.

For their part, LU members avoided focusing on Mexican culture too much in their programming. During a meeting Cristina, the president of Latinos Unidos, asked the group what they thought about creating club t-shirts. They then talked about designs. Selena said, "We could do Black and white negative image with Chente" (Vicente Fernandez, an iconic Mexican singer). Walter chimed in and suggested, "We could have that circle that the Latino cultural center has on their logo." Genova interrupted, "You mean the Aztec calendar?" A few members laughed because Walter did not know what the "circle" was, but then Genova continued, "I don't want an Aztec calendar because it's Mexican centered." Ana and Cristina agreed. Janelle said that she liked "the cube design." Cristina described the cube: "It's a cube with different kinds of skin and hair with LU printed in the middle." Selena seemed confused and asked, "Different types of skin and hair?" Cristina clarified "Yeah, like different types of people." Janelle added, "You know to show diversity among Latinos."

In another instance, Latinos Unidos students discussed a wall they would be painting on campus for Latino Heritage Month. They spent quite a bit of time deciding whether to paint the flags of all Latin American countries or select only a few. Rafael suggested randomly assigning each flag a number and drawing them from a hat. Cristina was concerned: "What if the main ones don't get picked?" Javier added "Yeah, like Mexico." Rafael said, "Yeah, but we can't leave anyone else out and we can't do all of them." Finally, Marina said, "Ok, let's paint the ones that are most represented on campus and then send an email to the school that others can come paint their flag." They all agreed this was the best strategy to ensure all groups felt included.

It is notable that while a majority of the students in LU are of Mexican origin, they place great importance on being open. I asked Ana, the only East Coast Latina in the group (of Puerto Rican descent), if she felt comfortable talking to the group about inclusivity. She responded, "I've always felt comfortable to speak up and remind the group that they're becoming Mexican-centric. I get it though for a lot of the members that's their background. I think we've done a good job with our events, like our music for parties. I had never heard *banda* before college, but we also play *reggaeton, merengue,* and *bachata*."

This is not to say that no one ever draws boundaries within or around Latinidad on the LAC campus. On a few occasions, I heard members of Latino Links and Latinos Unidos use the term "box checkers." When I asked Ana to explain this term, she said: "We have a specific joke to talk about people, who are Latino that we know don't identify. We call them box checkers. I think it's sort of confusing, like we don't know why they don't really identify. I think we are aware that it's bad that we're doing it." "Box checkers" were usually brought up when members discussed the reasons why some individuals of Latino origins did not join a Latino-specific organization on campus. However, as Ana's remark reveals, even as they drew this distinction, students at LAC were self-reflexive and critical about it.[3]

Constructing Identities at LAC

Liberal Arts College students not only established highly inclusive boundaries of "Latinidad" in their interactions, but also expressed them in their definitions of identity labels during their interviews. Recall Selena in the opening of the chapter: she held a broad understanding of "Latino" as including people across national borders and emphasized heterogeneity within the Latino population. Josiana similarly stated, "Latino has kind of become this thing about solidarity in the US. We have a similar story, like we were all colonized by the Spanish. Latina is someone who was born in Latin America or the US with parents from Latin America." Natalie likewise explained her identity-label preference as rooted in its broad basis for solidarity: "Latina is more accepted and encompasses a group experience of colonialism, neocolonialism, and exploitation." Adalberto, a member of Latino Links, expressed similar sentiments about embracing multiple, overlapping identities:

> I identify as Chicano, Mexican American, and the broader term "Latino." Chicano is not from Mexico, born in America but not completely American and you still have Mexican origins. Mexican Americans are those born here. All four of my grandparents were from Mexico. My grandparents on my mother's side were part of a migrant cycle following crops from Florida to Nebraska to Bakersfield. My grandparents on my father's side were also migratory but just migrated up and down California following crops. "Latino" means from Latin America. It's a really broad term. People tend to think that Latinos are just Mexicans so Latino helps include others.

Adalberto, like other members of Latino Links and Latino Unidos, privileges solidarity and explained that "Latino" is an appropriate term because it "helps include others." But he also combines this identification with that of Chicano and Mexican American.

Cassandra, a member of Latino Links, also identified with more than one category and explained how doing so was context-dependent: "Usually, in general, I identify as Latina but in contextual terms, where my more specific identity is more important I identify as Mexican like with my friends. For my race and politics class, I would say it's a more general term like 'Latina.' I feel like in the classroom it's a more general identification and it's very significant because I'm talking about politics so I say 'Latinos,' it's more general. I think that identity changes from place to place." This process of switching, as needed, from general to specific identities was one that many students at LAC described. Ana, a member of Latinos Unidos, similarly identified in both broad and specific terms: "I identify as Latina, Puerto Rican and Boriqua. My mom and dad would definitely identify as a Puerto Rican and Latino and they are very proud of their background." She then explained what "Latino" means to her: "Latino is definitely related to a panethnic awareness and an affinity with other peoples. I think it's about being different racially and some have different experiences with discrimination and prejudice. Some people identify as Afro-Latino, some Latinos are more light and have long hair." Cristina, a member of Latino Unidos, also uses both general and specific identities but in different contexts, as she explained: "I say 'Mexican American' because I was born here. My parents are from Mexico. Sometimes I just say 'Latina,' when I speak in general. . . . So, I kind of just use words depending on what other people say."

The one category LAC students rejected almost across the board, however, was "Hispanic." Many explained that the term "Hispanic" is a politically incorrect, artificial imposition by the U.S. government, created for the 1980 Census. Paloma described the process by which she came to understand the term as problematic: "I really didn't have a problem with the word Hispanic growing up because of the Census and different surveys used it. I was always told to mark it because I'm not white or Asian. But here, I learned it's very disrespectful because the Spanish took over these countries. But I know that we are not seen as Spanish in the color hierarchy. We are not seen as European so I think using Hispanic and being discriminated against at the same time, it just doesn't work." Paloma learned at LAC, in the classroom, and among her peers that "Hispanic" is not the "right" identity label to use. Adalberto put it this way: "'Hispanic' is not a word that should be used. It means of Spain. I know we have Spanish influences in Mexico but it's still Mexico, not Spain." Cristina, on the other hand, did not object personally to the term "Hispanic," but she did not use it much out of respect for her peers' preferences, as she explained: "I say 'Latino' not 'Hispanic.' I know that we're not Hispanic because we're not from Spain and we were colonized but I really don't have a negative connotation toward it."

In summary, processes of ethnic identification at LAC appear to be shaped by experiences of racial marginalization, which produce particularly cooperative relations among Latino student organizations and inclusive understandings of Latino identity more generally. Students faced initial culture shock, tokenization, racial microaggressions and overt racism at LAC, and these experiences are consequential. This racial climate led students to focus on solidarity and cohesion across different "types" of Latinidad and across Latino student organizations. Both the low numbers of Latinos on campus in general and the presence of Latinos of various origins, including international students, seem to foster a definition of Latinidad at LAC that combines heterogeneity and unity and perhaps provides the strength in numbers. A similar dynamic is found in Okamoto's (2003) research of pan-Asian coalitions—namely, that when specific national-origin groups are marginalized they reach out to panethnics for solidarity. In my observations of organizational meetings over the course of two academic years, LAC students never drew boundaries around ethnic authenticity. Rather than seeking to define the behaviors or characteristics that make one "Latino," they emphasized Latino diversity and embraced a range of cultural consumption patterns or identities.

Research University: Qualified Panethnic Identification and Competition

At Research University, Latino student organizations play a central role in students' experiences on campus. The relationship between the two organizations I studied was competitive and sometimes even contentious—something I explore further in Chapters 3 and 6; in this chapter, however, the focus is on the importance that members of Latinos United for Action (LUA) and Latino Fellowship (LF) ascribe to their organizations and their role in campus life. In both organizations, co-members form students' primary community and friend groups. Many call their respective organization "a home away from home." They serve as ethnic refuges or safe spaces. Recall that the ethnic breakdown of the student body at RU is approximately 50 percent Asian American, 25 percent white, 11 percent Latino, and 2 percent African American; thus, not unlike students at LAC, Latino students at RU reported feeling racially isolated and experiencing culture shock on campus.

Kenya, a member of LUA, described her freshmen year: "It was a big culture shock coming here. I didn't see any brown faces, I'm not too brown but you know. I remember saying that what I miss the most was pulling up at a stop sign and hearing someone bump *banda*." Lissandra, a member of LF, likewise described missing having more co-ethnics around: "I am the only person from my high school here. I didn't really know anyone and I was used to being around only Latino and black people so it was really weird." She felt disoriented in the new racial landscape of RU, where Latinos and blacks are in the minority. For Gilda, a member of LUA, even having a non-white roommate was not enough to ease the sense of isolation; she shared that "freshman year I was friends with my roommate but not people in my dorm. I felt very ostracized because I felt that no one really understood me. My roommate was ethnically Indian, but adopted by a white Jewish mother. Most of my schooling was really diverse."

The underrepresentation of Latinos gave my respondents a feeling of not belonging. Externally ascribed as "other" on campus, they found refuge in Latino organizations. Joining a Latino student organization helped ameliorate the feeling of being out of place. Mireya, a member of LF, described her transition to life at RU in the following manner: "It was really different because I was used to a really strong Mexican community, and here, you could count the Mexicans. So, I really wanted to find those people, find people that come from my background. . . . I found the Latino organizations and that helped me the most. It was familiar to me." Finding other students with the same background was crucial to finding one's "place" on campus. During one LUA meeting, a freshman stated, "I don't really fit in, I mean most of my high school was Latino. So, I like coming to this organization because I feel at home." Deidra, a member of both LF and LUA, explained her transition to RU: "My dad really wanted me to go to a closer college and not move. I would really cry on the phone. I just felt like that quarter was so long. I didn't relate to the Asians in my hall. I just felt really different. I was excited to find anyone like me in LUA and LF." Jennifer, of LUA, also stressed the importance of the organization in her transition: "I think that LUA has helped me meet people and create a little family. If I didn't have LUA, I think I would not have as many friends or as good as a time. It's really kind of bland here and there aren't enough Latinos." Gloria, a member of LF, took it a step further and described the empowering effects of being among co-ethnics:

> We are a minority on campus and our population is not that big. If there weren't any Latino organizations on campus, I don't think we would know that there are so many Latinos on campus. That's the way we feel comfortable, if you want to speak Spanish, come and speak Spanish. Being a minority in such a big campus and actually having a little place where you can come and hang out with all the Latinos. It's reassuring like . . . yeah, we can party but we're here for a reason. And it's like, if you can make it, then I can make it, and we can do it together. We are going to graduate and do all these things and that's why we are here.

Gloria's words make it clear that these Latino organizations play an important role in students' lives at RU.

Although Latinos are a minority at RU, as they are at LAC, RU students did not report experiencing with microaggressions. Indeed, Belinda, a member of LUA, was the only respondent at Research University who disclosed encountering overt racist remarks from non-Latino peers on campus: "I felt really, really lost when I first got here, especially in housing where it was mainly Asian. They would make a lot of remarks that didn't make me feel good at all—very racist remarks against Latinos. They would say things like 'The only Mexicans in our school are retarded like the janitors' and things like that." That students at RU did not talk much about such experiences in meetings or interviews should not be taken to mean that there are no microaggressions or overt racism on the RU campus; rather, it speaks to the intensity of simply feeling isolated and out of place, though not necessarily negatively stereotyped or invalidated per se. At the same time, the circumstances wherein racial microaggression, tokenization, and marginalization were *not* identified as frequent occurrences at RU seemed to produce a difference in how Latino students themselves thus engaged in drawing ethnic boundaries when compared to LAC student boundary deployment. Recall that in the face of racial hostility, LAC students drew broad and inclusive boundaries among each other whereas RU students ended up creating more narrow intragroup boundaries. Latinos respondents at RU focused on finding a space that felt like "home" on campus and these "homes" became sites for constant boundary deployment.

Drawing Latino Boundaries around Culture and Color

In their quest for a "home," both student organizations engaged in processes of marking and patrolling ethnic boundaries. Cristina Beltran (2010) theorizes that as political groups seek to create a sense of home, they often misread this home as a presence of homogeneity and agreement. Quoting Bernice Johnson Reagon (1983), she argues that home is seen as a "refuge—the space of sameness, a potentially nurturing place where you act out community and decide who you really are" (Beltran 2010, 65). Thus, it is not surprising that as students come to see these organizations as homes, they actively define the boundaries of belonging. They did so in different ways and to different degrees, but collectively, their doing so differentiated both RU organizations from those at LAC.

During my interviews, members of both LUA and LF described LUA as a site where the boundaries of Latino authenticity are carefully guarded and deployed according to such criteria as cultural consumption, Spanish fluency, and even skin color. Tania, a member of LF, recounted her experience with LUA:

> I tried LUA once, and I felt completely out of place. Everyone told me that I'm whitewashed, which I am. I didn't really grow up around a lot of Hispanics and we always had financial stability and stuff, so I never had to deal with that kind of thing. I just had a lot of white friends, Asian friends—I don't know I just didn't have the vocabulary and stuff—I don't speak Spanish, which is like a big thing. I'm a Latina, but I'm not, I don't fit the characteristics or whatever like I don't speak Spanish, you know I

haven't eaten all the Hispanic foods, that kind of stuff, like in a lot of the other clubs they integrate a lot of Spanish.

Tania's remarks reveal several indicators used to define and patrol Latinidad: language, culture, social class, and friendship circles. Several other students also felt that Latinos United for Action members judged their Latino authenticity by evaluating their social relationships (whom they dated, whom they were friends with, and so on). Gloria, a member of LF, used a Spanish-language proverb to describe the process: "Dime con quien andas, y te dire quien eres [Tell me who your friends are, and I will tell you who you are]."

Deidra and Gilda shared the experience of having LUA members draw boundaries around skin color. Deidra, who has fair skin and green eyes, reported: "Sometimes people think you have to be brown to be Latina. Sometimes LUA members say, 'Brown is beautiful and brown pride,' but I'm not brown. I want to say 'Hey, we're not all brown, maybe inside we're brown and culturally we're brown, but like, I'm not brown.'" When she first joined LUA Deidra felt that her presence was constantly questioned and she was mistaken for "the white friend" of other members. Deidra described feeling like she had to "prove that I could be there." Gilda also claimed skin color was used as an indicator for Latino identity at LUA. She described her girlfriend's experience attending a meeting: "At one point, she did go to a meeting, but I guess she had really bad experience when the co-chair at the time said, 'Wow! You're dark! That's good for the organization.' And her friend didn't know Spanish so they told the co-chair, and she kept speaking Spanish." Gilda went on to explain that the leadership believed darker skin would amplify their claims that Latinos are an oppressed ethnic minority. At LUA, skin color became a proxy for experiences with discrimination and racism and a political commitment to racial-ethnic equality and justice. In this way, skin color is constructed as a relevant boundary of Latinidad.

Pablo, a member of LF, shared: "Sometimes I warn people about LUA, because I know people who have gone and they say they are not Latino enough to go there." When I asked whether members of LUA explicitly told people they were "not Latino enough," Pablo responded: "I think so, or they just say other things." Even when members of Latino Fellowship could not describe exactly how LUA members restricted the boundaries of Latinidad, they felt excluded nonetheless.

But aside from the perceptions of Latino Fellowship members, *were* such efforts to patrol and restrict ethnic boundaries indeed going on in Latinos United for Action? In my observations of LUA gatherings, I did see these processes at work, but I also saw and heard about LUA problematizing such practices and trying to remain open to different ways of being Latino. Every LUA meeting consisted of a discussion of political and/or social issues. These discussions created many opportunities for members to voice their opinions about Latinidad and its boundaries. For example, during one meeting in the fall of 2009, the leadership decided to have a discussion about Teatro[4] and how it can be used as a tool for liberation. They opted to have groups discuss a topic first—immigration—and then imagine a play that would highlight the main issues that emerge. The goal of the session was to have members understand how Teatro could be empowering and raise awareness around important issues. Giovanna began the meeting by asking the group to talk freely about the issue of immigration. The conversation did not go as expected. Gustavo began by saying, "I think it's really hard to be an undocumented student, like a lot of them are called white-washed from their families and friends for succeeding in school." Miriam quickly jumped in and steered the conversation in a different direction: "Yeah, like when I go to Mexico, my family and their friends make fun of my accent." Giovanna and a few other members exchanged looks. She cautioned, "I want to remind everyone that there are privileges that we have being in this country, and we need to check ourselves." Carlos, another member of the leadership, said, "All this talk reminds me of authenticity, which is always problematic. I've experienced this a lot because I don't speak Spanish." In this exchange, Giovanna attempted to remind members to think about how their experiences are shaped by their own privileges, such as being born in this country; specifically, she was implying that Miriam should remember that privilege when she's "made fun of for not speaking Spanish" in Mexico. Carlos also reminded the group that it is problematic to draw boundaries around Latino identity on the basis of language.

Although Gilda, a member of LUA, described an incident when the leadership continued to speak Spanish even when non-Spanish speakers were present, at least some members were determined to keep the space accessible to audience members who spoke only English. For example, when an artist from a local community center came to a LUA meeting to discuss *son jarocho* (folk music) and began by speaking in Spanish, Kenya and Lalo quickly interrupted him and asked if he could switch to English. They said, "Thank you, we know that not everyone understands Spanish." LUA members were, nonetheless, aware of and sought to dispel perceptions that they were Mexican-centric and exclusive to Spanish-speakers. Jennifer said, "I know some people think LUA is predominantly a Mexican space. But in my experience it is not. Not everyone in LUA is Mexican. We do deal with issues that pertain to Mexico but I'm not full Mexican. Also, I don't speak Spanish and nobody cares." Still, whether accurate or not, the prevailing understanding of LUA is that it is a site where ethnic boundaries are drawn around language and even national origins.

Yet patrolling ethnic boundaries is something that happens at Latino Fellowship as well, only there it happens in a very different manner—one that, ironically, is much harder to explicitly address. In Latino Fellowship, members frequently draw ethnic boundaries through jokes and banter. This was particularly common during cultural presentations, which happen several times a semester. During these presentations, students showcase the culture of a particular nation in Latin America. The official rationale for the presentations is to expose members to each other's cultures, with each presentation being led by students whose heritage is the particular country. Suyeli explained, "I think we do cultural presentations to spread our culture. A lot of people think, 'Oh, she's Latina, oh, she must be Mexican.' People don't know that there are other countries besides Mexico in the Latino culture. Latino Fellowship is a place to come and learn about culture." During one meeting, Suyeli and Thalia, both of whose parents are from El Salvador, were presenting about Salvadoran culture. I sat next to Pablo and a young woman I did not know. Pablo asked, "Who is presenting today?" The woman responded, "El Salvador." "Oh, Salvis. It must be *negrita*,"[5] Pablo replied. The young woman exclaimed "Racist!" and then chuckled. When the presentation started twenty-five minutes late, Pablo noted, "Yeah, we're on Latino time." Suyeli and Thalia stood in front of the room with a Salvadoran flag, some *pupusas* (a Salvadoran dish), and an indigenous artifact. There were about forty members at the meeting, and a few men were teasing in a flirtatious fashion. One young man asked Suyeli if they could "have a *pupusa* before the presentation." She quickly and sternly replied "No." Pablo said, "Damn! She is Salvadoran!" As they began to talk about El Salvador, one member bellowed something about Mexico being better than El Salvador in soccer. There were laughs.

Suyeli continued to explain that "El Salvador is part of Central America, it is not part of Mexico like Cruz says all the time." Cruz responded, "Yo, it's smaller than LA." Suyeli continued to tell the group about the structure of the government and the civil war and briefly mentioned US involvement in the war. When Pablo asked what tribe people of El Salvador come from, Suyeli responded, "The Mayans and they call themselves *pipil*." Thalia and Suyeli spent more time talking about food; they mentioned *pan con chumpe* (turkey sandwiches), *pupusas* and *horchata* (rice-based drink), emphasizing that "[the horchata is] different from the Mexican one and it's served in a bag usually." Cruz interrupted, "I forgot, what part of Mexico is El Salvador?" More laughter. Suyeli then asked a young man to come up and recite a poem that described common words and slang used by Salvadorans. The young man concluded by saying, "Salvadorans are better looking than Mexicans, it's a proven fact." The room exploded in laughter, and they all ran up to the front of the room to eat *pupusas* and *platanos fritos* (fried plantains).

Students laughed as they joked about each other's national origins. It was a common occurrence during presentations for groups to make jokes with ethnocentric undertones. The collective mood of the room always remained light during these discussions. At LF meetings there are many instances of boundary deployment between Salvadorans and Mexicans. But there are also racial comments, such as when Pablo referenced Suyeli's dark skin by calling her "negrita." Recall Deidra, a member of both LUA and LF, who said LUA members did not think she was Latina. At LF, she found attitudes that were even more intrusive, with members asking, "Are you sure you're not a little bit white?" Although students have a perception that the boundaries of Latinidad are foreclosed only in LUA, the difference between the two organizations lies more in *how* boundaries are established and patrolled.

In general, ethnic boundary deployment is constant at Research University. This is reminiscent of processes Beltran (2010) identified among the Chicano activists of the 1960s, when they questioned each other's allegiances to the movement. She quotes a poem by Audre Lorde, "Between Ourselves," to describe the conflictual process amongst co-ethnics. Lorde's words resonate here too:

> Once when I walked into a room
> My eyes would seek out the one or two faces
> For contact or reassurance or a sign
> I was not alone
> Now walking into rooms full of black faces
> That would destroy me for any difference
> Where shall my eyes look?
> Once it was easy to know
> Who are my people.

Lorde's poem speaks to the perceptions that many students held about interpersonal relations at LUA and between LUA and other Latino organizations on campus. The specter of "acting Latino enough" is palpable on this campus. Although members of both organizations describe LUA as a place where ethnic boundaries are delineated, my ethnographic observations reveal that leaders and members of LUA often work to keep the boundaries open by explicitly noting whenever ethnic lines are drawn and seeking to address the issue. Conversely, at LF, where such boundary maintenance is achieved through ethnic banter and humor, such processes are more likely to fly "under the radar," allowing the group to appear more neutral and inclusive.

Constructing Identities at RU

When asked to discuss their own self-identification, students at RU overwhelmingly used the "Latino" label, but their rationales for using it were different from LAC students, who chose "Latino" because of its unifying potential. Members of both organizations chose to identify as Latino, while some LUA members also identified as Chicano. Cruz, a leader of Latino Fellowship, explained his identity-label preference: "I identify myself as Latino. My parents are from Mexico; however, I'm not. To identify myself as Mexican, I feel is inaccurate. I think the term 'Latino' kind of includes people from all over Latin America, including the United States. I am from California, I was born here, but I'm not Caucasian, but at the same time, I'm not from Mexico. A lot of people identify themselves as

Mexican—I can't say that." Cruz highlights the complexities that many Latino youth grapple with as they try to understand who they are, in light of their own and their parents' birthplaces. Similarly, Thalia, another member of LF, sees herself as Latina rather than Salvadoran; she explained, "I'm Latina. I don't say I'm Salvadoran or Salvadoran American. I will say my parents are from El Salvador. And I'm definitely not going to say I'm American." Both Cruz and Thalia consider the place where they were born and where they reside as part of their identity. Similarly, Pablo said, "I'm Latino. Latino is anyone who is from the continent from Mexico and under."

For some students, however, identifying as Latino was more problematic. For instance, Mireya, a member of LUA, said, "My parents are from Mexico. I'm Mexican American. But I also always say that I'm Latina. But all of this is just an ethnicity, it doesn't define me. It's just a name. I'm just me." Like Mireya, others expressed some uneasiness with the "Latino" label. Tania, a member of LF, said, "I identify as Latina but I don't fit all the characteristics, like I don't speak Spanish and I haven't eaten all the Latino foods." Both Tania's signaling that she is not representative and Mireya's refusal to allow Latina to define her are rhetorical strategies used to distance the speaker from some imagined "ideal" Latino/a. Such strategies both acknowledge that others patrol the boundaries of "authentic" Latinidad and seek to preempt potential questions about the speaker's claims to the category.

Still, for many of these students, the term "Latino" was preferred precisely because it was perceived as more inclusive and unifying. When I asked Gloria, a member of Latino Fellowship, "How do you identify?" she replied "Latina . . . I'm Latina because I am from Latin American and I don't want to differentiate myself." Kenya of LUA similarly explained, "I call myself 'Latina.' I use it when including myself with Central Americans." And Gilda of LUA put it this way: "I think the word 'Latino' is more about a Latin America type of idea. I don't really think about it as an imposing, it's more descriptive. I like Latino because it's a Spanish word and it's more reflective of the culture." For Gilda, the Latina label is not an imposition, unlike the perception many students held of the term Hispanic, which was created by government officials (discussed later in the chapter).

In addition to identifying as Latino, several student members of LUA also identify as Chicanos. These Chicano-identifiers have been part of the organization for several years. In my survey and interviews, I did not encounter any first-year members who identified as Chicanos, which is consistent with students' understanding of this identity as volitional and something one grows into. Students in this historically political group saw claiming a Chicano identity as a state of consciousness. As Lalo, a leader at LUA, described it: "It wasn't until my third year that I started to call myself 'Chicano.' It was a slow transition to call myself 'Chicano' and it happened because we read the founding organizational documents of the 1960s. And I know at least in this chapter, we think about it [Chicano identity] as a political ideology not a nationality." When I asked Lalo to say more about what it meant for Chicano to be a political ideology, he elaborated: "I'm conscious about the social injustices that our communities have gone through. And I believe in giving back to our communities who identify as Chicano or Latino. My brother says he's Chicano and I tell him, 'No, you aren't.' He doesn't know what he wants to do yet. I ask him questions like 'Why do you identify this way?' Sometimes he says things like 'I thought Chicano meant being born here.'" For Lalo, one has to grow into an identification as Chicano—more specifically, one has to understand the history and political consciousness that comes with the category. Lalo expects his brother to have a clear idea of what he wants to do and how he wants to contribute to the Latino community before he adopts a Chicano identity.

This idea of "Chicano" as a political term was reinforced through interactions. Recall in Chapter 3, where I described a workshop in which members were directed to discuss what it meant to be Chicano. There, while it became clear that the term and even LUA itself were sometimes perceived as being "only about Mexicans," members were also pleased to learn otherwise as students of non-Mexican origins disclosed relating to the Chicano label. Kenya addressed such perceptions head-on: "'Chicano' has different definitions depending on who you talk to, it doesn't just mean Mexican born here. I think people of other ethnicities get turned off by it. We tell people that it's not just for Mexicans it's for people who want to address inequalities. . . . Chicano means to me to have the heart to sympathize but also have action and work to better the community. Chicano means that I'm close to my indigenous roots and that I don't forget about them." These students often simultaneously identified as Latino.

Finally, like students at LAC, students in both organizations at Research University almost universally disliked the label "Hispanic." Evelyn, a member of LUA, explained:

> I use "Latino" or "Chicano" depending on the context. Latino is being from Latin America. I think it's more like a nationality like where you're from. I think Chicano is more than just a nationality or not nationality at all because you don't have to be Mexican American. Being Chicano means that you're active and that you're politically conscious. "Hispanic," I don't like it because of the history of the word and Reagan and how he tried to make himself a friend of the immigrants and that was bullshit, he could care less.

Here, Evelyn echoes commonly held perspective about the origins of the word "Hispanic," noting its connection to the government and a seemingly disingenuous effort to connect with immigrants. Kenya made the same point: "I think 'Hispanic' was created by the government to put some sort of number on us. So, I really don't call myself 'Hispanic' and when someone calls himself Hispanic I feel like it's a really strange." For Gloria, the term's connection to the Spanish language is too restrictive: "I feel 'Hispanic' is just like a word that the government uses for the Spanish speaking but not everyone in Latin America speaks Spanish." She also reacted strongly against it: "I cringe when I hear it. I read all these articles about where the word 'Hispanic' came from. I think of it as an imposed identity. It's a way of defining all these people. I think that it homogenizes everyone. I really don't like the word. From my understanding the word 'Hispanic' comes from the U.S. government."

Aside from the consensus among LAC and RU students regarding the problematic nature of the label "Hispanic," the identity process varied between these two campuses. The competition and conflict between Latino Fellowship and LUA further shaped the identification patterns. First, members of LF felt the need to qualify their identification preferences. They often claimed a term, but then listed presumed requirements they did not meet. And members of both organizations perceived LUA to be the space where ethnic boundaries were more carefully patrolled, even though, as I noted above, similar processes were at work in LF, only in different ways. LF was a space where ethnic boundary deployment happened constantly, albeit with humor. The term 'Chicano' differentiated LUA and LF members because it as associated with the realm of politics, and it came to belong to LUA (further discussed in Chapter 6).

Regional Public University: National Origin Identification and Missing Interactions

As explained in Chapter 4, Regional Public University is quite different from both Liberal Arts College and Research University in many ways. First and foremost, RPU is a commuter campus. Students spend little time on campus beyond the classroom and interact very little with other students outside of the classroom. The two organizations I studied at RPU, Latinos United for Action (LUA) and Hispanics for Economics (HE), didn't interact at all—they neither *cooperated* as at LAC, nor *competed* as at RU; rather, the organizations were autonomous and simply *coexisted*. Second, recall this campus is a Hispanic-serving institution, where over 45 percent of students are Latino; the next largest group are Asian Americans at 20 percent, followed by whites and African Americans at 8 percent. The Latino majority at RPU makes it quite distinct from Liberal Arts College and Research University.

This difference became especially clear when I asked RPU respondents to discuss their transition to college. In stark contrast to LAC and RU students, who described experiences of culture shock, racial isolation, and microaggression,

RPU students reported no such experiences, even when probed further to discuss instances of discrimination or prejudice. They also did not express the need for a Latino space or a "home away from home" on campus. Instead, when prompted to discuss race, many members of Hispanics for Economics, in particular, emphasized the organization's openness to non-Latinos and deemphasized the importance of ethnic identity on campus. As noted at the start of the chapter, these findings should not be taken as evidence that students at RPU have *no* experience with racism on campus; the findings suggest, rather, that such experiences are not a predominant characteristic of RPU students' experience. In other words, though RPU students, like students at LAC and RU, are learning about who they are and where they belong, they are not doing so through experiences of racial discrimination and marginalization on campus.

Keeping Ethnic Boundaries Open at RPU

A common narrative reiterated by members and leaders of Hispanics for Economics was the importance of keeping their organization open to all students on campus regardless of their ethnic background. For example, during my interview with Yvette, the president of HE, I asked her to tell me why she joined the organization. She discussed the first meeting she attended: "I sat down and met people! I thought, 'Oh, this is pretty cool.' You know, they weren't all Latinos so for me it was kind of like, it's called Hispanic for Economics, but the diversity of the group really encouraged me. Even though segregation isn't really big deal, you do see how certain groups are like, 'Oh, here are the Asians, here's the blacks, and here's the Latinos.' So, knowing that we can interact in a business kind of way, it really impacted me." Members continuously described HE as a diverse organization. Of the approximately fifty registered members that HE had every term, about ten were not Latino.

According to Yvette, this openness was a central and long-standing feature of the organization: "We've been here since 1986 and it was predominantly Latino, obviously it was the eighties. I think in the early nineties we opened it up to non-Latino students on campus." When I asked how that came about, she replied: "I'm not too sure about that but I'm assuming it's because, you know racism wasn't such a big deal anymore. We were more open to different cultures and we really try not to discriminate against other races and plus, I'm assuming like other organizations were not biased towards a certain race or anything like that." Yvette's narrative of HE's history reveals a colorblind approach toward race relations. She implies that discrimination has dissipated and the organization seeks to remain open to all ethnic-racial groups. Her narrative treats ethnic and racial diversity as if it is disconnected from power and resources; all groups are simply and unproblematically equal.

Many other HE students reiterated this type of narrative. For example, Yareli, a member of HE, explained:

I think when the organization used that word [Hispanic] it was important to have a place where Latinos had a place to claim as their own. I really like that they're open to other ethnicities but I do get a sense that it's a Latino business organization because it's called that. I think it's good and it's bad. I can see where it was born and the need for it. I think that maybe the founders needed to call it that but I think that it takes away from the business part. And I think if anything we should know better than to exclude anyone.

Yareli emphasized the importance of remaining open to all and questioned whether a Latino-specific organization was even necessary. Lucy, another member, said, "HE is open to all minorities and ethnicities. Some people think it's only for Mexicans and Latinos. When they started it, they did want some sort of club for minorities. We do have an African American member but he says he joined because there is no black business organization. Our media officer is Filipina!" This message about diversity was expressed not only during interviews but also during meetings. For example, at the beginning of one, Yvette stood at the front the room and said, "I know Hispanic is not the politically correct word but that's how we started and we want to honor that. Plus, we are very happy that there are people here who are not Latino. We are open to all students, so please keep coming."

Despite, the official narrative focusing on openness, some of the guest speakers did address the organization as being specifically Latino. For example, when a senior executive at Telemundo came to discuss jobs in broadcasting, before mentioning the type of work available in broadcasting, he discussed his upbringing and occupational trajectory. He shared that he grew up in Compton and went to community college. He asked the group, "Does anyone know what Affirmative Action is?" No one in the room reacted. He quickly said, "It's a negative word now but it wasn't then. I was the first class of Affirmative Action that transferred to UCLA." He then urged the group, "Become bilingual if you are not. We need Latinos everywhere. We even need them to help fix the problems in Wall Street." Although the speaker felt he was being empowering and encouraging, this was lost on some of the members. Yareli, for one, said of the speakers: "I really do not care if they are Latino; I want them to tell me something I don't know. Like this person from Hollywood came to tell her story, which is fine, she was Latina but she didn't really have anything to offer me." For Yareli, the ethnic background of the speakers was secondary; she wanted to know what useful information they could provide to *all* students.

For others, such as Sandra, the secretary of HE, the problem with speakers addressing Latinos specifically in the organization was the potential of alienating other members. As she put it, "It makes me really sad when our speakers talk to only Latinos. We are open to all ethnicities and we try to emphasize that to all our members. I don't want any of our members to feel discriminated against. Last semester, we actually had a black member who was very proud of her race." Sandra worried about the non-Latino members' feelings of belonging. Her remarks also speak to the transitory nature of HE's membership (as she mentions the membership changes semester by semester), which results from RPU's status as a commuter campus and a place that attracts transfer students (as discussed in Chapter 4). They tend not to relocate for college and often spend less than four years at RPU given their previous work at community college.

While Latinos United for Action was characterized by the same quick member turnover as well, they lacked the organizational structure to keep operations running. They often canceled meetings and spent less time together overall. When they did meet, they tended to focus on organizing events. Occasionally, they did discuss ways to present the LUA message to the student body. They valued honoring the indigenous roots of Latinos, in particular Mexicans, and thus kept this as an important boundary. For example, when planning a celebration of the Mexica New Year, Josefina suggested they have *salseros* perform. Monica countered by suggesting they include *cumbia* rather than salsa, because it has "more indigenous-type rhythms."

Given RPU students' tendency to deemphasize the importance of race on campus, I asked them to discuss what it was they saw themselves and other Latino students as having in common. They consistently responded "culture." When pushed to define that "culture," men emphasized the goal of supporting their families financially, while women mentioned the expectation that they live at home while in college and before marriage. Jackie said, "When I think of Latinos, for example, our parents won't let us leave the house until we get married. My mom won't let me move out until I get married and I have a curfew." Mayra, a member of HE, described her perception of traditional Mexican culture as consisting of strong gender norms and obedience to a patriarch: "I've had a few friends that their parents, especially the father, didn't let them leave. I would say I didn't grow up traditional to a certain extent. I didn't grow up traditionally Mexican. My dad hates makeup and really girly stuff and I told him I wanted to do cosmetology and he never questioned it." Mayra described her father, who let her undertake a subject of study he "hated" as exceptional, but she also referred to Mexican culture as involving family systems where fathers control their daughters' life choices. Respondents at LAC and RU did not give any examples of an imagined "traditional" Latino family when asked to describe what it meant to be Latino and what Latinos had in common. Only RPU respondents' referenced commonalities among families when defining the boundaries of Latinidad. This tendency was probably a result of differences in residential patterns and the fact that RPU students lived with their families in predominantly Latino communities. At times, members even colloquially mentioned stereotypes about Latinos. For example, Yvette, the president during the 2008–2009 school year, approached me after one of the first meetings I attended. She apologized because the meeting started late. She said, "I'm sorry the speakers are usually not so disorganized or late." I eased her concerns and told her that HE was one of the most organized student organizations I had seen. She answered, "Well, Latinos tend to be *cohibidos* [shy] so we bring people to them so they get used to talking to others," suggesting that being shy is a Latino trait.

Choosing Identities at RPU

As many of the quotes in the last section reveal, HE members do use panethnic terms such as "Latino" in conversation. But when it comes to their own self-identification, they overwhelmingly choose not to use such terms, in contrast to students at the other two schools. Regional Public University respondents rejected *both* "Latino" and "Hispanic" panethnic labels, despite their membership in organizations named "Hispanics for Economics" and "Latinos United for Action." Indeed, some RPU students viewed all panethnic labels as problematic and even racist. For example, Vanessa explained: "I don't use the words 'Hispanic' or 'Latino' at all. I've always thought that people from Spain came over and raped our mothers and then just left, so why would I use that word ['Hispanic']? And I always think of the word 'Latino' as derogatory to dark-skinned people. I don't use words that are about the physical. For example, people say, 'Oh, she has dark hair, she must be Hispanic or Latino.'"

Like Vanessa, Alex also found both terms disempowering, saying, "I identify as Mexican. I don't like the word 'Hispanic' it is like recolonizing yourself. 'Latino,' I say, 'What does that word mean?' 'Latino' means 'Latin.' Mexicans are not Latins. 'Latino,' it's just a word to categorize us." Inter-ethnic dynamics, specifically relations between Mexican and Central American populations, were another reason for rejecting panethnic terms, as Alex further explained: "Like I know Salvadorans don't like to be called Mexican, so I think 'Latino' and 'Hispanic' are not the words to use." Teresa echoed Alex's concern, "Some people think 'Hispanic' and 'Latino' are the right things to say. They say 'I don't want to call a Salvadoran Mexican or a Mexican Salvadoran.' I tell them to ask people what they want to be called." Several members of HE expressed this preference for labels that specified national origins: Sandra was typical in saying, "I consider myself Mexican because my ancestors are from Mexico." Yvette similarly explained, "I'm half-Cuban and my mother is Salvadoran so that's what I say."

Despite their preference for national-origin identities, a few RPU students did indicate they used panethnic identification if necessary. When I asked Lucy, "Do you call yourself 'Hispanic' or 'Latina?'" she replied: "No. I call myself 'Mexican American.' People are getting the hang of 'Mexican American.' But that doesn't include people whose parents are not from Mexico, [it] doesn't include Central America or South America. I call myself 'Mexican American' or 'Chicana.' 'Chicano' means I'm not Mexican or white American. 'Hispanic' sounds

like Spanish or European. If I have to I'm more comfortable calling myself 'Latina.'"
Lucy identified foremost as Mexican American and even Chicana, though her
understanding of the latter did not have the political undertones that it had for
members of LUA at Research University. Thus, terms have distinct meanings
in different institutional contexts. She conceded that she might call herself
"Latina," but only if she "had to."

Students offered two other reasons for not identifying panethnically at
RPU. First, some were not born in this country; theirs is commonly referred to
as the "1.5 generation." Sara, a member of HE, explained, "I say I'm 'Mexican.' I
never say 'Hispanic' but if some people say 'Are you Hispanic or Latina?' I'll say
yes but it will not come from my mouth. And I have never ever said 'Mexican
American.' I was born in Mexico and migrated at the age of ten. I don't think
'Chicana' is a word for a person of my generation in the United States." Jerry, a
member of LUA, called himself 'Mexicano' or 'Mexican' because he was born in
Mexico. He did not use 'Chicano' because for him, it meant "someone who thought
they knew more about being Mexican than everyone else." Jerry, a member of
LUA, had very distinct ideas about the label 'Chicano' compared to his peers at
Research University who are also members of LUA. Jerry also spoke at length
about tensions between U.S.-born Mexicans and immigrants in his high school,
noting that "they used to call me wetback. There was a lot of brown on brown
friction."

Second, some members were mixed race. For example, Marta, a member of
HE, said, "I'm half Mexican and half Filipina. I'm Flipxican." When I asked her "Do
you use words like 'Latina' or 'Hispanic' to identify yourself or other people?," she
responded: "I think I use 'Latino' sometimes. Like I say, 'Do you like Latin men
or do you like Latin women?'" Jesus, also in HE, similarly indicated that he used
the term 'Latino' but he also usually qualified this: "I primarily say 'Latino.' But
I am mixed ethnicity. I do let people know that I'm not just Mexican, I am also
Armenian and Native American. I do say 'Latino' but if we do get into conversation that I do emphasize that I'm not just Latino."

Only one student whom I interviewed at RPU indicated a preference for
panethnic terms, 'Latino' in particular. Yareli is a member of Hispanics for Economics, but she spent the first two years of college at the University of California, Santa Barbara. Medical issues forced her to return home and transfer to
RPU. When I asked her how she identified, she responded: "I say 'Latina.' I sup-
pose sometimes I may say 'Hispanic.' For a while I would say 'Salvadoran' and
then people ask me exactly from where. I would have to emphasize that I was
born here so I don't say that anymore. I think 'Latina' is what I'm comfortable
with. I don't say 'Hispanic' too much because 'Latino' sounds more Spanish.
Anyway and 'Hispanic' reminds me of 'spick.' I don't say 'Salvadoran American'
because I don't say 'American.'"

As a Hispanic-serving institution, RPU has a critical mass of Latinos. There are both panethnic and national-origin based organizations on campus. However, both LUA and HE had members from Central America and Mexico. The large Latino population on campus draws student attention to interethnic difference rather than panethnic similarities. When asked to discuss coalitions between Salvadoran and Mexican organizations and label these coalitions, students emphasized that panethnic labels were unnecessary. RPU Latino respondents were less likely to identify panethnically. Like my respondents at LAC and RU, most of my RU respondents are the first in their families to go to college. Yet, as college students who continue to live at home, they did not confront culture shock or racial microaggressions in college. Unlike the racial climate at LAC and RU, in which student identities were ascribed externally on campus, RPU's racial climate did not appear to "other" Latino students categorically. They were part of a majority Latino, working-class student body. Again, this is not to suggest that there is no racial inequality on campus; it is to say only that none of my respondents reported instances of perceiving racial animus.

RPU's commuter campus dynamics also make organizational involvement less salient than at Liberal Arts College and Research University. Students spend most of their time off campus with friends and family not associated with their university, not dealing with co-ethnics on campus. When I prompted my respondents to discuss the ethnic boundaries of Latinidad, they identified family and gender arrangements as shared commonalities. The racial climate is predominantly Latino, but characterized by little interaction among the student body in general. Respondents did not disclose a process of renegotiating ethnic boundaries and identities, perhaps because they feel little need to do such negotiation. As the majority, they did not face a new racial environment on campus that forced them to re-process their ethnic identities.

Conclusion

Latino students' experiences varied across the three campuses studied, in part because of the following constellation of institutional factors: (1) the percentage of Latino students on campus, (2) the economic origins of the student body, (3) student residential patterns, (4) diversity programming and policy, and (5) interorganizational relations. These institutional characteristics create the racial climate in which Latinos learn, interact, construct panethnic boundaries, and choose to self-identify.

At Liberal Arts College, the racialized organizational setting is characterized by an institutional prioritization of diversity coupled with affluence and privilege among the predominantly white student body. This fosters cooperation and solidarity among Latino students. Research University similarly promotes diversity but its organizational structures unintentionally foster competition for resources among Latino student organizations, as demonstrated by the differential treatment LUA and LF receive from the Multicultural Center (as described in Chapter 3). One consequence of this competition is that Latinos at RU draw intra-ethnic boundaries and question their peers' panethnic authenticity. In contrast, Regional Public University, located in a Latino enclave, serves mostly local Latino students. This Hispanic-serving institution's racialized organizational setting matches the adjacent community outside the campus gates; thus Latino students do little re-learning or "discursive reinterpretation" (Brown and Jones 2015) of their ethnic-racial knowledge when compared to LAC and RU students.

Respondents at Liberal Arts College disclose experiences with culture shock, racial microaggressions, and tokenization, in line with processes of external ascription. The large gap between the experiences of the mostly affluent student body and those of the first-generation working-class Latino students creates a sense of marginalization for the latter, which, in turn, fosters their panethnic identification on campus. LAC students live on campus among affluent peers, and they choose to prioritize solidarity with other Latinos in this environment. This elite institution draws students from all over the country; thus, LAC's Latino population, though mostly local, Mexican, and Central American, includes some Puerto Ricans and Dominicans from the East Coast as well.[6] In planning Latino cultural events, students were careful to be inclusive of all national-origin groups' cultures. This national-origin diversity also fostered an inclusive and broad perspective about who exactly is Latino and what Latinos look like. Through a mutually constitutive process of ascription and identification, LAC Latino students come together to form a collective sense of being that focuses on embracing heterogeneity to establish solidarity.

In contrast, students at Research University perceive that ethnic boundaries are deployed at LUA in particular around skin color and Spanish language fluency. Even some members of Latino Fellowship shared anecdotes about friends who decided not to join LUA because they were made to feel not "Latino enough." Students described LUA as exclusionary, although my observations indicate instances where LUA attempts to be open and avoid authenticity discussions. Also, LF is not immune from deploying ethnic boundaries, but its members use banter and humor in doing so. Organizational competition and division at RU resulted in intra-ethnic boundary deployment. Students thought that Latinos Unidos for Action, the political organization, defines the parameters of both belonging to the organization and representing authentic Latinidad by questioning participants' political commitments, Spanish fluency, and skin color. Issues of ethnic authenticity were significant factors in the division between LUA and LF at Research University; no such division was present between the organizations at Regional Public University or Liberal Arts College.

Though there are large differences between Research University and Liberal Arts College, there are also some similarities in the ways that Latino students identify at these schools. Latino students are in the minority at both institutions, accounting for 11 percent of all students on each campus. Latinos in ethnic organizations at both LAC and RU have a heightened sense of ethnic identity because of their underrepresentation. Respondents at both institutions overwhelmingly identify as Latino and use national-origin identities secondarily, with a subgroup of LUA members also adopting the Chicano label.

Like to the students in other studies (Umaña-Taylor 2004; Tovar and Feliciano 2009), my respondents at LAC and RU became hyperaware of their *panethnic* similarities and the power that identifying as Latinos afforded them on campus. There, where Latinos are a small minority of the population, their experiences with isolation, a new culture, and discrimination remind them that they do not belong and cannot identify simply as Americans. Instead, students discovered the potential for solidarity in defining themselves as Latinos, even though some RU students felt the need to justify and defensively qualify this identification.

In contrast, RPU respondents overwhelmingly rejected all panethnic identities. They were reluctant to identify with broad terms such as "Latino" and "Hispanic." In the Latino-majority classrooms at RPU, students highlighted their specific national origins instead of their panethnic similarities. Even in panethnic organizations, students specified their Mexican, Salvadoran, and Guatemalan uniqueness. RPU students, unlike LAC and RU students, mentioned intra-ethnic relations and differences among Latino groups and cite these differences as reasons to avoid panethnic identification. Moreover, many HE students downplayed the significance of race while emphasizing the need to keep the organization open to all groups. Latino students' identity preferences at RPU are consistent with Dina Okamoto's (2003) theory of segregation among ethnic groups. Like the Asian Americans she studied, the critical mass of Latinos at this Hispanic-serving institution meant that student could separate and form national-origin groups, which ultimately highlighted differences between groups rather than similarities.

What this comparative analysis shows is twofold. First, ethnoracial identities are locally negotiated. The fact that students in two chapters of the same organization (at RU and RPU), Latinos United for Action, drew ethnic boundaries and adopted different identity labels demonstrates that the campus environment is formative. Second, identity-formation processes are *activated* by different conditions on each campus. Residential patterns mattered on all three campuses, but for Latino respondents at LAC, they mattered because they were interacting with predominantly affluent white peers with whom they lived for four years. At RPU, not living on campus foreclosed students' opportunities to interact in a new racial environment. And at RU, living in a new setting, coupled with scarce resources, created an optimal environment for competition between Latino student organizations. What this analysis demonstrates is that it is important to avoid making blanket statements. Institutional characteristics create unique settings across campuses. The boundaries of Latinidad are fluid in some contexts and rigid in others, externally deployed in some settings while mainly internally deployed in others. And thus choosing identities can have a significant impact on interpersonal relationships on some campuses while being inconsequential on others.

Within, these college organizational dynamics Latinos are learning and creating ideas about who they are ethnically and panethnically. As such, racial understanding may be part of the hidden curriculum of college—a curriculum that teaches students distinct lessons. In the next chapter, I turn to another "unit" in the hidden curriculum of college: learning how to engage in politics.

6

What We Do

Defining and Performing
Latino Politics

FABIAN: Oh my God, I was so mad with the commencement speaker decisions made this week by the committee. I think we need to talk about an action because they totally disregarded Latino students. It's disrespectful to us because we have families that are undocumented and this speaker is anti-immigrant.

BERNARDO: Well, is the decision final? Can we change it?

FABIAN: I talked to them and they said the announcement is official so they can't take it back.

MARCUS: Well maybe we can have noisemakers and when she comes up we can make noise?

VANYA: Or maybe we can stand up and give her our back?

FABIAN: Yeah, I like that!

JANELLE: I like that too!

BERNARDO: Well, I think that's a little disrespectful.

FABIAN: Maybe you're right, and the school might get mad at Latinos Unidos, and we don't want that.

MARCUS: So, maybe we can wear like white sashes in solidarity with immigrants.

This discussion took place during a 2010 Latinos Unidos meeting at Liberal Arts College.[1] Members were frustrated with the commencement speaker chosen by the college, whose immigration views they found abhorrent. They chose to react deliberatively and symbolically rather than contentiously, opting out of protest and ultimately deciding to wear white sashes at commencement. The insulated, supportive, and communal aspects of LAC foster deliberation and discourage contention as students consider their relationships with administrators in making tactical choices. Although this is only one example of how LAC Latino students engaged politically, it is emblematic of their deliberative political style.

In addition to distinct racialized experiences and identity preferences (as discussed in Chapter 5), Latino students also defined and engaged in political action in quite distinct ways on each campus: LAC students talked, while RU students quarreled with each other, and RPU students protested off campus. In this chapter, I explain the process by which Latino students learn how to engage in politics within the organizational culture of their campuses and demonstrate how institutions of higher education mediate collective action. Students make political selves and choose specific tactics depending upon the context, according to the institutional, organizational, and cultural settings in which they live and study. To illustrate this process, I build on inhabited institutional theory, which posits that cultural schemas are implemented, modified, or inhabited within each specific setting (Hallet and Ventresca 2006; Nunn 2014). As Latino students pick ways to do Latino politics they are not only making calculations about what might work, but also considering the norms that surround them and suggest what is appropriate.

Latino politics, like other ethnic politics, constitute a cultural schema because actors subscribe to them, enact them, and imbue them with meaning. Latino politics are adopted at the local level but also on a broader scale—nationally and, increasingly, internationally, given the growing transnational ties and immigration policies that affect and connect Latinos across the globe (Abrego 2014; Golash-Boza 2012; Roth 2012; Smith 2006). By socially constructing politics within each campus, students give meaning to Latino politics and *inhabit* them in specific ways. In this chapter, I demonstrate how the contextual factors outlined in Table 6.1 interactively influence students' political understandings and decisions.

For example, I show that just as the all-encompassing bubble of LAC shaped students' ideas of Latinidad, it also shaped politics by keeping students committed to on-campus politics. Residential arrangements also influence how much time students engage in life outside of the campus gates by reinforcing or weakening the boundaries between the campus community and the outside world. Furthermore, the extent of cooperation or competition among student organizations, largely a function of resources and contact, affect the development of their political programs. And, of course, each campus has its own political culture or sense of how to go about engaging and trying to effect change. Within each of these unique institutional dynamics, members of student organizations crafted political understanding and actions. In the sections that follow, I show how these dynamics cultivate three distinct political approaches among Latino students.

TABLE 6.1

Summary of contextual factors shaping political styles

	Liberal Arts College	Research University	Regional Public University
Strength of student social ties to campus at large	High	Medium	Low
Description of external campus boundaries	Rigid and enclosed	Semi-permeable	Open and permeable
Description of internal organizational boundaries	Minimal and nonexclusive	Differentiated and exclusive	Minimal and nonexclusive
Role of organization for members	Contributing to diversity on campus	Family away from home; identity	Instrumental connections
Political style	Deliberative politics as campus ethos	Politics as a divisive boundary between organizations	Issue-oriented and contentious politics
How Latino politics are inhabited	Political talk and event planning	Political talk and event planning exclusively by one organization	Protest

Liberal Arts College and Institution-Making

Liberal Arts College is a residential campus. The strong LAC community boundary that encloses students' lives keeps them almost totally engaged within the campus gates, and the student organizations studied for this book rarely participated in events off campus. There is a vibrant student life on campus, and social ties among the LAC community are strong. Members of both Latino Links and Latinos Unidos actively participated on campus and regularly reiterated their commitment to bringing and representing Latino culture to the LAC community.

LAC's political legacy skews left of center. Several LL members described the campus culture as critical of government, liberal, and "hipster." "The LAC bubble is a hippie culture," as Tamara put it. But, she said, "My parents were not part of the sixties movement and eating green doesn't really resonate with me. Being green is really expensive and eating organic food is really expensive." Many respondents described the campus culture as leftist and environmentalist, and they attributed this culture to an institutional legacy and the politics of the parents of the broader student body. Like Tamara, other Latino students reported that their views often differed from those dominant in the larger campus culture, which complicated their ability to relate to peers.

Despite Latino students' initial feelings of alienation from their mainly white peers' politics, they absorbed their political tactics and styles of expression. They practiced and inhabited Latino politics mainly through political conversation, deliberation, and event planning for the LAC community—activities that I refer to as "institution-making," Although Latinos Unidos' and Latino Links' institution-making mainly took the form of programming, such as hosting speakers or cultural festivities, and creating a Latino presence on campus.

Members of Latino Unidos revealed their impulse for institution-making on several occasions. During their election for new leadership, for example, Renata advertised during her campaign for co-president: "I will expand our culture to the rest of the student body." Fabian offered similar visions in a campaign email to the entire organization:

> My work has focused on building sustainable relationships with professors, deans, student groups and staff; my past programing has included student dinners, cultural and political trips, the execution of Latina/o Graduation, volunteer service work, retreats, and numerous conversations with deans and professors about the state of Latina/o students at LAC in an effort to increase outreach. As a co-president, I would continue my efforts to build community and assure that we are providing efficient and critical programing that promotes our mission statement. I hope to build a democratic space that builds on the diverse backgrounds of our community so that we may all find empowerment. In solidarity.[2]

Fabian's campaign narrative is packed with the political language of institution-making. He highlights his experience "building sustainable relationships with professors, deans, and student groups" and his "numerous conversations with deans and professors about the state of Latina/o students at LAC in an effort to increase outreach." He is internally focused on community building, relationships, dialogue, and conciliation on campus. Moreover, his goal is "to build a democratic space that builds on the diverse backgrounds of our community." Here, while he seeks to persuade LU members to vote for him by pledging to fight for their representation on campus, he does so by using the most open definition of what it means to be Latino, emphasizing diversity.

In line with these politics of institution-making, members of Latino Unidos were also concerned with changing the organizational culture and focus of the Latino Cultural Center (LCC), especially during the 2008–2010 academic years. During a meeting, Fabian said, "We are very disappointed that LCC has not taken a more active role in responding to the hateful incidents that occurred across campus. These incidents have created an unwelcoming, to say the least, environment for students of color and we sincerely regret that the LCC did not take a more active role, within the administration, representing the concerns of Latino/a students." Here Fabian is referring to some of the instances of racism detailed in Chapter 5. LU spent a significant amount of meeting time brainstorming ways to reform the LCC, as well as criticizing the staff and programming. Their preferred solutions were hiring a new director and expanding LCC workshop topics.

LAC Latino students were even concerned with faculty hiring, another form of institution-making politics. Both LL and LU discussed the retirement of a senior Latino Studies faculty member. During an LU meeting Genova said, "I think it's really important that Latino Studies gets to keep the line and that we are involved. We are one of the oldest departments in the nation and students started it forty years ago." In dedicating meeting time to discuss faculty hiring, LL and LU members signaled their interest institution-making at the departmental level and some understanding of the academy.

Beyond reforming the LCC and influencing hiring in the Latino Studies department, both LL and LU had an extensive list of events, political in nature, that they invested time in developing. Many of these events embodied a kind of symbolic politics designed to represent Latinos yet also build up the impact of Latinos within the institution. For example, both organizations regularly hosted events for Hispanic Heritage Month, the Day of the Dead, and Cesar Chavez Day. Every year both LU and LL created an altar for Día de los Muertos on November first. During a meeting, Fabian suggested they dedicate the altar to Luis Ramirez, an undocumented Mexican immigrant who was murdered in Shenandoah, Pennsylvania, by two white teenagers. Cristina suggested they dedicate their altar to Mercedes Sosa, an Argentine folk singer who explicitly sang about leftist political issues in Latin America. After much discussion, the students ultimately dedicated their altar to immigrants who died in the desert crossing the U.S.-Mexico border. The Día de los Muertos *altares* have become an institutionalized ritual on campus, and even non-Latino organizations participate in the activity by creating their own altars.

Latino Links and Latinos Unidos regularly support the efforts of other organizations on campus, especially when they are related to Latino issues. Nonmembers regularly asked LL and LU for funds to support their Latino-related activism and research. For example, a white student (not a member of LL) once asked LL to help fund her trip to Fort Benning, Georgia, to protest the School of the Americas for its role in Central American civil wars; LL provided funding. Some members also attended a vigil hosted by this student upon her return from her protest. In addition, members of both organizations attended a vigil organized by a human rights organization to support the Dream Act. These vigils are clear examples of the symbolic politics that LAC students regularly participated in.

Deliberative Politics at LAC

In addition to institution-making and symbolic politics, LAC students also engaged in deliberative politics. Latino students initially expressed feeling disconnected from the leftist political culture of LAC, but as they became acculturated, they began to express an elaborate understanding of that culture. LAC respondents held expansive views of what it meant to be political and articulated them mainly through deliberation. Members of the politically oriented LU constantly questioned what it meant to be political and how political they should be. For example, in one meeting, students debated having weekly lunches that would be dedicated to political discussions:

JANELLE: I would like to avoid heavy conversations during my hour break.

MANUEL: Then we need to think about it, should LU be more political?

JANELLE: Well, Fabian likes to say that having a table of Latinos in the dining hall is political because there are so few of us, so if we get together then that says something.

No one responded to Janelle's comment and the conversation continued, with some members expressing the desire to be more political without alienating current or potential members who were uninterested in focused political discussions.

MANUEL: How about more group volunteering?

MARIBEL: Can we get involved with the Dream Act?

No one responded to Maribel's comment, and the group finally decided to organize weekly dinners to show their presence on campus. The students considered their discussion intrinsically political. In their expansive view of politics, anything, including dining together, could be considered political—an attitude that underscored the value of symbolism at LAC. Moreover, they saw their presence in the dining hall together to be significant, a type of symbolically representative politics that was common at LAC. Maribel and Manuel suggested alternative, more community-oriented actions, but the group decided not to pursue them, reflecting the ethos of their university by inhabiting Latino politics through symbolism, political conversation, and deliberation.

Political deliberation was constant especially among the expressly political group, Latinos Unidos. A few weeks before Columbus Day,[3] the students discussed their plan to commemorate an alternative celebration on campus, Día de la Raza. Fabian argued, "We should organize a talk about the word *raza* because the National Council for La Raza always gets a lot of pressure from conservatives. They are called racist. I think we should be prepared to talk about this." During this same meeting Fabian shared that the campus groundskeepers, janitors, and dining hall employees had received permission to paint a common wall on campus. This wall is regularly painted by different student clubs and then painted over by a new group every week. The workers would be painting the wall orange for their cause of improving working conditions. The next group in line to paint the wall was an LGBTQ student group who would paint a rainbow over it. Fabian shared during an LU meeting that he was trying to convince the latter group to use only part of the wall so that the workers' cause would remain highlighted. But, he reported, "Gay students want to paint over it, drama!" Selena said, "I love oppression Olympics."

LU's discussions spanned a broad range of political subjects—those affecting Latino students at LAC and Latinos beyond the campus gates. During a meeting Fabian asked the group, "Should we discuss the [University of California] budget cuts and fee increases? Although we're privileged to be at this institution, we gain from the UC system. Like Manuel and I did a summer program at Berkeley. Many of our professors and the work we read come out of those schools. And unfortunately most of our Latino brothers and sisters get funneled into that system." Genova asked, "Are there actions of students on those campuses that we can join or maybe we can think about ways to show our support?" Fabian responded, "Maybe we can all keep our eyes open and think about this." I followed up with LU leaders about this: they never made connections to collaborate with students in the UC system.

Deliberation occurred amongst Latino Links members during a meeting at which members discussed the purpose and mission of their organization. This discussion was prompted by a question posed by Ines, a nontraditional student, probably in her early fifties, who was attending an LL meeting for the first time. She sat quietly as the leadership ran through a list of planning items for the next two weeks, which consisted mainly of speakers and events on campus. Ines finally interjected and asked, "What is this organization doing? What is your purpose? What kind of progress are you pushing for? When I was at local community college in the 1970s, we were pushing for so much." Tomas responded, "Latino clubs can't be political if there isn't the need to be political. There's always need, but not as much as there has been historically; therefore, we can be a social rather than political club for now. This means we are an outlet for Latinos to hang out, a place to feel safe, get to know people like each other. But at the same time I know there is always the political side—it's not as hard as it was in the 1960s for Latinos to get into college, but it's still not easy."

This kind of deliberation was typical at LAC: students talked about whether there was a need in the present to have a political Latino organization on campus. Tomas suggests that there is but that some of the progress made to date had given Latino students the space to also engage in social activities. In this conversation, as students touched on the issue of racial progress and its relationship to politics, they extended their perspective beyond the campus.

The commencement discussion quoted at the beginning of the chapter, along with another discussion about whether to attend the May Day march in the local community or an alumni dinner that conflicted with it, shows that members of LU chose not to engage in contentious politics out of deference to their relationships with the college administration.

CRISTINA: So we need to talk about the May Day protests because Dean Marlo planned the alumni dinner the same day. What should we do?

SELENA: Well, Dean Marlo has been really helpful to Latinos Unidos and I don't think we should skip it. I think LU should show up to the dinner.

FABIAN: Yeah, I can always attend May Day.

Students entertained the idea of participating in contentious action but ultimately chose not to; they wanted to keep close, personalized relationships with administrators. That LU members wanted to keep these relationships amicable demonstrates how they negotiated their campus commitments with their allegiances to a broader Latino community. Within the communitarian context of LAC, students inhabited Latino politics through deliberation, dialogue, and even pre-professional pursuits like meeting alumni. In other words, LAC's culture created a "bubble" for students, which filtered their engagement in ethnic political action.

Although LAC students were concerned about national issues affecting Latinos, especially immigration policy, they expressed this concern in ways that reflected the LAC ethos. They discussed immigrant rights and justice, but they did not protest or engage in advocacy. For example, Angel began an LL meeting in April of 2010 by reading a *Los Angeles Times* article that explained Arizona's SB 1070,[4] and he asserted that it was important to fight the policy. He then introduced one of the student leaders of the Young Democrats, who asked LL to join a protest outside the office of a local congressperson who was working to end birthright citizenship. Angel responded to this call, saying "Well, I interned for [Congressperson] even though he's Republican and I'm Democrat. Obviously, I can't protest because of conflict of interests, but I'll tell you that this summer some people came into the building and protested inside. This got some serious news coverage and he was forced to speak to them. So if you do protest, don't just do it outside." Angel offered the Young Democrat advice on how best to protest but did not endorse the protest himself. The Young Democrat passed around a sign-up sheet and received four signatures. The following week, I asked the LL students if they attended the protest and was told that, due to time constraints, they were unable to do so. Despite this opportunity to engage in contentious politics, Angel chose to protect his relationship with the congressman, and LL as an organization declined to endorse the protest. In this instance, students engaged in reproductive agency, choosing to act in accordance with the patterns of LL and the ever-present script at LAC of talking about issues while avoiding conflict.

The above example also highlights another aspect of politics that was more present on the LAC campus than at RU and RPU—students' engagement in and connections to conventional politics. It is not a far stretch for students who attend an elite liberal arts college, accustomed to talking politics, to also be involved in conventional politics. Students' ties and alliances to local politicians were revealed on several occasions, like Angel's in the scenario above. Another student, David, a member of LL, consistently offered to bring U.S. Representatives Linda and Loretta Sanchez to campus because they had just written a book and wanted to speak at the school. David emphasized that they were family friends. In another case, during a meeting students discussed a Latino political candidate because he is an alumnus of LAC who had served in the state assembly. Natalie said, "All Latino politicians sell out like Mayor Villaraigosa. But I know that he advocates for the Dream Act." Lorena asked, "Why do you think he sold out?" Natalie responded, "He's been using money for dinners and stuff." "Well he can use as much money as he wants as long as he passes the Dream Act," said Lorena. In these instances, we see that LL and LU students at times did have direct links to politicians, which they could pursue if interested. However, I did not see any of these representatives on campus during the 2008–2010 academic years.

Communitarian Impulse at LAC

Although the primary form of political engagement at LAC is through institution-making and deliberation, some students tried to get their peers involved in community projects off campus. However, they failed in almost every case. For example, during a Latino Links meeting, Adal made several suggestions:

ADAL: I think we should take a border trip with a community studies class. They go every semester.

TAMARA: I've never been and I think it would be a great thing to do as a group.

ADAL: Also, we can do a toxic tour of the city, which is relevant to Latino issues because Latino communities is where we find the most environmental injustices.

TAMARA: Another great idea.

Despite the enthusiasm expressed by Adal and Tamara, there was no major buy-in to either of these tours, and Adal went on his own. He was constantly trying to mobilize his classmates to take more action in the local community. Towards the end of another meeting he said, "I know you are all itching to leave the meeting but I would like everyone to think about how LL is doing as a club in the Latino community and LAC? Maybe we should do other things like go to ICE checkpoints? I know organizing as Latinos today is hard because issues aren't blatant and it's hard to see them, and act on them." There was no response and the meeting was quickly adjourned.

Adal was not the only voice in LL to express disappointment. Bianca shared, "The other day I bumped into an alumnus who was a member of LL years ago. She asked me, 'What kind of significant action is the organization doing this year?' I said, 'Not much.' I guess during the first years of LL they did meaningful action like translated financial aid forms." The involvement of LL in "meaningful action" became the topic of conversation on several occasions especially in relation to several faculty-led community engagement projects with local Latino populations, related to worker rights, immigration justice, and educational inequalities. Some of the members of LL and LU participated individually in the programs, either through research credits or paid employment. However, much of the LAC student involvement was non-Latino. This was discussed on several occasions.

SANDRA: Professor Jimenez came up to me; he's wondering why there isn't a larger Latino student presence when there are protests in the community about immigrant raids.

TOMAS: There are more non-Latino students participating in immigrant rights, even though it's a human right. But we would expect more Latinos to be motivated. But how do we get people motivated—if it doesn't happen on campus, it's hard to get the students to care.

CASSANDRA: The problem is that these programs aren't here.

TOMAS: They're dealing with a Latino population, concerning immigrants' rights. Let's organize across Latino groups.

MARCO: I will go to meetings of other Latino organizations to get more students to sign up for events.

LORENA: But people need to follow up on what they commit to, if you put your name down you have to go.

MARCO: I know. I saw people in dining hall and they aren't motivated to come. Let's get people to commit and stay committed.

The discussion above shows students' interest in being involved in programs and initiatives that serve Latinos outside of campus. However, as Lorena points out, students sign up to attend and do not follow up. This was a constant struggle and not unique to LL or LU. This is the problem that most social movements deal with—the problem of recruitment.

An iteration of the same discussion occurred at LU. Another student organization, the Worker-Student Alliance, gives the janitorial workers breakfast once a week. LU participates once a year in this breakfast but does not lead the effort. At one meeting members reflected on the breakfast, to which they had brought *pan y chocolate*. Fabian said, "They [the workers] don't think we're Latinos! They say, 'Oh, you speak Spanish.' I think we need to increase our efforts with the Worker-Student Alliance, so they can know there are Latinos on campus too!" LU reached out to the Worker-Student Alliance and asked if they could possibly organize a hike with the workers to bond with them. Fabian reported back, "We just heard back from the workers and they would not like to go on a hike with the students because they are tired enough. I think we should have a spa night for them instead. You know how the school brings a masseuse for the students during finals." There was an echo of agreement in the room. But the spa night did not take place.

Students seem to want to be involved with Latino communities outside of campus, but despite the presence of community engagement programs on campus run by faculty, most of the involvement is by non-Latino students. The students in LL and LU are concerned with social justice issues affecting Latinos, but they choose time and time again to engage in deliberation versus action and advocacy. They cite fears of losing the support of administrators when they think about protesting, but mainly they focus on talking about issues that affect Latinos and organizing speakers and cultural events on campus.

Research University: Politics as a Symbolic Boundary

Most of my Latino respondents at RU were living away from home in a new environment, and RU does not provide the integration and cloistering that LAC's residential experience does. For example, RU Latino students are not paired up with a Latino peer advisor and do not have a faculty advisor. RU could be quite isolating especially for first-generation college-goers, who tend not to seek resources or community. For members of Latinos United for Action and Latino Fellowship, organizational membership is particularly significant. Students repeatedly referred to their organization as a "home away from home," a statement not used to describe organizations at LAC or RPU. But these two "homes" had quite distinct identities due mostly to opposing perspectives on politics. Politics was the defining symbolic boundary between LUA and LF. LUA actively engaged in politics mainly through consciousness-raising workshops and event-planning, while LF avoided engaging in anything political.

Students viewed the organizations as incompatible and membership was exclusive—simultaneous membership was difficult to sustain As mentioned in Chapter 3, three young women tried to join both groups, which members of both organizations considered strange. Within both organizations these three women were constantly questioned about their membership in the other group and reminded that no student was able to balance membership in both. Deidra described the perceptions that members of each organization held about the other:

> Some LF members do make fun of us [LUA members] sometimes. And one LUA girl did say, "Oh it's really cool that you're bringing people together." We were always asking questions about the divide. People told us that it was old beef that's continued, so people continue to be separated. But I guess at the beginning, people always go to both meetings and it's natural that they choose one; they never choose both. The LF people always said, "LUA people are always like *fight the power.*" And then there was a LUA girl that would say, "LF doesn't do anything and LUA does so much, so what's the purpose and what's the point of LF?"

Members of Latinos United for Action saw their group as "doing so much" in contrast to Latino Fellowship, which "doesn't do anything." Members of LUA who attended an LF meeting while shopping for an organization criticized the content of LF meetings, which typically consisted of introductions, announcements about upcoming social events, and either a cultural presentation about a specific Latin American country or a game. In comparison, a typical LUA meeting involved a workshop about an issue, such as immigration, gay rights, or Latino identity, which was intended to spark discussion. LUA regularly held political discussions and events on campus, but unlike chapters of LUA on other campuses, such as RPU, the organization was not involved in contentious politics, especially off campus. LUA focused mainly on talking and holding consciousness-raising workshops about political issues. They felt they were "doing something," which meant engaging politically, as opposed to LF members, who played games or ate ethnic food.

Some RU Latino students had attended high schools with Latinos United for Action chapters, so they were drawn to the LUA welcome meeting upon arriving on campus. However, not all of the attendees ultimately joined the organization. For most, electing to join Latinos United for Action also meant explicitly choosing *not* to be part of Latino Fellowship. Their choices demonstrated an allegiance to a particular political Latino identity on campus. This division was historical and fostered through structural arrangements and access to resources on campus. LUA and LF had differential access to resources at the Multicultural Center on campus, which I discussed in Chapter 3.

Latino Fellowship: Avoiding Politics

In choosing LF over LUA, students effectively chose a nonpoliticized Latino identity over a politicized one. During LF meetings members did not discuss political issues whereas LUA frequently explored a variety of political issues. In fact, politics was deflected by LF leadership and members.

LF's active avoidance of politics became most clear when Cruz, president of Latino Fellowship, shifted away from organizational norms in 2008. During the national presidential campaign, he invited members of the Young Democrats and Young Republicans to attend an LF meeting and speak about Obama's and McCain's political campaigns. This event went smoothly, with LF members asking questions about each party's stand on immigration and education and receiving straightforward answers. Yet afterward, LF alumni and other officers reprimanded Cruz for organizing the event, reminding him that LF avoided political activities in order to appeal to Latino students who were uninterested in politics. Their reprimands reinforced an organizational identity distinct from that of LUA. In the following year, this political debate was frequently cited by LF leaders, who emphasized the importance of remaining apolitical. Lissandra, the organization's president from 2009 to 2010, explained, "Last year Cruz organized a presidential political campaign debate. Most of the alumni and us didn't like it. Old members found out and they didn't like it; they said, 'Latino Fellowship is not political.' They told us not to do anything so extreme." Lissandra's statement recapitulated the collective and historical perspective that political engagement was too "extreme" for LF. Cruz's actions revealed transformative agency as he tried something new and attempted to change the organization's approach, but other members challenged him and steered their organization in a way that reproduced LF's cultural script. LF's organizational identity was firmly entrenched on the RU campus.

Although Cruz broke protocol by allowing space for discussion of the 2008 political campaign, he did voice LF's apolitical emphasis in many other instances. When I first attended an LF meeting, Cruz told me that "LF is a no-commitment, no-obligation organization. There are many organizations on campus that either have fees or are political. We like to create a very open space. We require nothing from our members." Cruz emphasized this point in several meetings. For example, recall that during LF's first meeting (discussed in Chapter 3), a young woman made an announcement about collecting money for the local Boys and Girls Club to buy soccer equipment, and Cruz quickly interjected, "It's not mandatory." As the young woman passed around a collection box, Cruz again proclaimed, "It's not mandatory." During another meeting, an officer of external affairs explained that LF was going to try to do more community service. Again, Cruz interjected, "There's no obligation to participate." Donating money or volunteering is not necessarily political, but Cruz still felt compelled to give members a way out.

Members of LF shared similar preferences for avoiding engaging in politics and gave several reasons for doing so: it was not their interest, they were much more reserved, and they did not understand the reasons for engaging. For example, I asked Pablo to discuss politics and its place in LF.

PABLO: We're not a political group and we don't want to turn off our members who don't want to be political. Like, for example, last year two people running for positions in the student government wanted to talk to the LF members and the board said "no" because it's not in the interest of the members.

DVR: How do you feel about politics?

PABLO: I'm not opposed to politics, but I rather not take part because they don't interest me."

Suyeli voiced similar sentiments.

DVR: How do you feel about politics?

SUYELI: I'm not very political and I'm not into news. I don't really care about politics. It's not me.

DVR: How do you define political?

SUYELI: Political is like into laws and the Chicano thing. I know it's important because I'm also Latina but it's just not for me. Everyone is here for a reason. People do politics but I'm a scientist.

For Suyeli, politics is equal to science in that it is an area of study and she does not have to like or take interest in both. Mireya also saw politics as a language she did not know. She explained, "I'm not very involved in politics besides voting. I lean more towards liberal. I don't really know a lot about politics. I don't really follow politics. It's boring. It's like Chinese to me; it's like another language for me, I don't know." Mireya equates politics to a foreign language: hard to learn.

During the 2009–2010 academic year, college students across the state staged protests against the cuts in education funding. I talked to Deidra, who was temporarily part of both organizations, but ultimately chose LF. She explained, "I really want to support the protests. My brother asked me if I went to class because of the protests happening today. He told me, 'You're not supposed to go to class!' My brother has a little bit of the LUA mentality; he likes history. I told him, 'I have class. Why would I leave class to protest? I don't see the logic. I'm trying to avoid getting more costs for education because I value my education. Why would I ditch class to protest?'" Deidra seems to agree that the rising cost of college is a problem, but she does not think it's a smart strategy to skip class in protest. She believes that if she truly values education, she should focus on her academics by going to class.

Other students thought that engaging politically did not match their personalities, like Gloria, who explained, "It seems that LUA is to express yourself and be able to come up and not keep yourself as a minority. But I'm not that type of person so I don't feel comfortable." Gloria not only explains how she is not comfortable with politics, but does so by highlighting LUA's political foci. Lissandra also discussed her ideas about politics in reference to LUA, explaining,

> I think that LUA is very political because they are on top of things and on top of issues. I've been around them when they're not in their meetings. I went to my friend's house, who lives with a bunch of people from LUA. She just made a comment like "I don't like Sarah Palin." Everyone asked her, "Why do you say that?" They asked her if she's read everything. They were already attacking her. They wanted to know if her sources were good. She said a small comment and they were all jumping on her. It really bothered me.

It is clear from LF members' comments that they perceived LUA to be not only political, but *the* Latino political voice on campus. But how did LUA members think about their role on campus? Did they agree? And how did they engage in politics?

Politics within Latinos United for Action

LUA members' perspectives on politics were quite different from those of LF members. For example, in an interview, Kenya, the 2009–2010 LUA president, explained the organization's position on campus: "I look at the Black Student Union; they have the support of their Greek organizations. And if you look at LUA, we don't really have the support of anyone else. It's just us doing all this active stuff on campus. Latinos or Chicanos[5] on this campus, they will avoid us because we are political." Kenya communicates an understanding of LUA's position among the Latino student community on campus as one that stands alone among the other organizations. Moreover, she sees more unity among the black student organizations.

LUA members expressed opinions about politics with ease. Gilda, a member of LUA and a former president, explained:

GILDA: I think politics is in your everyday life; it is in everything. I remember the first LUA meeting of the year: I told people not to be scared to be political because being on this campus is a political statement. I think there's a fear of politics on campus.

DVR: Why do you think that is?

GILDA: Campus is so apathetic. I think a lot of students come in with pressure from their families to do good in school. And then they have scholarships and they depend on their GPA. So they get scared or they think they don't have time.

DVR: What do you think makes LUA different from other groups?

GILDA: I think our programs help us stay consistent and political so that we don't become *pan dulce* [sweet bread], just like some social groups. I think as long as we have the programs we run, we will keep our responsibility to have politically conscious workshops for the students. I think having a close relationship with each other is good because we feel comfortable around each other but we can challenge each other.

Gilda brings several issues to light. First, she underlines what she perceives as the political climate on campus. She thinks that students are "apathetic" and attributes this to the pressures of keeping a high enough GPA to maintain their scholarships. Second, when I asked her to reflect on how LUA is different from other organizations, she quickly mentioned the programs and "consciousness raising" workshops LUA runs and contrasted them to what social groups do, calling socially groups' programs *pan dulce*. Gilda's estimation of LUA's actions is correct. The political actions that LUA mainly engaged in were workshops intended to raise consciousness among members. They covered many topics: labor rights, immigration, militarization of the U.S.-Mexico border, white supremacy, feminism, LGBTQ issues, legislative proposals at the state and federal levels, HIV, educational inequalities, and human trafficking.

One meeting a year was dedicated to discussing the origins of LUA and its role on campus. This meeting began with a reading of the foundational documents of LUA. Foremost, members discussed reclaiming their ethnic identity and empowering students. They mentioned the need to keep the Chicano movement alive and away from opportunists who sought to divert it, including some administrators. They discussed working with other organizations, but believe they should not do so just for the sake of unity. Franky mentioned United Latino Organizations (an umbrella group of which all Latino organizations on campus are members) and explained that LUA does not work with them because of ideological differences. They also discussed competition with other organizations for members. Max proclaimed that "fraternities come to LUA flaunting their Greek letters and recruit the straight men."

Several students raised concerns about LUA having few straight male Latino members. One working theory was, as Franky mentioned, that other organizations did a better job recruiting straight Latinos. However, other members hypothesized that it was the LGBTQ-friendly workshops LUA sponsored that turned off straight men. There were several such workshops each year. During one, Carlos, Jennifer, and Maximiliano went to the front of the room at the beginning of the meeting and announced that this meeting would be about Queer Aztlan. They began by distributing sheets of paper with either a term or a definition on it. They asked people to find their match (definition and term). At this time all the students stood up and started to talk to each other. Their papers had terms such as "queer," "gender," "transgender," and "androgynous." This activity took about ten minutes. The workshop leaders then asked everyone to take a seat and started calling out terms. They asked whoever had that term if they found their definition. Maximiliano and Jennifer defined most of the terms because many students did not find their definition. These terms included "intersex," "gender-queer," "queer," "transgender," "transsexual," "bisexual," "questioning," "fluid," "transvestite," "drag," and "androgynous."

The workshop leaders spent a little more time describing *joteria*, or the study of Latino people whose lives include dissident practices of gender and sexuality,[6] and Queer Aztlan. Carlos elaborated:

> Homophobia is a fear that is not logical—a lot like racism. In the 1960s, heterosexual men dominated the [Chicano] movement and there were problems with sexism and heterosexism. The feminists and gay members of the Chicano movement struggled to get equal recognition within the Chicano movement. They had to learn to deal with intersectionality, which was their simultaneous struggles against racism, sexism, and heterosexism. This struggle was difficult because people thought they were infiltrators! But they succeeded and added to the organizational constitution that all future chapters are required to address gender and queer issues by having workshops. It gave us a place in the mythical history of Aztlan.

He then asked all the members to walk to each of the corners of the room where a print of a painting hung. These pictures played with classic Mexican images and transformed them into LGBTQ portraits. For example, there was a print of an Aztec *guerrillero* (warrior) holding another *guerrillero*. This picture traditionally features a man and a woman. This activity took about five minutes. Then Carlos asked everyone to sit in a circle.

Carlos, Max, and Jennifer asked the members to talk about their reactions to the pictures. Liliana said that she really liked the picture of the two Aztec warriors (one carrying the other) because usually it's a woman being carried and the new image challenges that. She added that society is more comfortable with female homosexuality and that this was also being challenged. Alicia said she liked the *sirena* (mermaid) image, which was transposed on the portrait of the virgin of Guadalupe. "I like it because it places a sexual object with the religious," she Alicia. Carlos interjected: "*Sirenas* symbolize infertility and the virgin is asexual."

The conversation developed into a discussion about terminology and what words are acceptable to use.

CARLOS: Many words that used to be offensive have been re-appropriated and politicized, like the word "Chicano." It's not offensive anymore; you can say it.

JENNIFER: I used to think "queer" was an offensive word.

LILIANA: I felt the same way about *joto.*

GILDA: Some students that used to be part of LUA called each other *joto* very casually. I thought it was so offensive at first. Now I think it is beautiful because they re-appropriating the word.

LILIANA: But, who decides what words are ok?

No one addressed Liliana's question because Lalo pointed out that they were out of time. But several other meetings were about LGBT issues. LUA also held workshops about many other issues, including one about white supremacy and the prison industrial complex, in which they discussed the three strikes law, crack and cocaine sentencing disparities, racial profiling, capitalism and poverty. LUA members engaged in politics through consciousness-raising.

To sum up, at RU, my Latino respondents' choice of organization determined their participation in politics. Whereas LF avoided politics wholesale, and LUA claimed to be the only Latino political organization on campus. How Latino students at RU were incorporated shaped this firm division between the two organizations. First, because the campus and its classes were large, students felt a need to find a sense of belonging within a particular Latino organization. Second, RU afforded these groups different resources and recognized LUA's historical legitimacy on campus, creating a disparity between the organizations. These factors contributed to a situation in which Latino organizations were constituted as mutually exclusive. In this context of competition, students inhabited Latino politics in different ways.

Regional Public University: Not a Bubble nor an Incubator for Organizational Conflict

Regional Public University lacks a particularly vibrant student life; as discussed in Chapter 4, fewer than 10 percent of students live on campus, and most students leave when they are not in class. With little to no student activity on campus, students report few strong social ties to their peers and professors, and no salient school identity. The average RPU student spends most of the time off campus; many work and commute from the communities in which they grew up. Thus, in stark contrast to LAC, RPU is the opposite of a bubble and does not keep the outside world, including politics, outside the campus gates. Unlike the organizations at the other two campuses, Hispanics for Economics (HE) and LUA were not primed to consider their organizational reputation, relationships with administrators, or the political culture of their campus when choosing how to react to political threats directed at Latinos. Unlike Liberal Arts College, which has a long-standing culture of being politically left of center, RPU does not have a salient political cultural identity, although during the Chicano movement of the 1960s and 1970s, students were very active at RPU. Gilma, leader of LUA, shared that few current students had any knowledge of the activism of their antecedents. Because there was no transmission of a political legacy, RPU students' actions were unrestrained and unfiltered by the campus culture. RPU's porous nature, with a weak boundary between the outside world and campus life, also provided no filtering of intra-organizational boundaries. Unlike organizations at Research University, RPU organizations were not in competition or conflict; they did not even have contact. Neither organization exercised a monopoly on Latino politics on campus, as did the LUA chapter at Research University.

Since politics was not a hard line or a boundary at RPU, members of both LUA and HE expressed some interest in politics. For example, both Yareli and Yvette discussed its importance to them:

DVR: Do you consider yourself a political person?

YARELI: Yes.

DVR: What does that mean to you?

YARELI: I think it means to be informed and to form an opinion. I may be wrong and not have all the facts but I know what I feel and I know what I believe. What I read might be biased because almost everything is biased, but I try to be informed and try to form an opinion. And I may not be correct because I don't have all the facts, but I think if I stand with something and I defend it, then I am political. I live with that Republican and she finds holes in what I say and we go back and forth. But I find holes in what she says, but I don't shoot it down for no reason. I think there are fundamental things that are not going to change. I think you have an opinion and you state the opinion; that makes it political. If you have an opinion and you don't state it, then you're not political. The point of politics is debate. I think political means you let people know how you feel and you take a chance of being wrong.

Yareli's ideas about what it means to be political do not seem to be filtered by campus culture. Her narrative does not mention her peers on campus or her professors. Recall that LUA and HE members' paths rarely crossed. The organizations held meetings on opposite sides of campus, and members almost never took courses together. Administrators had limited interaction with student organizations, and Latino groups were not concerned with each other. Instead of on-campus politics, Yareli, like other RPU respondents, was vested in local, statewide, and national politics. Yvette, an HE member, told me, "I just make sure that whatever I decide, as far as politics, I always make sure that it benefits me and what I'm going to be doing in the future. I think it's really important that we follow politics because, really, if you don't, you're just blind. If you don't practice politics, then please just don't complain about what happens in your economy or your world or your community." At first glance Yvette may sound like a typical market-oriented student, but her comments show she had a more expansive view of "me" that encompassed "the other" and looked beyond herself to the needs of her community at large.

The following sections show how the missing filtering process at RPU allowed organizations and individual student members to participate in politics off campus in the local environment, reacting to national issues and engaging in a politics of contention.

Outside Politics Enter the RPU Campus Gates

It was not solely RPU student organizations that discussed politics happening in the world outside of campus. Students across all three campuses discussed political issues relevant to Latino communities. At RPU, however, I saw outsiders come into the organizations from time to time, as well as students becoming collectively involved in political actions off campus. For example, a Latino candidate for state senate came to discuss his candidacy with members of HE during a meeting. Mayra introduced him: "Hi everyone. We are very lucky to have Adan Mendoza today, founder of a huge Latino professional network in the area. He's going to talk to us about his campaign." She turned the floor over to Adan, who said, "Hi everyone! Thank you for giving me the chance to talk to all of you. This organization holds a really special place in my heart. I was part of an organization just like this when I was in college. I am an attorney and the founder of a Latino professional network. How many of you have been to our parties?" A handful of students cheered and about two-thirds of those in the room raised their hands. Adan continued, "I built that network because I think we can create something powerful together as Latinos. I'm here to talk to you about my campaign for state senate." Adan gave a ten-minute pitch about his family's trajectory in the United States, his experiences in college, and the American Dream. Students seemed relatively engaged, and when he was done, Mayra thanked him and encouraged those who could to vote for him. The presence of Adan on RPU's campus contrasts with the discussion of political candidates at LAC's Latino Links, whose members, despite their connection to political leaders, were suspicious of candidates and never sought the opportunity to invite them on campus.

Adan's speech was not the only time that outside politics penetrated HE. For a few weeks in a row, Mayra and a few other leaders urged members to vote on a local initiative that would tax oil companies at a higher rate to fund the public higher education system in California. And another time, Mayra urged members to volunteer at a local food bank. She said, "We're in a recession so a lot of people are struggling. The food banks are running out of food so let's get involved." HE pushed its members to participate in politics, by endorsing candidates and initiatives and, especially, volunteering. This contrasts with LF at RU. Recall Cruz's constant reminder to members that volunteering was not mandatory.

Latinos United for Action at RPU were also visited by outsiders on several occasions. However, the visitors were not businessmen or political leaders but rather grassroots activists and community members. Some of the visitors included a leader of a local LGBTQ organization who spoke to group about Proposition 8, a statewide ballot initiative that eliminated same-sex couples' right to marry. Other times, the visitors came with random requests. For example, one day a man in his later twenties walked into a meeting and introduced himself as someone involved in real estate. He said, "I am here because I want information about the Treaty of Guadalupe Hidalgo because I thinks it relates to my business." Most members looked stunned, and Jerry suggested he go to the library. Another meeting was attended by an MBA student who was asking LUA to host a commemoration of Ruben Salazar, a Mexican American journalist who died during the National Chicano Moratorium March against the Vietnam War in 1970. Several members agreed to discuss this as an option, but they never hosted such a commemoration.

The make-up of LUA meetings was never as random as on the day the members discussed the meaning of LUA. At this meeting, there was a female member of the local Brown Berets in full costume and some graduate students. Gilma asked members to explain their organization to the guests.

ALEX: It's about social justice and giving our communities the things they need to *sobresalir* [get ahead, succeed].

ADRIANA: We are a social movement organization that tries to mobilize people.

ERNESTO: Are we exclusively Latino or open?

ANTHONY: We accept anyone who cares about social justice.

RAFAEL: I think that we really have to understand our past, like in order to go forward.

JOSEFINA: Yes, it's empowering to know our past and fight for justice by any means necessary.

ALEX: Yes, but we have to make sure not to scare people, like when I was in high school; I thought it was too radical. Let's not be that militant.

GILMA: But maybe we need to remove the stigma from radical. We need to advocate for things against the status quo.

JOSEFINA: Yeah, I think that protesting and educating others is not radical.

ALEX: Yeah, I agree but we are not *guerreros* [warriors] or violent.

ANTHONY: Yes, you are right, but books are our bullets.

At this point the Brown Beret interrupted and said, "Actually LUA started with the Brown Berets, and it all started with pre-Columbian history and we were *guerreros*. We are from Aztlan, which is in Arizona, I think." Anthony lost his patience and exclaimed, "You can't actually find Aztlan. It is philosophical, not geographical. And you, *mujer* [woman], are infiltrating our organization and you need to leave!"[7] She responded, "I've been honest about who I am." Gilma jumped in, asking Anthony to be more respectful. Hector asked the woman, "Please give us more time as students to figure out who we [LUA] are as a collective." The meeting adjourned at this point, and the woman never returned, but Hector's comment about "figuring out who we [LUA] are" penetrated and shaped most meetings. Like LUA members at RU, those at RPU also discussed current political issues, including the plight of undocumented students, the killing of Oscar Grant (an unarmed man killed by a transit policeman in Oakland), and the meaning of Thanksgiving. However, they spent more time rethinking the organization. They read the founding documents as they charted a way forward. They discussed the meaning of radical versus nonradical politics. And they got involved in politics off campus.

HE and LUA members reacted to off-campus national and local provocations far more frequently than members of RU and LAC organizations. RPU organizations had more options to participate in contentious political action in the broader society because they did not have the pressures that Liberal Arts College students felt to appease administrators or the full agenda of events to organize that LUA did at Research University. The relative weakness of RPU's campus culture provided few constraints of or distractions for students, who staged protests off-campus to address salient political issues.

Inhabiting the Politics of Contention

In late May 2010, members of Latinos United for Action at RPU discussed the implications of Arizona's SB1070, a bill that gave police authority to inquire about an individual's legal status. But this was not the first time Arizona had been mentioned during an LUA meeting. In early 2009, Gilma had called for an entire meeting to be dedicated to discussion of Arizona. She said, "I have been watching Sheriff Joseph Arpaio on YouTube and it's really bad. He ties immigrants together and displays them on the street to humiliate them. This is dangerous because they serve as a model for other states." LUA organized a trip to Arizona to protest SB 1070. Vanessa, a first-year student member of the group, expressed her concern over the issue: "All the people who are there now are going to be stuck. What are they supposed to do? And you know they're going to profile anyone who looks Latino. We need to do something." The student members caravanned to Phoenix, Arizona, where they carried signs that read, "You are on stolen land" and "Immigration Reform Now." Meanwhile, individual members of Hispanics for Economics showed their opposition to SB 1070 by joining a local protest in California. Among all my respondents, RPU students were the only ones to engage collectively in protests off campus. This is not only because their campus culture did not control student action, but also because the institution provided no clear forum for students to express their grievances.

At RPU, both HE and LUA members were concerned about communities outside the campus gates. The college did not mediate my RPU respondents' reactions to local and national politics. Though the two organizations were not in contact with each other, members of both HE and LUA mobilized against statewide education budget cuts. HE member Jesús told me, "I made some flyers for the downtown LA march. I've seen a lot of changes, for example, the quality of the professors here is . . . declining. . . . I know that it's hitting people hard. They can't get in to classes." Josefina, a member of LUA, also discussed the protests: "I've been working a lot of ways, and I'm really focused on fighting against budget cuts. We organized a big rally in November. We want to have more classes added because we're paying more anyway. We been advocating for the march. All my classes are on furlough that day so I plan on being there." Neither Jesús nor Josefina saw political participation as incompatible with his or her organizational identity, unlike LF members at RU. The campus and the organizations failed to provide a foundation for students to seek redress, so they took their concerns to a broader platform, inhabiting Latino politics through contention.

The RPU campus was marked symbolically by permeable external boundaries and weak interorganizational boundaries. The RPU campus did not filter out the larger world; students were mainly embedded in their local environments and reacted to local and national Latino political issues. The college provided organizations with few campus resources, so LUA and HE both operated largely autonomously and were able to participate in political demonstrations off campus and react to issues affecting Latino communities broadly. The culture of RPU was weak and had little reach; it did not channel action, leaving students open to respond to the outside world.

Conclusion

Campuses mediate the way Latino student organizations engage in and respond to politics. The interaction of campus cultures, residential patterns, and relationships between student organizations explains why students at RPU protest and mobilize off-campus, while LAC and RU students do not. But what campus characteristics matter? Where do they matter? What are the operative mechanisms on each campus?

Liberal Arts College is a true residential "bubble." Students' social relationships are bounded by the campus. Latino Unidos and Latino Links see their actions as significant and consequential within their campus environment. They learn discursive and symbolic politics within the leftist campus culture at

LAC. When they do engage politically, they get responses on-campus and are rewarded by administrators and faculty for doing so with resources as well as with legitimacy. These type of politics keep them focused within the campus gates. They do not have the time to address concerns about anything larger or beyond their campus.

The size of Research University and the lack of programming that integrates students makes Latino student organizations critical in developing a sense of belonging on campus. Students search for a "home" and community within ethnic organizations. Meanwhile, however, the Multicultural Center allots unequal resources to Latinos United for Action and Latino Fellowship. The need for community, differential resources, and historical conflicts breed competition between the organizations studied. Students are focused mainly on maintaining their organization. Although Latinos United for Action claims a political identity, it is not really engaging outside the group; rather, it works to maintain boundaries and solidify its group identity. The recitation of political positions is a way to build identity on campus, and the expression of them is bound to the campus and to the organization. Notably, they advance LGBTQ politics, which LUA at Regional Public University does not even touch. This is evidence that different chapters of the same organization can vary by campus and that local contexts and actors really help shape political styles and approaches. LUA's political work is a vehicle for supporting their members and their own organizational survival. In an effort to maintain their identity, Latino Fellowship avoids politics wholesale.

Regional Public University's residential arrangements do not foster relationships or interactions between organizations. RPU offers no incentives or distractions, and no boundaries. The world gets in, the students get out, and they express their concerns in ways that they see as most promising. In this way, RPU is an open arena for mobilization.

Interestingly, the interactive process of forming political understanding looks quite different across institutional contexts. The interaction of the campus characteristics outlined in the chapter are dynamic and shape who stays engaged and how. Campus characteristics are all worth considering. These findings make a case for studying how Latinos learn to do politics across different types of colleges and universities. This is especially important because, after graduation, they will likely interact and engage in political work with other Latinos and individuals who learned how to be political in distinct settings.

7

Where We Are Going

Ideas about Racial Inequality and Mobility

How do students see the social and economic prospects for Latinos in America? How do they view racial inequality, mobility, and opportunity as they relate to Latinos? Do their perspectives vary by campus or organizational affiliations? In this chapter, I examine how students think about the first two questions. I asked each of the students interviewed if, in his or her view, Latinos were a disadvantaged group in the United States. I purposely chose the word "disadvantaged" instead of "oppressed" because I wanted to get a sense of the meaning systems through which students viewed race and inequalities without leading to one particular way of understanding. Natasha Warikoo (2016, 45) defines these meaning systems as racial frames, arguing that they are "lenses through which we observe, interpret, and respond to social phenomena that shape how we understand the world and act within it." Further, she explains that frames are not always explicit but rather that they can be implicit and unconsciously affect understandings of race, imbuing it with meaning.[1] By asking students to discuss the social location of Latinos in the United States, I was able to bring these (at times) unconscious ways of understanding race and inequality to the surface.

I think of students' narratives about Latino disadvantage as connected to cultural processes. Students' ideas about racial inequalities and mobility are drawn from their experiences before college, on their college campus, and within their peer groups, including in organizational settings. When thinking about the social location of Latinos, students draw on ideas found within their cultural toolkits, or cognitive frameworks used to interpret their experiences (Swidler 1986). The "toolkits" students have to understand mobility in America come from society at large, institutions, and organizations. Some students hold broader ideologies that shape their perspectives on inequality. These ideologies are understood as "systems of meaning that couple assertions and theories about the nature of social life with values and norms relevant to prompting or resisting social change" (Oliver and Johnston 2000, 43). More encompassing than cherry-picked ideas, ideologies give students a worldview that may appear to be coherent and consistent. Moreover, ideologies often lead individuals to question the origins of their assertions and theories (Oliver and Johnston, 2000).

Some students had an ideology for understanding racial inequality and thus a coherent narrative, while others espoused narratives that seemed undeveloped and at times contradictory. These differences varied by organizations and campus because each of these contexts mediated or filtered students' ideas about the world to varying degrees. Each campus has a distinct environment, shaped by the level of affluence among the student body, structure of courses, relationships with faculty, and the intensity of peer interactions. For example, as we learned in Chapter 2, attending Liberal Arts College is all-encompassing experience, as most students live within the "bubble" all four years, and their peer interactions are constant. In contrast, as a predominantly commuter school, Regional Public University offers few mechanisms for distilling ideas on campus. Student organizations also mediate and shape students' understandings about the social location of Latinos in the United States, albeit to varying degrees. For example, Latinos United for Action (LUA, a political organization) at Research University holds consciousness-raising workshops, as detailed in Chapter 3, while Latino Fellowship at the same institution holds no events or discussions about issues related to inequalities. The members of Latinos United for Action at Regional Public University discusses the political mission of the organization as they make plans for recruitment (as discussed in Chapter 4); in this way, they are advancing particular ways of knowing how inequality works. And Hispanics for Economics, a nonpolitical organization at RPU, does not address equity issues and focuses instead on holding professional workshops.

Members of the nonpolitical groups—Hispanics for Economics at Regional Public University and Latino Fellowship at Research University—expressed *meritocratic narratives* that at times downplayed the role of race, reinforced stereotypes, or claimed that Latinos were not quite disadvantaged, thus putting the onus and responsibility for the disparities plaguing Latino communities on Latinos themselves. These narratives sounded like "culture of poverty" explanations, which depict intergenerational poverty as a product of deficit worldviews and aspirations fostered at home. Some of the students who expressed meritocratic narratives acknowledged inequalities but then asserted their belief in merit and that the effort individuals exerted triumphs over any inequality. This perspective is reflected in the American Dream, the idea that in the United States individuals can start from the bottom social strata and, through hard work, rise. Neither nonpolitical group (Hispanics for Economics or Latino Fellowship) provided an ideology or a lens that countered the narrative of the American Dream, and neither the Research University nor the Regional Public University campus provided a context for the filtering the American Dream

narrative that dominates our national rhetoric. Thus, without campus or organizational filtering systems, the members of these two organizations reflected
ideas in society at large. No students at Liberal Arts College or members of
LUA, the political groups at Research University or Regional Public University,
expressed these perspectives.

Some students listed a variety of ways that Latinos are disadvantaged,
including educationally, economically, racially, and by immigration policy.
These were expressed in students' *oppression narratives*. There was variation,
however, in the how students discussed the origins of these inequalities and the
extent to which Latinos are affected. For example, some students merely noted
educational and economic disadvantages and spoke only implicitly about oppression, while others took their analysis further in explicitly considering historical
oppression and institutional inequalities. The perspective that explicitly articu-
lates oppression is most clearly related to the power analysis frame employed
by Warikoo's respondents at Brown University, who viewed "the significance
of race in society according to unequal power relations between groups" (2016, 54).
However, I found implicit and explicit expressions of the *oppression narrative*,
which alludes to the presence of systemic inequalities. Such narratives operate
on a scale from implicit to explicit. Virtually all Liberal Arts College students
employed *oppression narratives* explicitly, as did a few members of LUA at
Research University, while most members of LUA at Regional Public University
expressed them only implicitly.

Of course, not every member of these organizations espoused these views,
but a majority did. In the sections that follow, I look at the oppression and meritocratic narratives and the mechanisms that shape them, and indicate which
students espouse them. See Table 7.1 for a summary of narratives.

Meritocratic Narratives

The meritocratic narratives ranged from those that acknowledged structural
inequalities while simultaneously attaching some blame to Latinos, to those that
blamed Latinos entirely for their social location. Joel, a member of Hispanics for
Economics at RPU, said, "I guess what's happening in Arizona doesn't favor Latinos.
In other ways, too, like economic issues and knowledge, like financial knowledge.
I worked at a bank. I had so many experiences. Like people don't know when you
borrow money from the bank; they give you the money, but if it doesn't clear later
they try to get it back." Joel acknowledges that inequalities plague Latino communities through immigration policy and the economy. I was unclear which bank
procedure Joel was explaining but understood clearly what he implied: Latinos are
ignorant of this process. Joel, however, offered no solution for alleviating this
problem. Was it Latinos' responsibility to learn? Did the education system fail in
teaching them? Should understanding the banking system be in the curriculum?

TABLE 7.1

Narratives about Latino disadvantage and mechanisms for learning

Narrative type	Description	Who uses it	Location of filtering mechanisms
Meritocratic	Might acknowledge inequalities or not acknowledge them at all, but overwhelmingly believes that merit is rewarded across groups and individual effort triumphs	Members of nonpolitical groups at Research University and Regional Public University	Society at large; organizations do little to no filtering
Oppression Implicit	Acknowledges systemic inequalities without explicitly stating so or discussing origins of inequalities	Members of political groups at Research University and Regional Public University	Organizations filter ideas; LUA offers ideology for understanding the social location of Latinos in U.S.
Oppression Explicit	Explicitly acknowledges systemic inequalities connects them historically to the contemporary period	Members of both organizations at Liberal Arts College and some members of LUA at Research University	Campus at large; Liberal Arts College bubble filters ideas

Lissandra, a member of Latino Fellowship at Research University, similarly acknowledged disadvantages, but at the same time also denied them:

> I do not think they [Latinos] are in a disadvantage because there a lot of *opportunities to take*,[2] but I do feel that there a lot of walls. I think that if you're Latino there are a lot of stereotypes that come with it. I feel like sometimes people think that we are not that smart. I've only ever had one person tell me that I wasn't good enough because I was Latina and I got so mad. I think that sometimes *Latinos take it to heart too much.*

Sometimes we think, "I can't do this because people might think that we can't do it." And we did have teachers in our elementary school that would tell us that we couldn't do stuff, and I think that sometimes you believe what people tell you. *But it's up to us to change how we think because the opportunities are there.*

Lissandra acknowledges the outside forces that shape Latinos' economic trajectories, such as "walls," stereotypes, and negative messages from teachers, but she simultaneously says that there are "opportunities to take." Her view that "Latinos take it to heart too much" makes the issue psychological and effectively puts responsibility for change in the hands of Latinos themselves.

Thalia, a co-member of LF at RU, held similar view, acknowledging that "Latinos are disadvantaged," but adding that "you can't blame the system completely because Latinos don't want to do anything to advance, sometimes." Thalia assigns blame to Latinos more directly than Lissandra by accusing them of not wanting to advance. Mireya, also a member of LF at RU, said "I think we can overcome all stereotypes. We made it into a four-year university and we didn't get pregnant in high school. We're still here, and that's why we [members of LF] want to let people know that, you know, any stereotypes, they could overcome it." By positioning herself and her peers at RU as outliers who beat the odds and are breaking stereotypes, she both reinforces those stereotypes and delegitimizes the structural nature of inequalities.

Cruz, a member of LF at RU, also positioned himself as an outsider among other Latinos.

DVR: Do you think Latinos are a disadvantaged group in the U.S.?

CRUZ: Where I came from, the community (I still talk to them every now and then when I go back home), they—I guess the easiest way to put it is that they are content with being stuck.

DVR: Are they Latino?

CRUZ: Yes, you know, four years later—I used to be nostalgic. When I talk to the same people, they're working the same jobs, you know part-time, you know eight-dollar-an-hour jobs, still hanging out with the same friends, still going to the same parties, still you know, doing the same activities on the weekends and nothing much has changed. I mean, they get drunk and do drugs every weekend, it's kind of like—it was fun in high school but you know, you're twenty-two and you're about to have a kid, it's time to move on.

Cruz laments the behavior of his friends back home and he identifies himself in contrast to them. He blames them for their social realities, not acknowledging larger social forces at play.

Other students did discuss the social forces shaping the lives of Latinos, but they more forcefully espoused a *meritocratic narrative.* Mayra, a member of HE at RPU, responded to my question about whether she thought Latinos are disadvantaged in this country by saying:

> No, I think a lot of the time we feel that we are. *And I think that's our crutch.* But I think that it's more about the geographic thing. I think it's because *where I live, they don't foster education and don't highlight academic achievement.* I wouldn't say that Latinos as a whole are disadvantaged. Most of my family lives in another neighborhood and the public school system is better there. So, I think it's more about a geographic fact because that affects your education.

Mayra acknowledges that school districts differ and, by proxy, economics shape students' educational trajectories. However, as she continued to explain her experiences and the opinions of some Latino parents, her meritocratic mindset became clearer: "I used to volunteer at an elementary school. The teacher didn't speak Spanish. It was really difficult to tell the parents that the children were not up to par. *And it kind of went in one ear and out the other. I remember thinking if people tell me my children were not reading at the right level, I would reach out to them every day. I think it's ignorance and it's easier not to go find a better way.*" While acknowledging that school districts differ in resources, Mayra simultaneously blames some Spanish-speaking parents for not being more involved and others for choosing to remain ignorant about new and different ways to advance. She continued:

> I've kind of grown from not wanting to be a statistic and not letting my ethnicity or my background generate who am. *I know I'm an outsider for that reason. I don't fall into that category because I do not allow my past to dictate my future.* Just because you're female or just because you're a Latino, it does not mean you can't do what you want to do. And I tell people, if you think it's a little bit harder, then work harder. I've seen enough successful people to know that it's a possibility. A lot of times I see that a lot of people close the door before they even get there. Or sometimes they say, "I'm not economically able to study" and are set to live a certain standard. I always tell them, "Well, sure, if you tie yourself, you're not going make it there."

Mayra uses her success and that of others as evidence that Latinos can advance, that they are not totally disadvantaged. She positions herself as an outsider and "not wanting to be a statistic." She uses the word "crutch," which both implies a critique of the belief that inequalities exist at all and questions whether acknowledging them helps advance individual and group status.

Marta, a member of HE and RPU, also used the term "crutch" when she answered my question:

> To a point, I do. Not stereotypically. One problem that I've seen a lot here at RPU is people saying, "That's not fair, that's not fair." I can't take full advantage of internships because I have to support myself and a lot of students here have to work. If I had a parent that was rich, I could take advantage of unpaid internships. But I do come across people who have been cared for by mommy and daddy and you give them a simple problem and they can't solve it. Economically, Latinos are disadvantaged. Color of skin: and I don't think is an issue. I've heard people say things. But I don't like people to blame things on the race. I don't use the race card as a crutch. I've never had to pull it.

Marta unequivocally sees herself as economically disadvantaged, but she downplays the role of race. She also complains about her peers who claim things are not fair.

Yareli, also a member of HE, similarly lacked compassion for her co-ethnics:

> I do think we have a little bit of a disconnect between realizing that we are all on the same boat. For example, Arizona and immigration: you have uppity Latinos who have been successful and who are well incorporated, but they don't feel the need to say, "Hey, that's not cool." Or a couple years ago, when they tried to boycott stuff, I think our own people aren't as united as we should be. If someone says, "This is for a Latino cause," some people say, "Why would I need to go?" There are so many of us. I think the power is in the numbers, but if the numbers don't show up, then that's not cool.

Yareli blames Latinos' failure to advance on their inability or unwillingness to join forces and forge the solidarity necessary to push back on political issues. Yareli's words could sound like an oppression-oriented narrative critiquing the lack of mobilization among Latinos. However, she takes her analysis further by blaming Latino culture and individual Latinos for their disadvantages.

> I think Latinos are a disadvantaged group, but it's maybe our own doing, except for the currently undocumented students. I was given full opportunities in this world. I don't need to have a million dollars to have opportunities. With what my parents gave me, I had the tools in my hands and education was what I needed to make my own way. *If we are disadvantaged, it's because we do it ourselves.* As far as the workplace, obviously, there's discrimination against everyone. I'm a woman, I'll be discriminated against. I think we can rise above that and don't let it get to you. If someone really

hates Latinos, they are not going to hire me. I think all races deal with discrimination. *I think once we start getting an education and stop having babies at a young age, then we won't have this problem.* I feel like, "Why don't we have such a large Asian population of unwed mothers? Why are we in gangs?" My parents worked day and night, literally, so I don't understand when people say that absentee parents are making students not focused. I think that that's incredibly selfish. I wanted to go to college because my parents wanted it but also because it was the way out. I said if I can't afford to put my child in a car then I can't have a child. I knew that the only way I was going get out of my parents' house was to go to college.

Yareli's narrative exposes the most extreme version of the meritocratic narrative, overtly blaming Latino culture by juxtaposing it with Asian American culture.

Pablo, a member of LF at RU, also blamed individual Latinos for their socioeconomic status and denied the existence of inequalities.

In education, I know we have all kinds of opportunities. I was part of an early academic outreach program. Most Latinos were not in the program because it was based on your grades. They give you guaranteed admissions to RU. We can get loans and grants just like everyone else. I know a lot of people from USC who have graduated, like my cousin [who] is getting a double Masters and PhD and makes good money and is only twenty-six. I don't think there was any kind of disadvantage. They were given a chance and they succeeded. I think the only disadvantage is not being American enough. I think older generations that just came to the country are disadvantaged. I feel like I'm American compared to my mom. The language is an issue: she speaks broken English.

Pablo espouses a meritocratic perspective on life in the United States and sees only immigrant generations as disadvantaged.

The narratives shared by the members of the two nonpolitical groups, Hispanics for Economics and Latino Fellowship, are reflected in mainstream American national narratives about inequality. Students espouse beliefs in American meritocracy, holding that their successful efforts place them above other Latinos. At times, these students dismissed the structural challenges their co-ethnics faced. Was this an effort to exert agency over their futures or was it a defense mechanism against the negative portrayal of Latinos nationally? It appears that the students who use the meritocratic narratives at times contradict themselves by both acknowledging that inequalities exist and blaming their co-ethnics for their social location. Members of HE and LF lack organizational and institutional sites to process their ideas about mobility and inequality, since neither group dedicates time to discussing these issues and students receive little attention from faculty; nor do they have small seminar-style classes where these types of conversations might take place.

Oppression Narratives

Aside from members of Hispanics for Economics and Latino Fellowship, all other students explained Latinos' social location in the United States using *oppression narratives*. Their oppression narratives were deployed along a scale from implicit to explicit (see Figure 7.1). The explicit narratives seemed to be connected to an ideology for understanding how Latinos have come to occupy the social location they do in America.

Members of both organizations at Liberal Arts College spoke about the institutional, structural, and systemic origins of Latino disadvantage in explicit ways. Members of LUA at Regional Public University spoke of these systemic inequalities but did so in more muted language, while some members of LUA at Research University talked explicitly about oppression.

Implicit Oppression Narratives

When asked, "Do you think Latinos are disadvantaged?" Vanessa, a member of LUA at RPU said:

> Everything that's happening in Arizona, just because people came and wanted to work. People are in a disadvantaged . . . because it's hard. And I think that these people are trapped in Arizona. It's either go home or be trapped. I know fieldworkers will probably just stay there and the kids are probably the ones that are supposed to go to college. But nobody told me how to do it. I don't know if it's because of the color of my skin or no one really tells us how to get ahead. I've been told by many people, even here, that they were not told how to go to college or how to get hired or anything. I don't even think I have a counselor here. I think you can look at the positions of work that people do, and usually you see like housekeepers and babysitters. And it means they can't live in a house and they have to live in an apartment with twenty people. And I don't think they can be comfortable living.

Oppression Implicit   Oppression Explicit

FIGURE 7.1. Oppression narrative scale.

Vanessa touches on the many ways in which Latinos are disadvantaged economically, in housing and education and by race and migratory status. She has a broad scope yet does not quite connect all of these factors as operating under one system of inequality. Likewise, Hector, a member of LUA at RPU, said, "Based on personal experiences, there is poverty. There are laws, like, for example, Arizona's immigration law. I think that citizenship sets a lot of Latinos back. I think you can't have access to resources. You're also seen as criminal and when you are criminalized it's easy to exploit that population." While Hector touches on several issues—migratory status, economic disadvantage, and racial profiling—he offers no explicit explanation of the origins of these inequalities. Also of note is that Hector mentions Arizona's SB 1070, which was proposed when I was in the field and was on students' radar. Many students mentioned this legislation as one of the main ways that Latinos are disadvantaged.

Other students focused their attention on one specific way that Latinos are disadvantaged. For example, Alex, a LUA member at RPU, said, "Latinos lack the opportunities in society. If you want to see a Latino community, you know where to go: where there is a lower income community. Latinos lack resources and money to do certain things so Latinos are disadvantaged." While Alex was squarely focused on economics, other students connected economics and education. In response to my question "Are Latinos disadvantaged in the United States?," Antonietta, a LUA member at RPU, and I had the following exchange:

ANTONIETTA: Yeah. I think that they should provide workshops in schools. Financial aid workshops! Before they didn't have that. My brother was the first one to be provided the workshop for financial aid. They tell you what financial aid is, how you can apply, what are the benefits of applying, all that kind of stuff. He got the advantage of that workshop, even though I already knew the process because I already went through it. I think, they should announce it more on the TV. When I was going to college, they didn't, so now I think they try to do that like, "Oh, *no se le olvide* [don't forget]" to give information about financial aid, like, on Univision. It has to be Spanish channels like that.

DVR: So you think Latinos are disadvantaged in education, knowing about higher education. What else?

ANTONIETTA: The newspaper once in a while, they can try to tell us there. The only thing they tell you about is the Cal Grant; that's the only thing they tell, Cal Grant.

DVR: Do you think Latinos are disadvantaged in other places besides education?

ANTONIETTA: Like what you mean other places?

DVR: In other ways?

ANTONIETTA: Hmm . . . maybe. Like, they're not really aware about like different cultural events going on, for example, opera music: they don't know what it is. They don't know about musical plays, music cultural kind of things.

Antonietta's comments reveal an understandable fixation on financial aid. Possibly, it was the most relevant to her experience. She was resistant to thinking about other ways inequalities might cut across Latinos' experiences. When further questioned, she mentioned the lack of exposure to cultural events and forms, but she did not discuss systems of inequalities in an explicit way.

Ernesto, a LUA member at RPU, was more explicit than Antonietta in connecting economic status to educational trajectories:

I think they [Latinos] haven't been able to use resources. I feel a lot of families are not involved in the family. Like mom and dad worked two jobs and that is a disadvantage for kids because they don't get any attention. And the kids can do whatever they want. The economics is a disadvantage. I think education is another problem. I can't really generalize because educational systems are different, but where I live, I don't see much progress. The administrators and teachers are not affecting or influencing the students. They [administrators and teachers] see them [students] as just a paycheck. They just want to meet the time and go home. I don't think they are influencing kids. They don't try to impact the kids in a positive way. I do notice those things and it bothers me. It does put us at a disadvantage: they are getting paid and they're not making progress.

Ernesto implies that economic status shapes family life and the schools one attends. He has had some experience with the K–12 elementary system, and he aspires to join Teach for America.

Two members of Latinos United for Action at Regional Public University, Jerry and Amalia, had more explicit understandings of oppression. Jerry drew on his personal experiences in the workforce in a very elaborate discussion on inequality:

I think if you see the statistics, we are a working-class community. That's the reason our people value education: because they see it as a way to get out of poverty. Another barrier, for sure, is the language. Latinos that were born here may also have an accent and the language barrier. Sadly, sometimes people hear an accent or you can't develop your ideas right on the spot, they misjudge you. . . . Some people think that people that speak with an accent are not intelligent. I also want to say that race is a disadvantage, like when you go get a job. I have experienced that racism through my accent. I was applying for a position where I would have to answer the phone and I would be the first image for the company; it was a concierge. It was a very high-end place. He [the manager] did tell me that for that position he wanted a higher level of communication. He did say that some people didn't want to hear the accent. I remember thinking that he had an accent himself! He was this Jewish guy. I especially think lack of resources and information are a disadvantage. We lack information about how to follow your dreams to education. That's our disadvantage, like how to get financial aid. I have known people who graduate from high school and they don't know how to put an essay together. So, I think that the schools are bad sometimes.

Drawing from his personal experiences on the job market, Jerry provides an extensive view of how inequalities operate. He reflects on how his accent and racialization have put him at a disadvantage, points to a lack of financial aid information, like his peer Antonietta, and highlights educational inequalities, as so many other students did, including Amalia. Looking back to her time in high school, she discussed how discrimination plays out in some young Latinos' lives:

There is still stereotypes and discrimination. Like at my old school, the principal and the vice principal said that we couldn't wear blue or red. They said it was gang-related. I felt like they were targeting Latinos. But I saw this kid wearing a blue shirt: the vice principal was there and he didn't say anything! Later my friend was wearing red sweatshirt and she got in trouble. The vice principal told her to take it off. It wasn't fair. The other kid, was light-skinned, might've been white. And another day, they said we could wear the American colors on Flag Day. On Cinco de Mayo, I wore a red and green shirt, and this girl had a Mexican flag on her shirt. She had to take it off because it had red. It wasn't fair. Why do we get to wear blue and red on your day and we can't wear those colors on our day?

Both Jerry and Amalia draw on personal experiences to talk about how racism operates to oppress Latinos. From the words of Ernesto, Jerry, and Amalia, we can see that we are moving closer to the high end of the oppression narrative scale, as they more forcefully connect inequalities to systemic issues.

Deidra, who belonged for a time to both LF and LUA at Research University, made the similar systemic connections based on her and her sister's experiences at work. She said:

I think, yes, in the sense of our social environment. My older sister is a teacher so I feel like if it wasn't for her, a lot of her students wouldn't have school supplies. I feel like a lot of kids come from single homes and that puts them at a disadvantage. My sister pays out of her pocket for her students' school supplies. I don't think that's part of her job. Also, there are rats in the school and the kids laugh because they are used to it. When I compare that to the nursery school that I work with here. Some of the kids were coloring, and this kid was coloring outside of the lines and the teacher told me to give him a new piece of paper. I wanted her to use the back and the teacher said these kids pay to come here, so they can use another piece of paper. She said if they want to color on 50 pieces of paper then they can color on 50 pieces of paper.

In comparing two distinct settings—the school where her sister works and the nursery center on campus—,Deidra reflects on inequalities in the educational system and in so doing comes closer to explicitly articulating a narrative of oppression.

Explicit Oppression Narratives

Evelyn, also a member of LUA at RPU, was more explicit than Deidra. She said:

The system does not work in our favor. I had a conversation with a fellow student about how Chicano Studies courses are easier; and he gets better grades. I think it's because what we're learning is about ourselves versus in K–12, we're taught about different cultures. And I feel like a lot of times it has nothing to do with us. I feel like sometimes, you're in the school learning about other people's cultures and I think that that's a disadvantage. Even in the workplace, there's a lot of racism. It's not overt. It's more institutional.

Evelyn talks about "the system" and uses the word "institutional" to talk about the social location of Latinos. Some members of LUA at RU also used these words. This is not surprising given the political nature of LUA. The manifesto of this national organization espouses a framework for understanding the place of Latinos in the United States, and this framework uses the language of internal colonialism, explicitly arguing that Latinos/Chicanos belong in the United States. When I asked Alicia, a member of LUA at RU, if Latinos are disadvantaged, she said:

Yes, because of institutional racism. I think a lot of institutions work or don't work for the benefit of Latinos. The perception that people have of Latinos is that we're immigrants. I think most Latinos know people who are undocumented and I think that that puts us at a disadvantage. The best way to say it works is institutional racism. I would say that the educational system also: I think Latino students go to the worst schools. And the criminal system targets Latinos.

Kenya also talked about the institutional nature of racism, and Gilda, a member of LUA at RU, spoke about the role of history in the construction of Latino disadvantage. In response to my question as to whether Latinos are a disadvantaged group in the United States, she observed:

Within the United States, yes, and in terms of their histories of colonization in Latin American countries. But I also think there are [Latin Ameri-
can] subgroups that faced oppression in different ways. I think that
people are disadvantaged in terms of political representation and economically. I think our culture is also repressed because it's not the dominant culture. I think we're disadvantaged in the way that we are framed
as an enemy and in a way that keeps the country together.

Gilda's narrative is far-reaching, including history, politics, economics, and
even the role of cultural representation.

Why were members of LUA at Research University more likely to use words
like "institutional" and talk about the "system" than LUA members at RPU? Recall
from Chapter 3 that LUA at RU dedicated ample time to advancing a particular
political perspective through their consciousness-raising workshops. Some of
these workshops even advanced an oppositional consciousness, which sociologist Sharon Nepstad (2007, 63) defines as "an empowering mental state that
prepares members of an oppressed group to act to undermine, reform, or
overthrow a system of human domination. It is usually fueled by righteous
anger over injustices done to the group and prompted by personal indignities
and harms suffered though one's group membership." When discussing the
conquest and annexation of the Mexican southwest by the United States,
members of LUA at Research University connected these historical experiences to the social realities and the inequalities they face in the present. Thus, it
is not surprising that Evelyn, Gilda, and Kenya linked the origins of inequalities to institutional racism. Jane Mansbridge and Aldon Morris (2001, 238)
outline four steps in the creation of an oppositional consciousness: (1) identification with other members of a subordinate group, (2) recognition of the
injustices suffered by the group, (3) opposition to those injustices, and (4) an
awareness that the group has a shared interest in working to ameliorate those
injustices.[3] These steps are present in the workshops run by LUA at Research
University.

The students at Liberal Arts College also had expansive explanations, particularly regarding the origins and manifestations of the inequalities plaguing
Latino communities. Like Gilda, Valerie, a member of LL at Liberal Arts College,
acknowledged the role of history in Latino disadvantage. "We [my class] had a
discussion about the East LA schools and the walkouts in the 1960s. And if I think
about it, I don't think much has changed. My high school was mostly Latino. We
had a really small library. We competed with other schools and people had really
nice football fields. I would say that a lot of these schools that are in Latino
communities are really at a disadvantaged." Like students across the other two
campuses, Valerie and other LAC students used education as a primary example to discuss inequalities. Josiana, a member of LU at LAC, said, "Latinos are

disadvantaged. They are immigrating to the United States. They may not have the same educational resources for their kids. This has a pipeline effect because these kids don't have access to the same opportunities." Josiana's reference the education "pipeline" suggests that she understand the origins of the inequalities to have contemporary consequences.

Servino, a member of LU at LAC, connects the macro-level inequalities to the micro by discussing his experiences:

> Yes. Latinos have been marginalized historically, I'm learning about Latinos in contemporary society in my classes. A lot of us live in areas of poverty and don't have the same benefits that other people do. We get more debt. I think that in education we tend to get the worst. My middle school wasn't one of the best schools. There were a lot of fights and it was thought of as a dangerous place. My high school, where I was supposed to go, was considered a bad school. I didn't want to go there, so I went to a new charter school, which I know have their own controversies.

Servino has had the space to discuss these themes in his course on Latinos. He connects his personal experiences to historical processes. Karla, a member of Latino Links (LL) at LAC, talked about how education has shaped her perspectives:

> I'm learning a lot here. It's difficult because I can tell the difference in the educational system at my home and other students' homes. Last semester, I took a lot of math and science. I'm really good at that. But this semester I took humanities and it was really hard for me. These kids are just so smart and they analyze things really quickly. I feel like I have to catch up to their level. I think we are not given the same opportunities as other people. When I was in high school, I never really wrote essays only in literature class. A lot of the teachers gave up on the kids. They only focus on the kids they thought had a chance.

Exposure to classmates with drastically different socioeconomic origins has shaped Karla's perspective on inequalities. She sees that relative to her non-Latino peers, she is disadvantaged. Moreover, Karla talks about the role teachers play in perpetuating inequalities.

Genova, a member of LU at LAC, also talked about teachers: "We have been disenfranchised in general. Even if you control for economic variables, Latinos still receive less healthcare than any other group. Most of the students in low performing schools are Latinos. I think teachers still believe, they are not going see advancement in their students. For example, my cousin said his teacher would say, 'I don't care what you do.'" Genova talks about broad disenfranchisement and the role of individual teachers. Natalie, a member of Latino Links at LAC, also emphasized the dearth of mentors for Latinos:

I think we are at a disadvantage because we don't have any mentors. Beginning from the application process, we don't have people to help us. Not that many people read our personal statements. We don't have counselors look over applications. We come from overpopulated schools and communities. And we don't really have much social capital. We're not challenged to think critically because we don't really have ethnic studies classes or we don't talk about colonialism or really interesting things that you can talk about at a private high school. And I think education affects everything. It affects housing, financial stability, and all your opportunities. And there's racial discrimination: that's institutional.

Natalie's view is thorough and, in addition to discussing the role of mentors, she introduces the concept of social capital and its role in perpetuating inequalities. Tamara, a member of LL at LAC, used similar language, saying, "I think there are institutional apparatuses that are inherently racist. I think that it's in our historical foundation. I think that the way our society views 'the other' has made it so."

While Tamara introduces the concept of *the other*, Ana, a member of LU at LAC, introduced the concept of *redlining* in response to my question about Latinos as a disadvantaged group. "Yes, because of stereotypes, such as laziness and violence. In terms of housing there's redlining, excluding practices, like having a realtor showing you some communities only and getting only some bank loans approved. This keeps you from going to the schools that you want. A lot of the discrimination is historical and it does persist over time and its impacts do get built up across generations." Similarly, Fabian, a member of LU at LAC, talked about how inequalities compound over time:

Yes, historically we aren't in the position to accumulate the monetary wealth like other groups. We haven't had all that's required to access routes to gaining more wealth. And when I think about Latinos, I think about those who have recently migrated to the U.S and they don't have the English knowledge to navigate schools or how to create more wealth. And even those who have been here for a long time, there's racism. Microaggressions do exist.

Fabian, like his peers at LAC, introduces new terms to the narratives of inequality, including the concept of *microaggressions*. His peers talk about pipeline effects, disenfranchisement, social capital, redlining, and the "other." LAC students employ the most developed iteration of the *oppression narratives* among students at all three colleges and the most critical. Two students even had a problem with my wording. Lorena, a member of LL at LAC, responded sharply to my question "Do you think Latinos are disadvantaged in the U.S.?": "What do you mean? I think it's a very structural and institutional in terms of the issues that people of color face. There's a status quo that does not incorporate a large Latino population. I think there are class, racial, and gender differences. I would guess that that's a disadvantage but going beyond institutions, no." After our interview, Lorena wrote a follow-up email in which she apologized for her tone: "I took your question to allude to some type of cultural deficiency model," she wrote, introducing yet another concept.

Selena, a member of LU at LAC, likewise had a problem with my question:

> I think it depends on how you define disadvantage. I don't think there's anything inherent about being Latino that puts us at a disadvantage or a category that makes us inherently disadvantaged. I think there are structural forces in place that discriminate against Latinos and other people of color. I think that that maintains the social hierarchy that keeps Latinos in a low income bracket. And it keeps us unaware of even knowing how things work, like structural things—voting, healthcare, and rights, like renters' rights. I think Latinos are disadvantaged by stereotypes of being lazy and not being educated and things like that. I think those are forces; I think that those barriers have been structural and societal. People love Mexican food but they don't want Mexicans in California. There are lots of stereotypes about Latinos and in this context about Mexicans. I think that Latinos are strong and intelligent. I would not really identify myself as a disadvantaged person. I am incredibly grateful to be Latina. I would probably use the word "oppressed" much more than "disadvantaged."

Acknowledging the institutional nature of Latino inequalities and simultaneously asserting pride in her Latino heritage, Selena pushes back against my use of the word "disadvantage," since for her it implies some presumed deficiency in Latinos that is, as she says, "inherent." Instead, she makes it clear that the issue is oppression.

Thus Selena and the other students at Liberal Arts College voiced the most coherent oppression narratives, and they often used complex terminology to explain social phenomena. I attribute this to the impact of small seminar courses, interactions with and mentoring by faculty advisors, and the deliberative nature of social life within the "bubble of LAC." As we saw in Chapter 6, at LAC students are encouraged to have debate and discussion with peers, faculty, and administration, and through this process, they create cohesive oppression narratives.

Conclusion

Students employed two master narratives when explaining their understanding of Latinos as a disadvantaged group in the United States: meritocratic and oppression. Students at Liberal Arts College have the most coherent narratives about how to understand the social location of Latinos. This is likely connected to the residential environment of LAC, where students interact with more affluent and white peers. Through these interactions, they are likely to draw comparisons to their lives and see inequalities relative to their peers. Many of the students at LAC talked about learning new ways of understanding their social realities in their classes and through their experiences at the college, in general. They had thought about these issues before meeting me and developed their narratives. Their responses to my questions were elaborate and they introduced new concepts into our conversations. Two of the LAC students even problematized my wording. Certainly, students are learning about inequalities in courses across all three campuses, but it is only LAC students who attribute their learning about inequalities to their academic experience and environment. At Liberal Arts College ideas are filtered by student experience in the "bubble."

Research University and Regional Public University are not mediating students' understanding of inequality as much, and their students' narratives are more varied. That members of LUA (the political group) at both RU and RPU used oppression narratives can be attributed to the mission and purpose of LUA (discussed in Chapter 3), which offers a clear narrative and ideology for understanding Latinos' social location specifically through its overt political focus and its connections to the civil rights movement. But members of these two chapters varied on how implicit or explicit their oppression narratives were. Those in the Research University chapter articulated more explicit narratives, likely because of the consciousness-raising workshops they held (as we saw in Chapters 3 and 6). The LUA chapter at Regional Public University was rebuilding and focusing all energies on recruitment. Its members strategized about how best to recruit students and in doing so discussed the place of a political Latino organization on their campus. These discussions included thinking about inequalities, but they were more informal and not as developed as the workshops run by LUA at Research University. In short, the nationalized organization of LUA provides an ideology for understanding the world and some students espoused it clearly, while others implicitly narrated oppression. The local chapter played a role in shaping students' perspectives.

Members of the nonpolitical groups at RPU and RU had different narratives than the political groups on their campus. This suggests that these two campus contexts do not advance one dominant way of understanding inequality. The nonpolitical group members were more likely to use meritocratic explanations. As illustrated in Chapters 3 and 4, members of HE and LF are not offered an overt message from their organization through which they can understand inequalities. They espouse the dominant American narrative of meritocracy, appearing to get their ideas from society writ large.

Students' narratives are developed by discussions, whether it be in class, with faculty, or with their organizational peers. How much time students have to process these ideas determines how sophisticated and consistent their narratives are. In this way, the level of processing is filtered by campus life to different degrees. The question "Are Latinos a disadvantaged group in America?" is not easy to tackle if one has not thought about it. Are Latinos disadvantaged or not? What happens when you ask a group of students who are "making it" educationally, albeit to different places in our stratified system of higher education? Does their answer vary by where they go to college? How do they understand their path toward success while so many others are not succeeding? Do they see themselves as exceptional?

The narratives of Latino students at LAC, RU, and RPU tell us about how they grapple with understanding their own mobility despite their origins and the social location of the broader Latino community in the United States. At LAC students regularly receive the attention of faculty, and they interact intensely on a residential campus, which leads them to develop a sophisticated understanding of the social, economic, and political position of Latinos in the United States. However, there is a mismatch between students' visions of meritocracy and their actual economic prospects. Paradoxically, students at LAC develop a cynicism about the American system as they see affluence daily and have multiple opportunities to develop ideas and language to understand these inequalities. Students at Research University and Regional Public University have less exposure to affluence, yet members of Latino Fellowship and Hispanics for Economics subscribe to the ideals of a meritocracy. These organizations emphasize individual students' achievements and mobility, thus reinforcing the idea that Latinos who are not upwardly mobile are to blame for their disadvantage, while at the same time likely giving these students a sense of agency and self-efficacy.

These findings suggest that campus institutions and cultures play an important role in developing students' worldviews, as do some student organizations (although this is the only outcome that varied by organization). In the final chapter I suggest that examining how students' perspectives about inequalities develop as they graduate and search for jobs is important, follow-up research. Do the campus and organizational differences still hold among alumni?

8

How Higher Education Teaches Disparate Lessons to Latinos

Every fall Latino students enroll in four-year colleges across the country. Although social scientists use "college" as a catch all for a supposedly standard four-year experience, student experiences differ widely. To be sure, their expectations are similar—they want to take courses, socialize, develop personally, and acquire socioeconomic mobility—and they enter college with varying visions of how they will balance them. Generally, students expect to develop and grow by the end of the four to five years they will spend on campus; however, few predict they will change how they engage politically, identify ethnically, and think about inequality, especially in ways that are shaped by the particular college they attend.

Consider for example the experiences of two students, Josefina, a member of Latinos United for Action (the political organization) at Regional Public University, and Deidra, a member of Latinos United for Action (for a while) and Latino Fellowship at Research University. These two young women attended the same high school; both of their parents are Mexican immigrants and have the same median income. Josefina identified as Chicana and Mexican American, while Deidra identified as Latina foremost and then Mexican American specifically. As we saw in Chapter 5, Josefina believed the panethnic labels "Hispanic" and "Latino" were racist terms, while Deidra embraced the "Latino" label. Deidra talked about feeling racially isolated among Asian Americans in her residence hall and having her ethnic authenticity questioned by members of Latinos United for Action because of her light skin. Their experiences with co-ethnics and the campus at large shaped how they viewed their ethnic identities. They both joined LUA at their respective institutions, self-selecting into a political Latino group, but Deidra left the group, citing tensions around ethnic boundaries and the practice of contentious politics.

Josefina was actively engaged in contentious politics and was interested in protesting, as we saw in Chapter 6. Deidra, on the other hand, chose not to attend the education budget cut protests on campus. Recall that she said, "Why would I leave class to protest? I don't see the logic. I'm trying to avoid getting more costs for education because I value my education. Why would I ditch class to protest?" When asked to discuss Latino disadvantage, both women expressed the oppression narratives, but only Deidra drew on comparative experiences in her narratives about inequality. Deidra talked about preschoolers having ample sheets of paper in the town adjacent to Research University, in contrast to the preschoolers her sister teaches in a predominantly Latino neighborhood. Given the socioeconomic differences between Deidra's hometown and her college home, she saw deprivation. Josefina's and Deidra's college experiences varied in ways that mattered for their understandings of what it means to be Latino in America.

In this book, I have examined how campuses structure and shape students' interactions and have an impact on their experiences in a variety of ways. In this chapter, I outline how these findings can inform the sociology of education—including how to approach the study of institutional characteristics and how to expand the lens of college outcomes beyond the focus on academic attainment. I provide suggestions for administrators on how to support Latino undergraduates. I end the chapter with a discussion about how campuses' institutional differences might inform how we understand the formation of Latino communities.

Studying Institutional Characteristics

Sociologists of higher education are consistently concerned with the study of institutions and how characteristics within them shape the lives of students, albeit with an overwhelming emphasis on the academic and occupational impacts. Through my comparative ethnography of three types of higher education institutions, I discovered that each campus produces a particular context given its institutional characteristics. Rashawn Ray and Jason Rosow (2010) and Jenny Stuber (2016) talk about the "normative institutional arrangements" of higher education institutions as "the features of campus life shaped by structural constraints, demographics, and policies." In this book, I have shown how the normative institutional arrangements of each of the three campuses studied set the stage on which students *interacted* with each other, faculty, staff, administrators, and communities off campus (Chapters 2–4). I have also shown how these interactions created distinct experiences, shaping how students constructed and deployed ethnoracial boundaries and identity labels distinctly across campuses (Chapter 5), how they engaged in collective action behavior (Chapter 6), and how they understood inequality (Chapter 7). But which specific institutional characteristics shaped students' experiences?

The five main institutional characteristics that are relevant to Latino students' lives on each campus are: (1) school size, (2) the demographic profile of the student body (ethnic and socioeconomic composition, as well as proportion of first-generation college students), (3) residential arrangements, (4) the relationship between students and faculty and administrators, and (5) how well diversity programs integrate students through cultural centers and retention centers.

At Liberal Arts College (LAC) the interplay of several campus arrangements, including the wealth of the student body, the underrepresentation of Latinos on campus, and the residential arrangements (living on campus all four years), created an environment that initially felt shocking to my primarily first-generation college-going Latino student respondents. Of students from the three campuses studied, those at LAC reported the most incidents of racial microaggressions. However, the campus provides support to assist Latino students in their transition: peer mentors, a Latino cultural center, faculty advisors, first-year student experience classes, and Latino suitemate options. The college also supports Latino student organizations with ample funding, and administrators frequently attend their events. Both organizations studied had relationships with deans. Given these dynamics, students identified broadly as Latinos and espoused solidarity and open ethnic boundaries.

At RU, a combination of factors interact and leave students searching for a community: a dearth of programs designed to integrate Latino students, the underrepresentation of Latino students, and large classes. The members of the two organizations studied, Latinos United for Action and Latino Fellowship, find refuge in their group. These organizations become members' main communities on campus and a salient part of their identity. The two organizations studied had varied access to resources on campus, due mostly to the Multicultural Center's policies, and this difference not only fueled some competition between groups but also contributed to the antagonistic relationships and experiences that some students (like Deidra). Members of LF and LUA identified as Latino but felt the need to explain and authenticate their experiences. Unlike LAC students, RU students drew narrow ethnic boundaries.

In contrast, RPU's intersecting institutional arrangements, including its being a predominantly commuter campus whose students live where they grew up, its having little student life, and Latinos representing a majority minority on campus (45 percent), do not ignite or trigger a process of renegotiating ethnic identities. Not facing racial microaggressions, underrepresentation, or tension between co-ethnics over racial identities, students at RPU (like Josefina) downplay racism and are wary of panethnic identities. In effect, RPU students inhabit the same world they did before arriving at the university.

There is strong evidence that institutional characteristics matter, but different characteristics produce different outcomes. The all-encompassing "bubble-like" atmosphere on LAC ensures that students are on campus all the time. This means they focus their politics internally and have little time to exercise their political beliefs off campus. Additionally, the support of administration influences students to avoid contentious tactics as they care about maintaining their relationships. The leftist activist political culture of LAC also channels students' political styles toward deliberative tactics. At RU, the same institutional characteristics that shape Latino students' ethnic identity-formation shape their engagement in politics, and although only one Latino student organization has a political identity, students learn a divisive Latino politics on campus. The interplay of campus arrangements for RPU's largely commuter student body creates little to no filter for politics, so the politics of the outside world easily permeate campus life. Because students do not learn one single, generally accepted way to engage in campus political activity, they default to community tactics and protest.

There is a large wealth gap between the general student body and my Latino respondents at Liberal Arts College. Through this gap, Latino students learn about inequality on another level: they see first-hand what they did not have in their home communities. Through small seminars and relationships with faculty, however, they are able to develop their understandings of inequalities and their origins. One outcome of this exposure is that Latino students at LAC express the most elaborate oppression narratives compared to their peers on the other two campuses. At RU and RPU, students are divided on their views of inequality. The members of the nonpolitical groups at both Research University and Regional Public University espouse the meritocratic narrative, while members of LUA, the political group at both Research University and Regional Public University, use the oppression narrative. On both campuses LUA members see barriers in the life trajectories of Latinos.

Together, several characteristics create an environment that influences how Latino students interact, identify, and come to understand their place on campus. We need large-scale quantitative studies and qualitative comparative analysis of institutional characteristics to assess which characteristics shape which outcomes and how. Education scholar Sylvia Hurtado (1992) distinguishes between distal and proximal characteristics. Distal characteristics are contextual variables, such as size, type of institution, selectivity, racial composition of the student body, and campus expenditures. Proximal characteristics are students' perceptions of the campus environment, including their ideas about the institutional priority given to cultural diversity, the school's reputation, and how student-centered the campus is. The extent to which a student feels a college prioritizes its students versus its reputation is often the key difference between a research-oriented campus and a more teaching-focused institution. Because research universities push faculty to focus their energies on publishing and acquiring grants, teaching responsibilities and student relationships are often a lower priority. Recall how Evelyn reflected, in Chapter 3, about missing relationships with faculty. Liberal arts colleges vary quite a bit from research institutions in this regard. As Alexander Astin (1999) notes, they are likely to promote frequent student-faculty interactions, interdisciplinary and humanities courses, courses that emphasize writing, infrequent use of multiple-choice exams, and frequent involvement of students in independent research. Moreover, liberal arts colleges spend generously on student services and promote frequent student-student interactions. These practices create big differences in the collegiate experiences of students at large public institutions versus small residential colleges (Astin 1999). Most salient are the types of relationships that are fostered through the practices listed above between peers and students and faculty, as I observed at Liberal Arts College.

What Hurtado calls "proximal characteristics" many sociologists conceptualize as organizational culture. Natasha Warikoo and Sherry Deckman (2014) consider campuses to be "organizations and purveyors of culture," an idea that has gained increasing popularity among sociologists of education.[1] Campus cultures shape how particular understandings become taken for -granted, as being simply part of the landscape. The combination of organizational characteristics and interactions together create and shape campus cultures.

The characteristics I mention are not meant to be generalizable to all liberal arts colleges, research universities, or regional public universities but rather to offer suggestions for future studies. Also of note is that institutions and organizations change through the years—some more than others. This book captures how these campus organizations created shared meanings over one period of time. Recall that, in Chapter 3, I discussed how Latino Links (a nonpolitical group) was seeking to change its structure at the time I was exiting the field. During the second to last meeting of the 2010 school year, LL members did something that had never been done in my two years of observation there. They discussed the structure of their meetings and the tension felt during the meetings. They mentioned forming committees so that there would be less business to discuss during the meetings. Tomas said that forming committees would make the meetings less business-like and open up space to discuss other issues and get to know each other. He said, "This might remove some of the tension some people feel." Tomas also mentioned the various ways that he could shorten meetings by creating a list of resources to "pass the torch." They briefly mentioned LUA and how its members "were friends" and sought to create a less awkward, more comfortable space. Tamara suggested that the group should read the LL by-laws and consider changing the structure of the club, and Karla suggested holding consensus-building and decision-making workshops. They decided to have only a treasurer and secretary and remove all other hierarchies and even considered having bonding experiences. Such structural changes suggest that when studying peer cultures on campuses, it is also important to track cohorts to understand the effect of individuals on institutions.

Expanding the Study of College Outcomes

There are many types of college outcomes. The most common written and talked about are educational, such as the attainment of degrees and credentials. Recently, scholars have begun to expand the definition of educational college outcomes to include what is learned and what skills are developed. In their book, *Academically Adrift: Limited Learning on College Campuses* (2011), sociologists Richard Arum and Josipa Roksa track the learning outcomes of students enrolled in twenty-four four-year colleges nationwide. Their finding that students leave college with little improvement in their critical thinking and other higher learning skills has opened up the study of college outcomes beyond degree attainment.

Another college outcome is the development of career options. Amy Binder, Daniel Davis, and Nick Bloom (2015) look at how specific college campuses funnel students into the financial, consulting, and high-tech sectors.[2] Astin (1999) refers to some of these career trajectory outcomes as "fringe" advantages that students receive from having a degree from a specific college. He suggests that such benefits influence the networks, job placement, and overall economic trajectories of alumni.

When people worry about college outcomes, they rarely think beyond academic and career trajectories. Astin (1999), however, identifies another category of outcomes—the existential, which refers to the quality of the experiences that students have on campus and how they evaluate the meaning of these experiences. Astin (1999) argues that this existential dimension of college life can shape students' patterns of behavior, self-concepts, attitudes, values, and beliefs. Several studies have opened up new ways of thinking about these existential dimensions by focusing on culture. In their book, *Paying for the Party: How Colleges Maintain Inequality* (2013), Elizabeth Armstrong and Laura Hamilton show how college cultures shape peer cultures and students' social lives. They note how campuses set distinct pathways for low-income and middle-class women by facilitating their access to Greek life and party scenes. Through in-depth analysis, Armstrong and Hamilton highlight the significance of social scenes on campus and how access to these, too, is often unequal across class origins. In another study, Amy Binder and Kate Wood (2014) compare conservative students at two different universities and find that students engage in two distinct political styles: deliberative and contentious (as I similarly found among Latino students; see Chapter 6). They argue that these styles are shaped by the cultural and organizational norms of the respective universities. Thus, college has implications for the types of political engagement in which students will likely participate.

Ann Mullen (2010) compares Yale students and Southern Connecticut State University (SCSU) students and finds that one outcome of the particular college attended is the transmission of different types of cultural capital, specifically students' understandings of the school-to-work connection. Yale students learn to delay career choices and focus on self-discovery, while SCSU students focus on the immediacy of finding a job. This finding holds true across students from all social backgrounds. In other words, the schools transmit understandings of the school-to-work connection so effectively that even working-class students at Yale, for example, receive the same message about self-discovery. In a similar vein, Stuber's (2011) qualitative comparison of a liberal arts college and a public state college examines social and cultural capital cultivation as a significant outcome of college. Finally, Warikoo (2016) examines racial frames as a college outcome. She analyzes how organizational cultures at four elite colleges shape their approaches to multiculturalism and diversity and finds that different approaches cultivate distinct understandings of race among their students. I report similar patterns in Chapters 5 and 7.

Building on this wave of scholarship, I take an organizational-analytical approach and identify and trace Latino student peer relationships and their interactions with each other and the campus at large, noting the different types of learning that happen on campus. I identify what we might think of as a kind of hidden curriculum that greatly extends colleges' pedagogical effects. I show how each campus's particular organizational setting promotes different sorts of ethnic and racial identity development processes, political lessons, and understandings of the social position of Latinos. Future quantitative research could follow the tradition of the National Longitudinal Survey for Freshmen and the Cooperative Institutional Research Program (CIRP) Freshmen Survey at the University of California, Los Angeles,[3] to assess the ideas and identities that students walk into college with (using some of the outcomes identified in this book). Measuring these before college would help us understand the influence of college on a range of outcomes and on a broader scale.

What Administrators Can Do for Latino Students

What can administrators do to help alleviate some of the challenges that Latino students face on their college campus? There is no a one-size-fits-all solution. I believe LAC administrators are doing well in supporting Latino students by providing peer mentoring programs and fostering faculty-student relationships. However, administrators can work to avoid some of the feelings of not belonging and racial microaggressions that Latinos face on campus by increasing the percentage of Latino students on campus so that it is more representative of the national or local population. Some private liberal arts colleges are making strides on this effort. For example, Vassar received the Jack Kent Cooke Foundation's Prize for Equity in Educational Excellence, which comes with a $1 million award to further its commitments to enroll and retain more low-income and first-generation college-going students (Kosmacher 2015). Additionally, administrators could have the entire student population learn about educational inequalities and microaggressions on campus so that the weight of making a change does not rest mainly on Latino students' shoulders. Administrators could create pipelines that bring first-generation students to elite research institutes and graduate schools and guide them toward particular career paths. I believe most LAC students are already encouraged to apply to prestigious programs, but programs, for their part, could target Latinos specifically.

At Research University, there are many areas for improvement. First, the administration can treat all student organizations equally. This would mean removing any special access to resources that a group might have (even if gained historically through activism). One fear of taking these away is that the history of these organizations, which originated in the civil rights era, will be forgotten. Latino Studies departments across the country battle this as they shift from ethnic-specific "Puerto Rican" or "Chicano Studies" to a broader, panethnic classification as "Latino Studies." Administrators could honor that history by requiring that the history of ethnic organizing at that particular college be taught in the curriculum. Also, administrators could honor the historical activism on campus that led to the creation of certain institutional structures, such as ethnic studies and cultural centers. Such efforts could create more dialogue between groups and promote a similar view on the part of Latino students, whatever their organizational affiliation. In the absence of differential access to resources, students might also promote collaboration, and campus politics might not be as divisive.

Students at Regional Public University face inequalities in their communities and their college. There are clear disparities in resources between this campus and the other two studied. One outcome of this segregated (mostly minority) college experience is that students do not list microaggressions or feelings of "not belonging," and this is one positive aspect of the RPU experience. However, because graduating students take different jobs in contexts in which they may be a minority, administrators could prepare them by exposing them to professional settings through workshops that model this possibility. They could also create career-track programs to well-paid jobs in STEM fields, government, or policy. If administrators would like students to focus more of their energies on campus grounds, they could provide more resources to organizations. They could also require a first- or transfer-year experience class that requires students to spend more time on campus and exposes them to resources, student life programming, and politics on campus.

Campuses as Critical Sites for the Construction of Latino Communities

Given the growing representation of Latinos in higher education, it is important that we understand the experiences of Latino millennials in four-year colleges. Understanding how their college experiences shape their sense of self may shed light, in turn, on subsequent patterns and processes of Latino community development. What types of consequences might arise from students learning different ways of (1) defining what it means to be Latino, (2) engaging politically, and (3) viewing Latinos' place in American society? Will these disparate lessons carry over after college? How will they affect Latino communities?

Take, for instance, the broad understanding of Latinidad and sense of solidarity that students at LAC develop: these could serve them well as they leave college, organize, and work with Latinos who come from diverse national origins and economic means and differ in generational status. Having had college courses that nurture their abilities to deliberate about ethnic boundaries and navigate difficult conversations, LAC students may be better equipped than Research University students to organize broad coalitions of Latinos. At RU, the competitive environment between Latino organizations may teach students to distrust one another, and to the extent that they do, students might carry this attitude off campus and to the Latino organizations they encounter throughout society writ large.

The political lessons might also have consequences for organizing Latino communities. The Latino students attending Liberal Arts College are learning a politics of deliberation, which fits well within conventional politics. The skills they develop will serve them not only in their further careers, but also if they choose to advocate for change within institutional channels. At Research University, students who are not part of the explicitly political organization are being de-mobilized. They are shying away from politics and often avoid them wholesale. This avoidance could continue after college, resulting in a subset of the Latino college-educated population with an aversion to politics. If two groups of Latino students on one campus can come to view the world so differently that they are unable to work together on campus, what are the prospects of them working together as alumni? Future research can examine these college differences and their potential to develop or to fracture communities.

Regional Public University students remain embedded in their hometown communities, and this has mixed consequences. Thus, one strength of their connection to their communities is their willingness to engage in community collective action during college. At the same time, one limitation of focusing on external community engagement is that students do not have the time to "practice deliberation," as LAC students do, and since that is the way of institutional politics, RPU students' access to particular leadership positions may be impeded as a result.

LAC students have more academic attention, more access to elite networks, and more mentorship. Although seemingly advantaged, Latino students at Liberal Arts College are worlds away from their hometown communities (even if, most of the time, very close geographically). LAC students have a sobering view of inequality as they gain exposure to this new world. However, they are gaining these insights while they live in in the LAC bubble. As they graduate and gain access to prestigious careers, professional schools, and fellowships, their lives will take them further from home. What implications might this have for Latino communities? The LAC experience might be one of "social decapitalization," which Angela Valenzuela (1999, 21) defines as a process of severing ties and removing meaningful relationships and resources from communities. This process is exactly the opposite of what the student crafters of "El Plan de Santa Barbara" foresaw in 1969, when they sought to reform higher education to be inclusive and open to Chicano and Latino students. Quoting the Mexican Secretary of Education José Vasconcelos, they wrote, "At this moment we do not come to work for the university, but to demand that the university work for our people." They envisioned that Chicano and Latino students would create a bridge from Latino communities to the university and that the education of any Latino would benefit the community broadly. They imagined a relationship of solidarity wherein educated Latinos would return home and invest their energies in the cultivation of prosperity for all Latinos.

Unfortunately, their vision of higher education has not been fully realized. The elite and exclusive nature of higher education in America still plays a part in fracturing Latino communities in that it gives access only to a few and removes many from their communities, at least during the four years they attend college. Future research could examine the life trajectories of Latino alumni who attend colleges in different places in the stratified system of higher education. How do their lives develop after they graduate and search for jobs? Do the campus and organizational differences still hold among alumni?

This book is about Latino millennials who attended college from 2008 to 2010. During that time I captured one political moment characterized by Obama's election, budget cuts in state funding for education, and anti-immigrant legislation, most notably Arizona's SB 1070. It remains to be seen how Latino students today will organize, given a political climate characterized by the emergence of Black Lives Matter, the explosion of campus protests for racial justice after the University of Missouri football players threatened to boycott, the election of Donald Trump, and the seeming legitimation of racist and nativist rhetoric.

Now more than ever it is important to think about Latino students—who experience marginalization—and challenge institutions to meet their needs.

There is a huge impetus to increase Latinos enrollment in higher education, and in fact institutions vary quite a bit, and these differences can have consequences in every conceivable way.

METHODOLOGICAL APPENDIX: STUDYING STUDENT ORGANIZATIONS IN MULTIPLE INSTITUTIONS

I made a series of methodological decisions in the design of this research. First, I chose to examine Latino student life at three very different types of institutions of higher education: a public research university, a regional public university, and a private liberal arts college. Each occupies a different place in a stratified system of U.S. higher education and serves distinct segments of the population, although the Latino students in my sample were quite similar demographically.

Because I wanted to conduct simultaneous ethnographic observations during the 2008–2009 and 2009–2010 academic years, the campuses needed to be within a convenient driving distance; and so, they are located within a forty-mile radius of each other. In addition, given my research interest in how race and politics intersect, I chose to study one explicitly political organization on each campus and one nonpolitical group. Before contacting any student organizations, I obtained Institutional Review Board (IRB) approval from my home institution and the IRB office at each of the three campuses. As highlighted in Chapters 2–4, I worked to gain entry into six different organizations and had to negotiate my involvement and identity in each of these settings.

I attended over 150 meetings between 2008 and 2010. All organizations, with the exception of Latinos United for Action (LUA) at Research University (RU), allowed me to actively participate. I took a seat within the circle or in the back row of each meeting. I generally observed and remained quiet except when participating in the ice breakers at the beginnings of most meeting, which entailed introducing myself and answering an easy question like: How was your day? How do you feel today? What's your favorite ice cream flavor? During LUA meetings at RU, however, I sat in the back of the room and did not participate, respecting the students' stipulation for allowing me access to their meetings (described in Chapter 3). I maintained this position for two academic years.

I interviewed ten members of each organization and the leadership in all organizations. However, in groups like LUA at RU and Hispanics for Economics (HE) at Regional Public University (RPU), I made sure to interview rank-and-file members as well, given the many leadership positions existed. This way I balanced the ten interviews between rank and file members and leaders (see Table A.1 for respondents' information). I also interviewed a total of twelve Latino faculty and administrators formally as well as informally. In the last month of fieldwork, I conducted a survey of the existing organizational membership by distributing a questionnaire during a meeting. I asked students demographic questions as well as their reasons for joining the organization, and their perceived benefits of being part of the organization.

Data Analysis

There were several phases of analysis of the data. I began by transcribing each of the seventy-two interviews and typing up field notes after observing each meeting. I uploaded these notes and transcripts into Atlas.ti qualitative software to begin line-by-line open coding. Examining the data line by line, I looked for emerging concepts and codes (Hammersley and Atkinson 2007; Huberman and Miles, 1994; LeCompte and Schensul 2010). I was particularly attuned to themes related to identity, race, and politics and to ideas about inequality. I came up with an extensive list of broad codes including "identity labels," "definitions of Latinidad," "racial boundary," "type of politics," and "inequality idea." I then began second cycle coding, which consisted again of line-by-line coding, looking for these same concepts (Miles, Huberman, and Saldana 2014). In this second phase of open coding, I came up with more specific subcodes, such as "Hispanic label rejection," "panethnic solidarity," "political talk," and "belief in meritocracy." Then, in the third phase of line-by-line coding, I took a tally of all my subcodes. The patterns revealed particular outcomes for each campus and organization, as presented in this book.

Ethical Considerations

One of the greatest challenges in conducting this institutional research was hiding the identity of each school while providing enough information to tell the story. Maintaining the anonymity of the institutions was particularly important, given the vulnerability felt by some respondents and especially by students of color at the predominantly white Liberal Arts College. I worked to blur some of the campus characteristics while maintaining the integrity of the social reality. This practice is common, and in adopting it, I followed the suggestions of the editor and anonymous reviewers at the journal *Sociology of Education*.

In each setting, with each interaction, I negotiated my multiple identities: a first-generation college-going student, a second-generation Mexican American, a woman in her late twenties, and a Ph.D. candidate. We could say I was an "outsider within" (Collins 1986) in each student organization, fitting in with the students as a Latina student myself yet having a privileged position as a graduate student. Glenda Flores (2016) calls this a "hidden privilege" of the Ph.D., wherein particular status and respect is accorded given the credential. My graduate student status was treated with suspicion by the leadership of LUA at RU, who feared I would infiltrate their organization and co-opt it (as described in Chapter 3). However, individual students from LUA looked to me for advice about graduate school both informally and formally, and I reviewed some personal statements for graduate school. Members of the nonpolitical organization at RU and both organizations at RPU also asked for some mentorship. I offered to organize a graduate student panel for all organizations and three requested that I do so (Latino Fellowship at RU, LUA at RU and RPU). These panels consisted of my Latino colleagues and friends at the University of California, Irvine, who graciously agreed to participate.

The personal statement review, the panel, and talks about graduate school were the extent to which I served the students. A fellow Latino scholar once asked me, "How are you helping these students?" She further asked how I was helping them organize or think about some of the issues they were grappling with. This question was particularly difficult to hear as I wanted to make sure I was not exploiting my research respondents and that I was providing them a service. However, I took a tip from LUA at RU by deciding not to actively shape the organizational activities. I wanted student actions to emerge organically and freely, even if I did not always agree with what they were doing. I continue to believe that Latino students should be given the autonomy to engage politically and collectively as they see fit.

TABLE A.1
Respondents

	National Origins	Immigrant generation	Paternal education	Maternal education	Paternal occupation	Maternal occupation
Liberal Arts College						
Latinos Unidos						
Genova	Mexican	2nd	Middle school	Middle school	Production	Service
Vanya	Mexican	1.5	Middle school	High school	Maintenance	Manufacturing
Ana	Puerto Rican	2nd	Bachelor's	Master's	Professional	Professional
Selena	Mexican	2nd	Middle school	High school	Manufacturing	Homemaker
Josiana	Mexican	2nd	Middle school	High school	Maintenance	Service
Maribel	Mexican	2nd	Middle school	Middle school	Production	Homemaker
Servino	Mexican	1.5	Middle school	Elementary school	Unemployed	Service
Fabian	Mexican	2nd	Elementary school	Elementary school	Maintenance	Service
Cristina	Mexican	2nd	High school	Middle school	Manufacturing	Maintenance
Bernardo	Mexican/ Salvadoran	2nd	High school	Master's	Manufacturing	n/a

TABLE A.1. (CONTINUED)

	National Origins	Immigrant generation	Paternal education	Maternal education	Paternal occupation	Maternal occupation
Latino Links						
Martiza	Mexican	2nd	High school	Master's	Clerical	Professional
Adalberto	Mexican	3rd	Master's	n/a	Professional	Homemaker
Cassandra	Mexican	2nd	Middle school	Elementary school	Service	Service
Karla	Mexican	2nd	High school	Elementary school	Unemployed	Manufacturing
Natalie	Mexican	4th	High school	High school	Manufacturing	Clerical
Paloma	Mexican	2nd	Middle school	Middle school	Unemployed	Service
Tomas	Mexican	3rd	High school	High school	Maintenance	Manufacturing
Angel	Mexican	3rd	Bachelor's	High school	Professional	Homemaker
Lorena	Mexican	2nd	Middle school	Middle school	Manufacturing	Maintenance
Tamara	Nicaragua	2nd	High school	Bachelor's	Manufacturing	Professional
Research University						
Latinos United for Action						
Evelyn	Mexican	2nd	Middle school	Middle school	Manufacturing	Homemaker
Gilda	Mexican	2nd	High school	High school	Maintenance	Clerical
Carlos	Mexican	4th	Middle school	Middle school	Manufacturing	Maintenance
Kenya	Mexican	2nd	Elementary school	Bachelor's	Manufacturing	Professional

(Continued)

TABLE A.1. (CONTINUED)

	National Origins	Immigrant generation	Paternal education	Maternal education	Paternal occupation	Maternal occupation
Lalo	Mexican	1.5	High school	High school	Service	Service
Alicia	Mexican	2nd	High school	Middle school	Maintenance	Service
Liliana	Mexican	1.5	Elementary school	Elementary school	Maintenance	Service
Jennifer	Mexican/ Puerto Rican	2nd	Master's	Bachelor's	Professional	Professional
Belinda	Mexican	2nd	Middle school	High school	Maintenance	Service
Guadalupe	Mexican	2nd	Middle school	Middle school	Maintenance	Homemaker
Latino Fellowship						
Deidra	Mexican	2nd	Middle school	Middle school	Manufacturing	Homemaker
Gloria	Mexican/ Salvadoran	2nd	n/a	Middle school	n/a	Maintenance
Lissandra	Salvadoran	2nd	High school	High school	Manufacturing	Clerical
Cruz	Mexican	2nd	High school	High school	Unemployed	Service
Suyeli	Salvadoran	2nd	Associate's	Elementary	Manufacturing	Service
Mireya	Mexican	2nd	High school	High school	Clerical	Clerical
Pablo	Mexican/ Armenian	2nd	Middle school	Middle school	Maintenance	Service

TABLE A.1. (CONTINUED)

	National Origins	Immigrant generation	Paternal education	Maternal education	Paternal occupation	Maternal occupation
Thalia	Salvadoran	2nd	n/a	High school	n/a	Service
Micaela	Mexican	2nd	Middle school	Elementary	Manufacturing	Service
Tania	Mexican	3rd	Bachelor's	Bachelor's	Professional	Professional
Regional Public University						
Latinos United for Action						
Hector	Mexican	2nd	Elementary school	Elementary school	Manufacturing	Service
Alex	Mexican	1.5	High school	Middle school	Manufacturing	Manufacturing
Amalia	Mexican	2nd	Middle school	Elementary school	Service	Maintenance
Ernesto	Mexican	1.5	Elementary school	Elementary school	Manufacturing	Manufacturing
Josefina	Mexican	2nd	Master's	High school	Professional	Homemaker
Theresa	Mexican	1.5	Elementary	College	Business owner	Maintenance
Vanessa	Mexican	2nd	Middle school	High school	Maintenance	Service
Gilma	Mexico	2nd	Middle school	Middle school	Manufacturing	Service
Antonietta	Mexican	2nd	Elementary school	Elementary school	Service	Service
Jerry	Mexican	1.5	Middle school	Middle school	Manufacturing	Manufacturing

(Continued)

TABLE A.1. (CONTINUED)

	National Origins	Immigrant generation	Paternal education	Maternal education	Paternal occupation	Maternal occupation
Hispanics for Economics						
Yareli	Salvadoran	2nd	Middle school	Elementary school	Manufacturing	Maintenance
Marta	Mexican/ Filipina	2nd	High school	High school	Manufacturing	Sales
Jesus	Mexican/ Native American	3rd	High school	High school	Unemployed	Service
Lucy	Mexican	2nd	Elementary school	Middle school	Service	Service
Joel	Mexico/ Guatemala	2nd	Middle school	Middle school	n/a	Manufacturing
Mayra	Mexico	1.5	Elementary school	Middle school	Manufacturing	Service
Sara	Mexico	1.5	Elementary school	Elementary school	Manufacturing	n/a
Sandra	Mexico	5th	High school	High school	Service	Clerical
Jackie	Mexico	2nd	Middle school	Middle school	Business owner	Clerical
Yvette	Salvadoran/ Cuba	2nd	Associate's	Middle school	Service	Homemaker

ACKNOWLEDGMENTS

Foremost, I would like to thank the Latino students who allowed me to be part of their lives for two academic years. They welcomed me as if I were a part of their communities. I am grateful to have watched them create vibrant Latino spaces on their campuses and develop as individuals.

I was very fortunate to receive various grants that supported this study. I thank the Department of Sociology, the Center for Research on Latinos in a Global Society, the Center for Organizational Research, and the Center for the Study of Democracy at the University of California, Irvine, and the University of California All Campus Consortium on Research for Diversity (UC/ACCORD). At the University of Connecticut, I am grateful for support from El Instituto: Institute of Latina/o, Caribbean & Latin American Studies, the Department of Sociology, the Office of the Vice President for Research, and the College of Liberal Arts and Sciences' Fund for Interdisciplinary Research Endeavors (FIRE).

I would like to express the deepest appreciation to my dissertation committee: David S. Meyer, Cynthia Feliciano, and Belinda Robnett-Olsen, who supported this project from the idea stage to the completion of the dissertation. In addition, I thank Francesca Polletta, Michael Montoya, and David Snow, who provided direction during the research proposal stage.

I am particularly indebted to David Meyer, who has continuously and generously given his time, reading many, many drafts. Without his guidance and persistent encouragement, my career would not be where it is today. David has been a dedicated mentor, providing me with the vital professional socialization I needed as a first-generation college student.

I am grateful to my colleagues Marysol Asencio, Ruthie Braunstein, Elizabeth Holzer, Matthew Hughey, Nancy Naples, and Mark Overmyer-Velasquez for advice on navigating the book-writing process. Laura Hamilton and Amy Binder provided indispensable feedback on drafts of my book proposal. I received critical feedback during meetings at the University of Notre Dame's Center for Research of Educational Opportunity, the Sociology of Education Association, and the New England Consortium of Latino Studies. I workshopped several chapter drafts in the Social Movement working group at Smith College, where

Steve Boutcher, Mary Ann Clawson, Rick Fantasia, Jasmine Kerissey, Joya Misra, Marc Steinburg, and Nancy Whittier provided invaluable feedback. Jenny Stuber, Kelsy Kretschmer, and Diana Pan generously read several drafts of chapters. Kim Greenwell and Elizabeth Mahan copyedited several drafts of chapters.

I have benefited immensely from the informal mentorship of Nella Van Dyke, Irenee Beattie, Gilda Ochoa, Carlos Alamo, Mari Casteñeda, Ginetta Candelario, Silvia Spitta, and Lisa Nunn and from the encouragement of Janice McCabe, Glenda Flores, Leisy Abrego, Erica Morales, and Veronica Terriquez. I am appreciative of the friendships I have made with colleagues throughout the years. Diana Pan and Megan Thiele are my graduate school besties and are both like family. They are constant sounding boards.

I thank the National Center for Faculty Diversity Development and Kerry Ann Roquemoore. I participated in her boot camp during my first semester on the tenure-track, and the skills I learned have changed my life. Although not by any means perfect, I have some habits, skills, and even language to talk about the challenges academic writers face. Christin Munsch and I connected during our interview over the teachings of Kerry Ann Roquemoore. I am grateful for Christin's friendship. I wrote the bulk of this book in the library with Amanda Denes and at a Berkins Coffee Shop with Milagros Montoya-Castillo. I'm grateful to both scholar/friends for making an isolating experience feel communal. I'm especially grateful for Milagros—for a few years now, we've set goals, checked in once a week, cried/pouted over rejections, picked up each other's spirits, and celebrated victories.

I am thankful for the support I received from friends throughout the data collection and writing stages of this project. I am grateful to Irene Barajas, who provided me with warm meals and a place to stay in between campus visits. Jennifer Kalker let me stay at her house as I finished writing the dissertation. Jasmin Ramirez, Lesley Meza, Consuelo Hernandez, Rita Duarte, and Kavetha Sundaramoorthy provided much needed support, distractions, and laughs. Esteban Martinez is a dear friend and brainstormed some beautiful cover ideas for the book. Araceli López-Arenas and I talk weekly, and she has given me *ánimo y apoyo* for over a decade, especially as I wrote this book.

I am extremely lucky to be part of a *huge* Mexican family, with eighteen aunts and uncles and sixty-two first cousins. I dedicate this manuscript to all members of the Reyes and Verduzco clans. Our family story is one of migration, of so many members carving out their individual paths in the United States. I am indebted to my grandmother Elena Verduzco Abundiz, a widow and mother of nine who migrated to this country alone when in her thirties. I hope this book and my career are a testament that her efforts paid off. My life and career are indebted to my grandparents Mami Maria and Papi Pedro, who birthed a generation of children who migrated to the central coast of California a *piscar fresa*. The list would be too long if I mentioned everyone by name, but I thank my Tio

Chepe y Tia Adriana *por su cariño*. Nancy Reyes, Jessica Reyes, and Jairo Reyes have been like siblings. I still remember the day I got the courage to voice a crazy idea to Nancy: "I think I want a Ph.D." It was her unwavering encouragement and belief that I could do it that pushed me to apply to graduate school. *Mis primos* and plus-ones, Deyanira, Peps, Brian, Anthony, Jorge, and Sonia, fill my life with fun along with Francesca, Joaquin, Bianca, and Julieta, who provide a new generation filled with hope.

I have two wonderful siblings, Christy and Jesse, who are incredibly intelligent and thoughtful individuals. They remind me that life is always better when family is close. And lucky me: Christy *is close*, having left sunny California and relocated with me to Connecticut for my tenure track job. I can't imagine what the often-grey skies and winter days in New England would have been like without her wit, encouragement and hugs. I thank my parents, Isabel and Jesus Reyes, for their hard work and selfless love. Their perseverance and resolve has been a constant inspiration to me. Their sustained encouragement and affection has made me feel capable of anything. *Los adoro.* I became a sociologist because I questioned why things were the way they were—from gender norms to religious practices. I thank my parents for putting up with all my "whys," and my cousin Nancy for giving me spaces and outlets early on to explore those questions.

I had the fortune to find a wonderful partner as I wrote this book, Stanley Esteban Gromala III. Not an academic, Stanley read up on the process of writing an academic book and how to best support someone who was. I thank him for the coffee, daily meals, and unwavering patience as I talked constantly about the book. He showers me with encouragement and support daily. I am so grateful to have you and *Tiberius* in my life.

NOTES

PREFACE

1. I use the term "Latino" as a descriptor throughout the book but unpack student label preferences in Chapter 5. Since I conducted my fieldwork from 2008 to 2010 there has been a push to de-gender the Spanish language by Latino LGBTQ+activists. This move began with the use of Latina/o, then Latin@, and most recently Latinx. I recognize the shifting terminology, but use Latino throughout the book as this was the term used by my respondents at the time.

2. "La raza" literally translates to "the race"; however, when used by social movements or advocacy groups like the National Council for La Raza (now UnidosUS), it is intended to mean a community of Latino-origin individuals with a common destiny. The term was coined by Mexican scholar Jose Vasconcelos in his book *La Raza Cósmica* (1925), in which he espoused the idea that Mexicans were the product of a mixture of all races.

CHAPTER 1   HIGHER EDUCATION AND LATINO STUDENTS

1. Approximately half of all Latino students enrolled in higher education attend two-year institutions. According to a report by Excelencia in Education, "Almost half of Hispanics in higher education were enrolled in community colleges (46%) or private 2-year institutions (3%)" (2015, 8). This is disproportional when compared to other ethnic-racial groups.

2. This statistic includes graduates of all racial-ethnic groups.

3. To protect the identities of respondents, I gave every campus, organization, and individual a pseudonym.

4. Pell grants are a good proxy for the percentage of low-income students on campus.

5. I coded an organization as "political" if it explicitly said so in its mission statement, but I took a constructivist perspective that left the specific definition of politics to the students.

6. College campuses can vary in their diversity initiatives in many ways. Some may have broad programming, including cultural centers, residence halls, mentorship programs, counseling services, and academic programs focused on ethnic-racial minorities, while others may have only a few or none of these programs.

7. For more on racial identity shifts in college see Feliciano 2009; Tovar and Feliciano 2009; Umaña-Taylor 2004.

8. See de la Garza et al. 1992; DeSipio 1996; Lopez and Taylor 2009; Michelson 2005; Sanchez 2006; Segura and Santoro 2011.

9. See Geertz 1973.

10. In order to be considered a Hispanic-Serving Institution (HSI) at least 25 percent of a school's student population must be of Latino origin. HSIs are eligible for federal funds designed to help schools serve first-generation college-going and low-income Latino students.

CHAPTER 2   THE COMMUNAL BUBBLE
AT LIBERAL ARTS COLLEGE

1. As a reminder, this name along with every other name in the book is a pseudonym.

2. The remaining 16 percent are international students and those who report "other" as their racial-ethnic category.

3. Since there aren't many Latino faculty on campus, they are often overburdened.

4. Henceforth, DVR will be used to identify me as a speaker in sections of dialogue.

5. Minutemen patrol the U.S.-Mexico border, are often armed, and try to catch unauthorized people crossing the border.

6. I was granted access to all organizational emails by the leaders in 2008–2009 and 2009–2010 academic school years.

CHAPTER 3   CONFLICT AT RESEARCH UNIVERSITY

1. Latinos United for Action has historically had representation in Chicano-Latino Studies since its inception as an academic program. The creation of this program was a demand of Chicano student activists during the civil rights era, which is when student representation in the academic unit was established.

2. A few years prior to entering the field, a graduate student tried to get LUA involved in labor issues on campus, pleading for the organization to stand in solidarity with the groundskeepers and cafeteria workers as they tried to end the university's subcontracting practices. When LUA did not prioritize this issue, the graduate student and some undergraduates splintered and started a new organization.

3. The Zapatista Army of National Liberation (EZLN) is a revolutionary leftist group based in southern Mexico.

4. These bags are made from fiber material and are popular in Mexico. *Morrales* come in various colors.

5. This clap starts out slowly and increases in speed and tempo, and ends with cheering as well. It has been used by many movements but is associated with the United Farm Workers.

6. This Mexican folk music originates from the state of Veracruz.

7. In 1968, a Chicano high school student protest movement emerged, when students walked out of classes demanding better conditions within the Los Angeles Unified School District.

8. The "Dream Act" to which Gilda referred is formally titled the Development, Relief, and Education for Alien Minors Act. First introduced in the U.S. Senate in 2001, it stipulates several conditions under which individuals who migrated as children can be granted legal status.

CHAPTER 4   COEXISTING AT REGIONAL PUBLIC UNIVERSITY

1. Mexica New Year is based on the Aztec calendar.
2. Use of italics in interview quotes is my emphasis.

CHAPTER 5   WHO WE ARE: (PAN)ETHNIC IDENTITY
AND BOUNDARY FORMATION

1. A shorter version of the findings in this chapter are featured in my *Du Bois Review* article (2017).
2. Jim Gilchrist is the founder of the Minuteman project, a nativist vigilante group that patrols the U.S.-Mexico border with the aim of preventing unauthorized immigrants from entering the United States.
3. Most of the interactive data in this section comes from Latinos Unidos' meetings, which are quite unstructured and afford ample time for informal interaction, humor, and banter between members. Latino Links, in contrast, has a very formalized organizational style, with little informal interaction and banter between members during the meetings. I observed fewer interactions at Latino Links where boundaries were actively deployed. However, as the next section will show, interviews with Latino Links members revealed that their ideas about the boundaries of Latinidad were similar to those of LU members.
4. Teatro originates from Teatro Campesino, which was founded by Luis Valdez in the 1960s. Its mission was to bring drama and the arts to the people and to carry out a political mission of raising consciousness of history, particularly the struggles of farmworkers.
5. *Negrita* is the diminutive version of the word *negra*, which refer to a black woman in Spanish. In this context, Pablo is using it to ridicule Suyeli in a joking fashion. There is a historical denial of blackness in many parts of Latin America including El Salvador, Nicaragua, and Mexico (some of the countries that represent the origins of the students at this LF meeting).
6. I am not claiming that there are no East Coast Latinos at RPU or RU but rather that students at these campuses did not mention this factor, while LAC students made a point of doing so.

CHAPTER 6   WHAT WE DO: DEFINING AND
PERFORMING LATINO POLITICS

1. A shorter version of the findings in this chapter are featured in my *Sociology of Education* article (2015).
2. With permission of the organizational leadership, I was added to their listserv. With the understanding that I was conducting research and would use their communication to understand their organization, I was granted access to their emails.
3. A federal holiday observed by most states in the United States. However, California has removed the paid holiday status of this date, and some cities, such as Los Angeles, have replaced it with Indigenous People's Day.
4. Arizona's Support Our Law Enforcement and Safe Neighborhoods Act (SB 1070) mandated that noncitizens carry immigration documentation at all times and granted law enforcement the right to inquire about immigration status and demand appropriate paperwork.

5. Note that Kenya is using the term Chicano as a descriptor for Mexican Americans on campus rather than politically identifying Chicanos, who assert the identity as an agreement with the mission of the political movement.

6. See Bañales (2014) for a more thorough and critical analysis of *joteria*.

7. Anthony believed this woman was "infiltrating" because she was representing another organization and trying to shape their (LUA's) direction/understandings. The organization is open to people but I guess according to Anthony not open to other organizations promoting their separate missions.

CHAPTER 7   WHERE WE ARE GOING: IDEAS ABOUT RACIAL INEQUALITY AND MOBILITY

1. Unlike Warikoo, I refer to these ways of understanding as narratives rather than frames. Snow et. al (1986, 464) define frames as cognitive structures that individuals use "to locate, perceive, identify, and label occurrences." Moreover, they conceptualize frames as action-oriented. Coming from a social movement tradition, I understand frames as embodying three steps: the first identifies the problem, the second offers a solution, and the last one constructs a moral justification for the prior two (Benford and Snow 2000). When I asked students to think about disadvantage and whether it affected Latinos, most missed one of the three steps and had either no solution or no moral justification.

2. Use of italics in interview quotes is my emphasis.

3. See also Nepstad (2007, 662).

CHAPTER 8   HOW HIGHER EDUCATION TEACHES DISPARATE LESSONS TO LATINOS

1. See also Armstrong and Hamilton (2013); Binder and Wood (2013); Clark (1992); and Stevens 2007.

2. See also Rivera (2015).

3. The survey is given to incoming first-year college students to measure "background characteristics, high school experiences, attitudes, behaviors, and expectations for college." It was been conducted for fifty years.

REFERENCES

Abrego, Leisy. 2014. *Sacrificing Families: Navigating Laws, Labor, and Love across Borders*. Stanford, CA: Stanford University Press.

Acuña, Rodolfo. 1999 [1981]. *Occupied America: A History of Chicanos*. Boston: Pearson.

Armstrong, Elizabeth, and Laura Hamilton. 2013. *Paying for the Party: How Colleges Maintains Inequality*. Cambridge, MA: Harvard University Press.

Arum, Richard, and Josipa Roska. 2011. *Academically Adrift: Limited Learning on College Campuses*. Chicago: University of Chicago Press.

Astin, Alexander. 1999. "How Do Liberal Arts Colleges Affect Students?" *Daedalus* 128, no. 1: 77–100.

Bañales, Xamuel. 2014. "Jotería: A Decolonizing Political Project." *Aztlan: A Journal of Chicano Studies* 12, no. 1: 155–166.

Beattie, Irenee R. 2014. "Tracking Women's Transitions to Adulthood: Race, Curricular Tracking and Young Adult Outcomes." *Youth and Society* 49: 96–117.

Beltran, Cristina. 2010. *The Trouble with Unity: Latino Politics and the Creation of Identity*. Oxford: Oxford University Press.

Benford, Robert D., and Dave A. Snow. 2000. "Frame Processes and Social Movements: An Overview and Assessment." *Annual Review of Sociology* 26: 611–639.

Binder, Amy J., Daniel B. Davis, and Nick Bloom. 2015. "Career Funneling: How Elite Students Learn to Define and Desire 'Prestigious' Jobs." *Sociology of Education* 89: 20–39.

Binder, Amy, and Kate Wood. 2014. *Becoming Right: How Campuses Shape Young Conservatives*. Princeton, NJ: Princeton University Press.

Brown, Hana, and Jennifer A. Jones. 2015. "Rethinking Panethnicity and the Race-Immigration Divide: An Ethnoracialization Model of Group Formation." *Sociology of Race and Ethnicity* 1, no. 1: 181–191.

Bruni, Frank. 2015. *Where You Go Is Not Who You Will Be: An Antidote to the College Admissions Mania*. New York: Grand Central Publishing.

Clark, Burton R. 1992. *The Distinctive College*. New Brunswick, NJ: Transaction Publishers.

Collins, Patricia Hills. 1986. "Learning from the Outsider Within: The Sociological Significance of Black Feminist Thought." *Social Problems* 33, no. 6: 14–32.

de la Garza, Rodolfo, Louis DeSipio, F. Chris Garcia, John Garcia, and Angelo Falcon. 1992. *Latino Voices: Mexican, Puerto Rican, and Cuban Perspectives on American Politics*. Boulder, CO: Westview Press.

DeSipio, Louis. 1996. "More than the Sum of Its Parts: The Building Blocks of a Pan-Ethnic Latino Identity." In *The Politics of Minority Coalitions: Race, Ethnicity, and Shared Uncertainties*, edited by Wilbur C. Rich, pp. 177–189. Westport, CT: Praeger.

Excelencia in Education. 2015. *Factbook: The Conditions of Latinos in Education*. Washington, DC: Excelencia in Education.

Feliciano, Cynthia. 2009. "Education and Ethnic Identity Formation among Children of Latin American and Caribbean Immigrants." *Sociological Perspectives* 52: 135–158.

Flores, Glenda. 2016. "Discovering a Hidden Privilege: Ethnography in Multiracial Organizations as an Outsider Within." *Ethnography* 17: 190–212.

Flores-Gonzalez, Nilda. 2002. *School Kids/Street Kids: Identity Development in Latino Students.* New York: Teachers College Press.

Fox, Cybelle. 2012. *Three worlds of relief: Race, immigration, and the American welfare state from the progressive era to the new deal.* Princeton, NJ: Princeton University Press.

Geertz, Clifford. 1973. *The Interpretation of Cultures.* New York: Basic Books.

Golash-Boza, Tanya. 2012. *Immigration Nation: Raids, Detentions and Deportations in Post–9-11 America.* Boulder, CO: Paradigm.

Goldsmith, Pat Rubio. 2009. "Schools or Neighborhoods, or Both? Race and Ethnic Segregation and Educational Attainment." *Social Forces* 87, no. 4: 1913–1942.

Gurin, Patricia, Eric L Dey, Sylvia Hurtado, and Gerald Gurin. 2002. "Diversity in Higher Education: Theory and Impact on Educational Outcomes." *Harvard Educational Review.* 72, 3.

Hallett, Tim and Marc J. Ventresca. 2006. "Inhabited Institutions: Social Interactions and Organizational Forms in Gouldner's Patterns of Industrial Bureaucracy." *Theory and Society* 35: 216–236.

Hammersley, M., and P. Atkinson. 2007. "The Process of Analysis." In *Ethnography: Principles in Practice*, 3rd ed., pp. 158–190. New York: Routledge.

Harper, Shaun, and Sylvia Hurtado. 2007. "Nine Themes in Racial Campus Climate and Implications for Institutional Transformation." *New Directions for Student Services* 120: 7–24.

Hays, Sharon. 1994. "Structure and Agency and the Sticky Problem of Culture." *Sociological Theory* 12, no 1: 57–72.

Huberman, A. M., and M. B. Miles. 1994. "Data Management and Analysis Methods." In *Handbook of Qualitative Research*, edited by N. K. Denzin and Y. S. Lincoln. Thousand Oaks, CA: Sage.

Hurtado, Sylvia. 1992. "The Campus Racial Climate: Contexts of Conflict." *Journal of Higher Education* 63, no. 5: 539–569.

Hurtado, Sylvia, and Deborah Faye Carter. 1997. "Effects of College Transition and Perceptions of the Campus Racial Climate on Latino College Students' Sense of Belonging." *Sociology of Education* 70, no. 4: 324–345.

Hurtado, Sylvia, Adriana Ruiz-Alvarado, and Chelsea Guillermo-Wann. 2015. "Creating Inclusive Environments: The Mediating Effect of Faculty and Staff Validation on the Relationship of Discrimination/Bias to Students' Sense of Belonging." *Journal Committed to Social Change in Race and Ethnicity* 1, no. 1: 60–80.

Kosmacher, Jeff. 2015. "Vassar's $1 Million Prize to Support High-Performing Low-Income Students." *Vassar Today.* https://vq.vassar.edu/issues/2015/02/vassar-today/cooke-foundation .html.

LeCompte, M. D., and J. J. Schensul. 2010. *Designing and Conducting Ethnographic Research: An Introduction*, 2nd ed. Lanham, MD: AltaMira Press.

Lewis, Amanda E. 2003. *Race in the Schoolyard: Negotiating the Color Line in Classrooms and Communities.* New Brunswick, NJ: Rutgers University Press.

Lofland, J., David Snow, L. Anderson, and L. Lofland. 2006. *Analyzing Social Settings: A Guide to Qualitative Observation and Analysis*, 4th ed. Belmont, CA: Wadsworth Thompson Learning.

Lopez, M. H., and P. Taylor. 2009. *Dissecting the 2008 Electorate: Most Diverse in U.S. History.* Washington, DC: Pew Hispanic Center.

Mansbridge, Jane, and Aldon Morris. 2001. *Oppositional Consciousness: The Subjective Roots of Social Justice*. Chicago: University of Chicago Press.

Mariscal, George 2005. *Brown-Eyed Children of the Sun: Lessons from the Chicano Movement 1965–1975*: Albuquerque: University of New Mexico Press.

McCabe, Janice. 2016. *Connecting in College: How Friendship Networks Matter for Academic and Social Success*. Chicago: University of Chicago Press.

Michelson, Melissa. 2005. "Meeting the Challenge of Latino Voter Mobilization." *Annals of the American Academy of Political and Social Science* 601: 85–101.

Miles, M. B., A. M. Huberman, and J. Saldaña. 2014. *Qualitative Data Analysis: A Methods Sourcebook*, 3rd ed. Los Angeles: SAGE.

Mullen, Ann L. 2010. *Degrees of Inequality: Culture, Class, and Gender in American Higher Education*. Baltimore, MD: John Hopkins University Press.

Muñoz, Carlos. 1989. *Youth, Identity, and Power: The Chicano Movement*. London: Verso.

Nepstad, Sharon Erickson. 2007. "Oppositional Consciousness among the Privileged: Remaking Religion in the Central America Solidarity Movement." *Critical Sociology* 33: 661–688.

Nunn, Lisa M. 2014. *Defining Student Success: The Role of School and Culture*. New Brunswick, NJ: Rutgers University Press.

Ochoa, Gilda. 2013. *Academic Profiling: Latinos, Asians, and the Achievement Gap*. Minneapolis: University of Minnesota Press.

Okamoto, Dina. 2014. *Redefining Race: Asian American Panethnicity and Shifting Ethnic Boundaries*. New York: Russell Sage Foundation.

———. 2006. "Institutional Panethnicity: Boundary Formation in Asian-American Organizing." *Social Forces* 85: 1–25.

———. 2003. "Toward a Theory of Panethnicity: Explaining Asian American Collective Action." *American Sociological Review* 68: 811–842.

Okamoto, Dina G., and G. Cristina Mora. 2014. "Panethnicity." *Annual Review of Sociology* 40: 1–20.

Oliver, Pamela, and Hank Johnston. 2000. "What a Good Idea! Ideologies and Frames in Social Movement Research." *Mobilization: An International Quarterly* 5, no. 1: 37–54.

Perry, Pamela. 2002. *Shades of White: White Kids and Racial Identities in High School*. Durham, NC: Duke University Press.

Pew Research Center. 2012. "Nonvoters: Who They Are, What They Think." http://www.people-press.org/2012/11/01/nonvoters-who-they-are-what-they-think/.

———. 2014. "The Rising Cost of Not Going to College." http://www.pewsocialtrends.org/2014/02/11/the-rising-cost-of-not-going-to-college/.

Quiñones, Juan Gomez. 1990. *Chicano Politics: Reality and Promise, 1940–1990*. Albuquerque: University of New Mexico Press.

Radford, Alexandria Walton. 2014. *Top Student, Top School? How Social Class Shapes Where Valedictorian Go to College*. Chicago: University of Chicago Press.

Ray, Rashawn, and Jason A. Rosow. 2010. "Getting Off and Getting Intimate: How Normative Institutional Arrangements Structure Black and White Fraternity Men's Approaches toward Women." *Men and Masculinities* 12, no. 5: 523–546.

Reagon, Bernice Johnson. 1983. "Coalitions Politics: Turning the Century." In *Home Girls: A Black Feminist Anthology*, edited by Barbara Smith, pp. 356–368. New Brunswick, NJ: Rutgers University Press.

Reyes, Daisy Verduzco. 2017. "Disparate Lessons: Racial Climates and Identity Formation Processes Among Latino Students." *Du Bois Review: Social Science Research on Race* 14, no. 2: 1–24. doi:10.1017/S1742058X17000054.

———. 2015. "Inhabiting Latino Politics: How Colleges Shape Students' Political Styles." *Sociology of Education* 88, no. 4: 302–319.

Rojas, Fabio. 2007. *From Black Power to Black Studies: How a Radical Social Movement Became an Academic Discipline.* Baltimore, MD: John Hopkins University Press.

Roth, Wendy. 2012. *Race Migrations: Latinos and the Cultural Transformation of Race.* Stanford, CA: Stanford University Press.

Sanchez, Gabriel. 2006. "The Role of Group Consciousness in Political Participation among Latinos in the United States." *American Politics Research* 34, no. 4: 427–450.

Segura, Gary, and Wayne Santoro. 2011. "Assimilation, Incorporation, and Ethnic Identity in Understanding Latino Electoral and Non-Electoral Political Participation." *Political Research Quarterly* 64, no. 1: 172–184.

Smith, Robert C. 2006. *Mexican New York: Transnational Worlds of New Immigrants.* Berkeley: University of California Press.

Snow, David A., E. Burke Rochford, Steven K. Worden, and Robert D. Benford. 1986. "Frame Alignment Processes, Micromobilization, and Movement Participation." *American Sociological Review* 51, no. 4: 464–481.

Solórzano, Daniel, Miguel Ceja, and Tara Yosso. 2000. "Critical Race Theory, Racial Microaggressions, and Campus Racial Climate: The Experiences of African American College Students." *Journal of Negro Education* 69, nos. 1–2: 60–73.

Stevens, Mitchell. 2007. *Creating a Class: College Admissions and the Education of Elites.* Cambridge, MA: Harvard University Press.

Stuber, Jenny. 2016. "Normative Institutional Arrangements and the Mobility Pathway: How Campus-Level Forces Impact First-Generation Students." In *The Working Classes and Higher Education: Inequality of Access, Opportunity, and Outcome,* edited by Amy E. Stich and Carrie Freie, pp. 110–127. New York: Routledge.

———. 2011. *Inside the College Gates: How Class and Culture Matter in Higher Education.* Lanham, MD: Lexington Books.

Sue, Derald. 2010. *Microaggressions in Everyday Life: Race, Gender, and Sexual Orientation.* Hoboken, NJ: Wiley.

Swidler, Ann. 1986. "Culture in Action: Symbols and Strategies." *American Sociological Review* 51 (April): 273–286.

Tovar, Jessica, and Cynthia Feliciano. 2009 "'Not Mexican-American, but Mexican': Shifting Ethnic Self-Identifications among Children of Mexican Immigrants." *Latino Studies* 7, no. 2: 197–221.

Umaña-Taylor, Adriana. J. 2004. "Ethnic Identity and Self-Esteem: Examining the Role of Social Context." *Journal of Adolescence* 27: 139–146.

Valenzuela, Angela. 1999. *Subtractive Schooling: U.S. Mexican Youth and the Politics of Caring.* Albany: State University of New York Press.

Warikoo, Natasha. 2016. *The Diversity Bargain: And Other Dilemmas of Race, Admissions, and Meritocracy at Elite Universities.* Chicago: University of Chicago Press.

Warikoo, Natasha, and Sherry Deckman. 2014. "Beyond the Numbers: Institutional Influences on Experiences with Diversity on Elite College Campuses." *Sociological Forum* 29: 959–981.

INDEX

Page numbers followed by the letters f and t indicate figures and tables, respectively.

ABOUT THE AUTHOR

DAISY VERDUZCO REYES is an assistant professor in the Department of Sociology and El Instituto: The Institute of Latina/o, Caribbean, and Latin American Studies at the University of Connecticut. She conducts research at the intersections of Latino sociology, education, politics, and sexualities.